D1292824

Startup!

Beyond the Myths to the Reality of Starting a Company

KEVIN SCHEHRER

ROI Press
(www.ROIPress.com)

"A moment's insight is sometimes worth a life's experience."

Oliver Wendell Holmes Sr.

CONTENTS

PREFACE

Firstly, my confession: I don't like most business books. The reasons are that they overcomplicate what is really simple, they often give bad advice and their contents can not be put into action by the reader. A friend who does company valuations is frequently asked for investment advice, to which he always responds that it is best to buy low and sell high. He is kidding, of course, but that is the kind of advice I find in most business books—mostly accurate and mostly useless.

Why This Book?

I decided to write this book because, while there is a vast amount of information available to those who wish to start new companies, not much of it is useful or good. The quantity is there but the quality is not. There is a lot of "conventional wisdom" that continues to get repeated because it continues to get repeated. Entrepreneurs trying to educate themselves are faced with a lot of information that is so widely accepted that it "must be true". They often end up paying dearly—in time, money and lost opportunities—for believing the conventional wisdom.

There is a lot of "conventional wisdom" that continues to get repeated because it continues to get repeated.

What Are the Primary Themes of This Book?

There are two primary themes underlying this book:

➤ The first is that facts and experience are the bases for wisdom and insight. However, wisdom and insight are far more valuable than facts or experience alone. In this book I have tried to pass on some of the wisdom and insights that have come from working with hundreds of entrepreneurs—mostly in the early stages of company formation. This is in contrast to the many books that will cite experiences without taking the step to wisdom or insight. Experiences are used throughout this book to *support* the wisdom and insights.

… facts and experience are the bases for wisdom and insight.

➤ The second is that people are the most important part of your business. They are more important than capital, inventions, processes and vision. Without good people working well together you will have to be very lucky for your company to succeed. With good people you can create a great company that will create value for decades. Good people plus a mediocre idea will always beat a great idea with mediocre people. The people theme goes deeper still. Not only do you need good people, but they have to work well as a functional team, communicate well and have cultural similarities even though they might have disparate ideas.

Good people plus a mediocre idea will always beat a great idea with mediocre people.

How Does This Book Move Beyond Others in This Field?

Throughout this book I have taken a point of view. There are mountains of data and stories in other books or on the Internet for you to sift through if you choose. Rather than make that mountain taller or sift through the data and stories for you, I have drawn from my and others' real experiences to provide you with insights and wisdom—typically gained through much trial and error. In doing so I have taken a position rather than simply provided information or discussed all aspects of an issue.

Throughout this book I have inserted action-oriented tips—these allow you to take action to obtain desired results. I have also pointed out myths and dispelled them—there is no reason for you to have to waste time relearning what others have already learned.

What Is the Goal of This Book?

The goal of this book is to provide its audience with useful, common-sense information on how to:

➢ determine whether to start a business

➢ determine whether or not a business opportunity is a good one

➢ get it started.

How Will This Book Give You the Information You Need?

This book will talk to you in direct language and dispel some of the myths and misconceptions that are out there. I will appeal to your common sense, intelligence and ability to reason, rather than citing such-and-such an academic guru. My goal in writing this book is to allow you to determine your best path and make your best decisions while benefiting from my experience as an entrepreneur who has also worked with many entrepreneurs. Much of this experience is the result of missteps and learning the lessons these offered.

Who Will Benefit From Reading This Book?

The other reason I have written this book is that there seem to be two categories of books aimed at entrepreneurs. One category is of the "all you need is venture capital" variety. These books don't say much about starting or running a company and focus 80% of their pages on how to raise money from venture capitalists. I will share some secrets here in advance:

➢ Very few people are successful in raising venture capital (VC).

➢ Your lifelong return on investment can often be better by starting non-VC-backed companies.

The other category is of the "here is how to buy a fax machine" variety. My premise is that most real entrepreneurs are pretty smart and they can probably figure out how to buy a fax machine or get business cards printed.

While I do devote some of this book to the best ways to raise venture capital and much of what I talk about will help you in raising venture capital, this is not the focus of this book.

People who will benefit from this book are:

➢ those who are starting a company

➢ those who are thinking about starting a company

➢ those who are thinking about starting a new venture within an existing organization

➢ those who are thinking about investing in an early-stage company.

Much of the experience communicated here is as relevant to a one-person service-provider as to a 200-person, VC-backed startup.

Some Notes on Conventions

While most of the discussion in this book applies well to product, service or Internet companies, it is awkward to list all three in every instance. This is a book, not a legal document. Thus, I sometimes write "product" alone, realizing that the discussion applies more generally.

I want this book to read more smoothly than most business books, so I talk to *you* as an entrepreneur. If you are an investor, work at a large company or are reading this book out of general interest, it may take a few pages for you to get used to this.

Entrepreneurship knows no gender distinctions, of course, and I don't want to suggest otherwise. For this reason, while specific examples within this book feature male or female entrepreneurs alone, both genders are represented in equal measure within the book as a whole.

1. INTRODUCTION

There is a lot of romanticism swirling about the startup world, and with that comes conventional wisdom that would be better called myth. One such myth is that good people and good ideas can always find venture capital (VC). Venture capitalists and entrepreneurs who have received venture capital are always good for a quote to this effect. However, depending on where we are in the venture-capital cycle, there are typically only a few hundred seed-round venture-capital fundings per year. Is it possible that in a country with 280 million people there are only several hundred good ideas per year? Moreover, with a typical VC track-record, only 10-30% of those will succeed to their full potential. Were there really only 30 truly good ideas in a year?!

Is it possible that in a country with 280 million people there are only several hundred good ideas per year?

Since there are many more than a few hundred good ideas every year, the reality is that many, many good ideas do not get funded by venture capitalists. Moreover, your odds of getting funded by venture capitalists while you are at the idea stage, no matter how good your idea is, are pretty low.

So what do you do? Throw your hands up, keep your day job and put Dilbert cartoons on your cubicle walls in quiet protest? No, you can do what hundreds of thousands of entrepreneurs do every year—start your own company. But, unlike most of those hundreds of thousands, who will fail, you should prepare, plan, take action and be resourceful so that you greatly increase your probability of creating a successful company with or without venture capital.

This book was written from my experience of being involved with more than one hundred startups, seeing summaries or plans for many hundreds of startups, meeting hundreds of bright entrepreneurs, venture capitalists and other investors, and having equity in a number of companies. The discussions in this book are not based on surveys or statistical analyses. Throughout this book I will use real-world examples to illustrate my points—with particulars altered to respect confidentiality.

This book is about how to get from an idea or a list of ideas to the point at which you have made a commitment and started your company. Unlike most books on startups, this book isn't focused on raising venture capital and

This book is about how to get from an idea or a list of ideas to the point at which you have made a commitment and started your company.

going IPO (initial public offering). I do, of course, discuss financing, since in most cases you will need it at some point in your company's growth.

This book is about moving prudently through the stages of starting a company—and choosing which company to start—so that when you make that commitment you are more likely to succeed. As you probably also have guessed from the opening paragraph, I will not keep repeating conventional wisdom that flies in the face of reason and I will dispel these myths where appropriate.

Early-stage investors, entrepreneurs, team members and corporate intrapreneurs will benefit from this book. I start from the pre-startup stage—the stage at which the reader may be thinking of starting a company. There is a lot of information about this stage available on the Internet, in magazines and in books. Unfortunately, much of it is not very useful, is inaccurate or is trite. In this book I give the entrepreneur a from-the-trenches perspective. I cut through all the bromides and conventional wisdom to get at what matters. I try, wherever possible, to bring the reader to action. I assume that the reader is serious, wants to take action and wants to achieve results—this is not an academic exercise.

I make absolutely no effort to be politically correct. I have a point of view backed up by my experience of starting companies and I have no qualms about expressing that point of view. I try to save you, the reader, the trouble of following conventional wisdom, making the same errors that many others have made and then having to adjust course in response to reality.

Most startup books fall into one of three categories:

➢ They say they are about starting companies, but thumb through these books and you will find that they are really about raising money. Some of these books can be useful but they are not really about starting a company.

➢ They focus on the mechanics of starting a company: how to set up an office, how to do an operating agreement, how to buy business cards and letterhead—these books can be quite helpful but they won't have much impact on your ultimate success.

➢ They are somewhat academic studies of past results or compilations of quotations and interviews. The best among these can provide interesting insights but don't speak directly to the topic of starting a company.

I don't think you will find any other book that gives you such practical advice on which you can take action…

I don't think you will find any other book that gives you such practical advice on which you can take action, that takes a point of view, that cuts through the noise and that dispels some of the common myths.

In Chapter 2 we will take a close look at you. We'll do this so that you do some self-examination to determine the types of opportunities to which you will add the most value, and the opportunities you will find most satisfying. This section will also help you to think about how long you might stay with a company and how your transition within the company, or your exit from it, might look. A lot of this will tell you what it is really like so that you can imagine yourself in those entrepreneur-shoes. In this chapter, many questions are posed so you can determine whether being an entrepreneur will be an exhilarating source of energy (as it will be if it is a good fit), or a scary, destructive experience (which it could be if it is a bad fit).

In Chapter 3, we'll move on to discuss how to screen opportunities—both to find one that is right for you and to find one that will allow you to achieve your goals. The premise of this chapter is that you need to think like a good, but time-pressed, investor to determine quickly whether an opportunity warrants further due-diligence and detailed planning. Whether you ask anyone for money or not, you'll need to convince yourself, vendors, employees and customers that this is a great business-opportunity. Each section in this chapter ends with a series of questions and has some exercises that are best done quickly (in less than ten minutes) and will be useful both in the quick evaluation of an opportunity and as the basis for planning, if that is warranted.

Chapter 4 is about planning. It is not a "How to Write a Business Plan" chapter. It has four primary purposes:

➢ gathering the information you need as part of further due-diligence and doing analysis on an opportunity

➢ creating a blueprint for what you need to do to make your company successful

➢ finding the holes in your thinking

➢ making sure that the disparate thoughts and information that you have about an opportunity actually are consistent and reinforcing.

Of lesser importance, it can serve as the basis for creating a communication document that can be used internally, for investors, or simply to clarify your own thoughts.

Chapter 5 covers testing the model. Here you explore how to prove out—without spending a lot of time or money—the risky bits that you discovered in your planning and due-diligence phases. This is a step that entrepreneurs might be tempted to skip. Many do so because they think that they need money alone to succeed. Many others skip it because they fall in love with the potential before fully exploring the reality. To put this in perspective, this is the type of work that today's more cautious investors will expect you to have completed.

You will need help from other people and need to make other preparations before starting your company or asking serious investors for money. Chapter 6 will take you through some last-minute preparatory thinking so that when you make the commitment to start you have everything in place to allow you to hit the ground running—in the right direction.

Chapter 7 is about investors and their relationship to entrepreneurs. It discusses the various types of investors, the pros and cons of each and what to expect from them. It also, of course, discusses how to approach investors for financing. This chapter has a lot of hard-earned, experiential information that will save you learning your way past the myths on your own.

Chapter 8 comprises a series of tips and techniques that will help you in running your company from day one. It is an overview of what I call "foundation-setting", which is often neglected but can have a huge impact on the probability of success. Foundation-setting covers principles, culture, milestone setting, communication and keys to success. Also covered here is how to use process without it paralyzing your small enterprise.

In Chapter 9 we'll take a look at two entrepreneurs. We'll briefly take a look at their backgrounds, then at how they got into their current businesses. Each entrepreneur's story includes quotes from the entrepreneur in which they share their wisdom and lessons learned. This chapter will give you some insight into what it takes to be an entrepreneur and start a successful business. You will see that starting a company is something that you can do too if you so choose.

I will not give you any magic potions or foolproof rules to success because there are none.

Over and over in this book I will stress that you need to use your head, that you have it within you to do what you need to do but you need to take action and you need to take responsibility. I will not give you any magic potions or foolproof rules to success because there are none. There is an entire industry based on pretending that there is, but I would rather you were successful than simply felt good after reading this book. The planet is littered with consultants dispensing advice such as the following, which is an actual quotation from an anonymous source in a newsgroup:

> *Just make sure a declining economy doesn't pull your sales staff's morale down with it. Consider these attitude-enhancing tips:*
> **Stay positive**. *If your salespeople smell fear, they'll start to worry.*
> **Rev 'em up!** *In a soft market, salespeople are getting beaten up every day. It's your job to inject a*

positive attitude into their lives. Leave them encouraging voice mails or pager text messages.

Be a cheerleader. *Make a big deal out of every sale. Celebrate successes to motivate your team to keep on winning.*

This type of advice is only slightly better than a financial advisor telling his client to buy low and sell high. Good advice? Yes. True? Yes. Accurate? Yes. Useful, insightful or added value? I'll let you answer that.

This book will have achieved its goal if it helps you achieve *your* goals generally, but, more specifically, if it gives you a few key-insights, if it dispels some myths and if it helps you find a great opportunity to join or start.

I also very much hope that you find this an enjoyable read. Starting a company is one of the most enjoyable and rewarding things a person can do—I hope that I have conveyed my love of starting companies, while deliberately avoiding the content-free happy-talk found in many media about startups.

2. YOU

This chapter will help you have a clear-headed approach to being an entrepreneur so that even if this company does not succeed, you as an individual will not be devastated. Leave the startup romanticism to journalists, pundits, analysts and other voyeurs, i.e. people without anything at risk.

There are a number of considerations to bear in mind in deciding whether and how to take the leap:

➤ What are your strengths and tendencies and how do you best exploit them?

➤ What are your weaknesses and how do you either make them strengths or find a way to get those areas covered by someone else?

➤ How much time can you put into this—today, and a year from now?

➤ How will your family react?

➤ Do you really understand how this might affect your lifestyle?

➤ And, finally, a huge question: can you afford to fail?

These are some of the issues we will cover in this chapter.
Perhaps most important and before you put anything at risk you should do some self-discovery to determine:

➤ whether you really want to be an entrepreneur

➤ what type of entrepreneur you are

➤ what type of entrepreneur you want to be.

This will help you in determining what is a good entrepreneurial opportunity for *you*. This is the subject of the next chapter.

Warning!

There are so many stories of entrepreneurs who have gone to the brink of financial disaster and came out winners that they almost fall into the category of urban legend. You know, stories like the ones about the alligators in the New York sewers. No doubt many of these stories are true—the ones about the entrepreneurs, not the alligators. However, the fact that some people go to the brink of financial disaster and ultimately succeed is far from meaning that all entrepreneurs who go to the brink of disaster will succeed or that you must go to the brink in order to succeed. In reality, most near-death experiences end in death, i.e. most people that go to the brink of financial ruin do in fact end up in financial ruin.

If you are prepared to go to such extremes that's fine, but please do it with your eyes open. Better yet, realize that you don't need to do that and that most successful people do not push it that far. Preparation and goal setting will go a long way towards avoiding these extremes, though, of course, what is extreme to one person is prudent risk-taking to another—as we'll see below.

Skills and Aptitude

There are some things at which you are good—you have the skills. There are things for which you have an aptitude. Sometimes you have skills in areas for which you do not have an aptitude or which you do not enjoy.

As an entrepreneur, you will have to be good at a lot of things, some of which you do not like or for which you have no special aptitude. One of the keys to being a happy and successful entrepreneur is to stay close to your strengths. So, as you go through thinking about what might be a good opportunity for you or what type of entrepreneur you are, don't confuse being good at something with that thing being your strength. For example, I can be very good at selling when I set my mind to it and apply the skills I have learned. However, this is not my strength. I add more value elsewhere in a company.

Entrepreneurial Characteristics

Entrepreneurship can be extremely rewarding and simply fun when you are pursuing an opportunity that is a good fit for you. On the one hand, in instances in which the fit is good, the time will fly by and it will be easy to take the trials in your stride as just other aspects of this delightful and challenging game. On the other hand, it can be pure hell if there is not such a good fit. In these instances, the stress can be almost unbearable and your life and business can seem out of control.

Notice I have not said that there are some types of people who should be entrepreneurs and others who should not. I would not claim anything so foolish and contrary to the reality we see every day. But we can recognize types of entrepreneurs, whom we can "type" in three ways:

> background and history

> tendencies

> current characteristics.

Background and History

There are many books that have lists of the background characteristics of entrepreneurs. Among them are:
> offspring of immigrants

> first-born child

> one or both parents were entrepreneurs.

These are results from legitimate studies of the backgrounds of successful entrepreneurs and I don't question their veracity.

However, they confuse causation with that which is measurable and correlates. The people who did these studies focused on what could be unambiguously measured. There isn't much subjectivity to the order of your birth. Unfortunately, some books, investors and entrepreneurs have turned this data on its head and think that either you need this background to be successful or if you have this background you will be successful.

Neither is true. These studies refer to the average successful entrepreneur, which is a statistical entity, not a human being. The interpreters confuse statistically significant incidence of background characteristics with cause. Being born to entrepreneurial parents does not cause you to be a successful entrepreneur. However, it does expose you throughout your life to the concepts of risk, persistence and resourcefulness so that these are second nature to you by the time you are an adult. It is people's characteristics, such as persistence, that have causal relationships to entrepreneurial success, not the motherlands or activities of the people's parents.

Still, there are people who will turn this data on its head and use it as a "qualifier" for entrepreneurship. I have even seen venture-capital firms include this rubbish in their Web sites. They tell the reader what good entrepreneurs are

"I have been a lifelong entrepreneur ... my father emigrated from ... both parents were entrepreneurs ... and so on." Who cares?

really made of and what they are looking for in those entrepreneurs. But they are really investing in the parents of those entrepreneurs.

I have also seen many bios in business plans that read as though someone has taken the entrepreneurial traits checklist as an outline. For example: "I have been a lifelong entrepreneur ... my father emigrated from … both parents were entrepreneurs … and so on." Who cares? So have millions of other people who have absolutely no business starting a company.

Chances are that your background does not match the background checklists that you will see. This is largely irrelevant to your success as an individual entrepreneur. Your focus instead should be on what I call here "tendencies" and "current characteristics", which speak to your capabilities and preferences in action.

Tendencies

A good test for helping you think through what is a good fit is the Myers Briggs test. I use this test in my work with early entrepreneurs and find it a great tool for uncovering some fundamental traits and preferences. The more advanced versions of the test are the most useful but cost. There are many versions of this test online but, as they say, "results may vary". There are also some excellent books on interpreting the results. (Especially good is *Working Together* by Isachsen and Berens.)

The Myers Briggs types consist of four letters:
1   The first letter is an I or an E standing for introvert or extrovert. This characterizes your attitudes towards others and how you are energized. (Quotes in 1-4 are from *Working Together* by Isachsen and Berens.)

"The person who is energized by having interaction with other people is said to be extraverted, while a person who prefers introspection and solitude is said to be introverted."

2   The second letter is an S or an N standing for sensing or intuition. This characterizes through what means you attend to and take in data.

"Those who have a natural preference for sensing probably describe themselves as practical, while those who have a natural preference for intuition may describe themselves as innovative."

3   The third letter is a T or an F standing for thinking or feeling. This characterizes how you process data and make decisions.

"Persons who choose the impersonal basis of choice are called thinking types by Jung. Persons who choose the personal basis are called feeling types."

4   The fourth letter is a J or a P standing for judging or perceiving. This characterizes your modes of dealing with the world around you.

"Persons who choose closure over open options are likely to be the judging types. Persons preferring to keep things open and fluid are the perceiving types."

So now you have some background on the Myers Briggs test. Let's get beyond the surface to understand what this means. It is true that most entrepreneurs are INTP, INTJ, ENTP or ENTJ. The common elements among these four types are intuition and thinking. The importance of intuition is that it helps you to process data very quickly and get partway to a decision. It also allows you to fill in the data gaps that are almost always there when you are doing something new and moving quickly as you do it. The thinking trait also assists in moving through the available data, connecting it logically and reasoning to a decision. In many cases, the information needed for proof and making optimal decisions is simply unobtainable. Nonetheless, you need to decide and act quickly—even if you are wrong and have to make a course correction. The ability to make good, quick decisions is an invaluable asset when you are running the show. Another component of preferring intuition to sensing is that it will be easier for you to find creative solutions and be resourceful. Moreover, you will be able to visualize a future that no one else has ever seen.

The thinking component is important because you will need to use your head as much as possible. There are facts and there is logic and you will need them both to get as far as you can before making a decision, to learn the right lessons from your mistakes, to assess accurately your external environment and to hold yourself and others accountable. If you are a feeling decision-maker then you might not accurately assess a situation and you could find it difficult to hold yourself and others accountable.

Being introvert or extrovert has relatively little impact on whether you will find it natural to be an entrepreneur. Rather, it will determine how you operate within the company and what your role is. The extrovert entrepreneur is more likely to assist in sales and to have a very public role. Introvert entrepreneurs are likely to be more inwardly focused on their companies and hire top-notch salespeople to complement them.

Being judging or perceiving also has relatively little influence since either can be a strength to a startup and both have their drawbacks. The judge will be more likely to drive things to closure while the perceiver will find it easier to adapt to changing terrain—both of these qualities have value to a startup.

With all that emphasis on thinking and intuition, what if you are not an NT? First, one thing that the Myers Briggs does not tell you is how good someone is at any component. An idiot can be a T or an intuitive might have horrible intuition. The flip side of this is that people who are feeling decision-makers can be extremely intelligent and force themselves to make decisions as thinkers. The second point is that there are opportunities that may match your tendencies better than others. For example, if you are sensing and want to start a company, then accounting software or a quality assurance ASP might be good fits.

Current Characteristics

There are some real-time traits that are very useful to successful entrepreneurship. These traits are under your control to some extent or can be learned. Alternatively, you can get others to help you develop them or hire someone who complements you so that, as a team, you (plural) possess these traits. The top-ten list I would choose is:

1. resourcefulness
2. intuitiveness
3. results-orientation
4. integrity
5. clarity
6. accountability
7. self-assurance
8. humility
9. sense of urgency
10. drive
11. agility.

> *(The astute reader will have noticed this is a very special book—where top-ten lists go to eleven.)*

> *It pains me to put integrity fourth. I would really like to believe that it is number-one. However, I have seen many entrepreneurs who were "integrity-challenged" get quite far with resourcefulness, good intuition and results-orientation. The lack of integrity backfires at some point, but often that takes a while—as long as a year or two in some cases.*

A book could be written about why these traits are useful and important—in fact some books of that sort have been written. In particular, I highly recommend *The Five Temptations of a CEO* by Pat Lencioni. He covers results-orientation, accountability, clarity and two others—trust and conflict—that I have left off my list because, even though they are essential to leaders, they might or might not be essential to being an entrepreneur.

Intelligence is a definite asset and I take for granted that you are pretty smart, but you don't need to be a genius to succeed.

Some characteristics not on the list or perhaps noticeably absent are "being smart" and "having domain expertise". Intelligence is a definite asset and I take for granted that you are pretty smart, but you don't need to be a genius to succeed. Facility in the other traits, along with street smarts, can easily make up for raw conventional intelligence. I also think experience is sometimes overrated. Once you have done enough, have a broad background and have collected some wisdom, you are likely to find that most things are not terribly difficult to learn if you are motivated. What you might lack, however, and need to find some backup for, is the insider knowledge that comes from time spent in a domain; knowing who in the industry are crooks and who you can work with, knowing that you can't import that key component from that Taiwanese company into the US, and so on.

Really do some soul-searching to determine whether you have these traits; if you don't, then consciously plan to acquire them for yourself or get help from others who do have them. Your thoughts about whether or not you have these traits will be based on your reference point, so be a little hard on yourself.

Resourcefulness

You will never have enough money, enough time or enough people to do everything that you want to do. Resourcefulness is about finding non-traditional ways of getting things done. Consider:

Resourcefulness is about finding non-traditional ways of getting things done.

➤ Do you know someone who knows someone who can introduce you to that key strategic-partner?

➤ Can you test-market your service on the Internet to see if there really is a demand and test how to tailor your service and your message?

➤ Instead of getting financing, can you get your vendors to finance your company by billing you after you have received payment from your customers?

➤ If you have already started some planning or have started collecting some information, what have you done that was resourceful?

➤ Did you enjoy finding that clever solution?

Resourcefulness isn't the same as being cheap. Spending a half-day at a furniture auction so you can save $50 on a chair rather than calling four prospects is not resourceful. Resourcefulness implies that you understand your priorities and are efficient at meeting them.

Intuition

Again, good intuition is what will allow you to project (correctly or nearly so) into the future and to make good decisions in the face of uncertainty. For intuition to be of much use, you need to be good at it. Knowing whether your intuition is good takes some introspection. In past situations in which you have had a disagreement with a co-worker or boss about strategy, have you been right most of the time? Notice that this question doesn't count the instances in which you agreed with others and were right. That's too easy and would give you points for recognizing the obvious or going with conventional wisdom, which is often correct. Have you written a business plan or strategy that had to anticipate technology or market developments and been mostly right? These questions allow you to go back objectively and read something that you wrote and compare current reality to what you envisioned, based on your intuitive assimilation of the data, filling in of the blanks and drawing of a conclusion.

Are you comfortable making decisions in the absence of complete information? This isn't the same as shooting from the hip—you should by all means collect information that you have the time and money to gather. Some CEOs confuse the speed with which they make a decision with having good intuition. I have seen this lead to a lot of wasted energy within companies as they move in all directions before finding one that makes sense. Closing the feedback loop to test those quick decisions is a cure for this: does every meeting to make a decision end in a list of information that must be gathered or do you make a decision within the first one to three meetings?

Results Orientation

... the definition of insanity is doing the same thing over and over again and expecting to get different results.

A friend who is a CEO often tells his people that the definition of insanity is doing the same thing over and over again and expecting to get different results. Put another way, there is a tendency to confuse activity with results. Working yourself and your staff to death merely results in death or at least heart murmurs. Hard work will almost certainly be necessary but it is not in itself the goal and will not by itself lead to success. Instead, achieving results that are on the path to ultimate success is how you will succeed. Listen to yourself when you tell people what you did yesterday or last week.

> *Do you say: "I worked on project BusyWork and I wrote a white paper on Catapult technology." Or, do you say: "I completed the first phase of project FocusedPerson. We proved the technology and built a prototype that will be used in next week's meeting with investors to close our financing. I also completed the white paper that will be instrumental to closing the Catapult sale."*

Integrity

Being an entrepreneur is a long-term game. Even if you are very successful and never need to work again, you are unlikely to spend the rest of your life sitting on a beach and you can only play so much golf. Most entrepreneurs that I have seen hit it big take some time off and then get the itch again.

This is important with respect to integrity because you will see some people make short-term gains through questionable methods. You wouldn't be human if you didn't start to wonder if maybe doing whatever it takes to make a buck would be in your best interest. You may feel like a bit of a sucker when you see another entrepreneur get investment by lying through his teeth or taking a customer from you using a bait-and-switch tactic.

If you have integrity, you will build relationships that will last a lifetime. You will be able to call on someone five or ten years into the future and they'll gladly take your call and try to help you in whatever new venture you are starting. You will have a reputation even among people you have never met so that it will be easier to make things happen in the future. Other businesspeople will respect you and investors will trust you. You will need to spend less time with lawyers because people will not feel the need to put you in a legal straightjacket before they do business with you. This is about branding yourself in a genuine way as a person with integrity.

If you have integrity, you will build relationships that will last a lifetime.

If you do business without integrity, you will have the opposite trajectory. Your bad reputation will make people wary of you. People will write you off and avoid you. Rather than getting easier over time, it will actually get harder—even harder than starting your first venture.

Integrity is about being honest and direct, having principles and a point of view and being consistent.

Having integrity does not mean you have to be a wimp—being direct and honest is anything but wimpy. Integrity is about being honest and direct, having principles and a point of view and being consistent.

Clarity

You will be bombarded with information and ideas from outside the company, within the company and between your ears. You don't need to know it all but you need to be clear on what you do and don't know and on where you are going. You need to be able to communicate this clarity to employees, vendors, investors and customers.

Do you tend to peal away an issue to understand what the fundamental principle is? Do you think in terms of second-, third- and fourth-order effects? These questions are asking whether you can get really clear in your mind why something is happening or what the sequence of consequences will be for a given action. Can you define success for yourself or your company in one to three sentences? Do you know where you need to be in one, three and five years to have succeeded in your mind's eye?

If you are like most people, you may not be able to answer all of these questions. However, the more important question, in considering these questions, is: Do you find it satisfying to have that clarity? Do your answers tend to be short but substantive or do they tend to be long and vague? If the latter, you don't have clarity. Do you tend to think that extracting several key bullet-points from a meeting is oversimplification? If so, then you might be emphasizing completeness over clarity. When you make charts, are they short lists of bullet points or paragraphs of text?

> *The art of the bullet point is to find the fundamentals. A good bullet-point might say:*
> ➢ *Doubled sales at Spanish and German distributors.*
>
> *A bad bullet-point might say:*
> ➢ *Positively involved in multiple geographies.*

Accountability

Accountability is closely linked to results and clarity. If you have clarity about your strategy and vision and you know what results are needed to be successful, then the missing ingredient is making sure that those results are achieved. This means holding yourself and others accountable, which sometimes means being unpopular with others or admitting your own errors.

> *Assuming that you are results oriented, think back to a result that you failed to achieve. Whose fault was it? Imagine two entrepreneurs whose companies failed when the Internet-bubble burst and who might have responded in different ways to these failures:*
> *__Entrepreneur A__: "The market crashed in April and the venture capitalists were running scared so we didn't have a chance to raise venture money or to IPO."*
> *__Entrepreneur B__: "We all knew that there was a bubble but we didn't know when it would burst. I screwed up by not having plans B and C. If I had it to do*

over again, plan B would have had us laying off employees and cutting low margin customers so that we would have a profitable business. For plan C I would have started raising money early when I knew I could get it, rather than holding out so long because I wanted to increase valuation and lower the team's dilution.

Entrepreneur A has not held himself accountable: he blames his company's demise on the market and scared venture-capitalists. The market *did* crash and venture capitalists *did* get skittish but these were not the real causes of his company's failure. Another huge error this entrepreneur has made is that, by not holding himself accountable, he hasn't learned anything. If he hasn't learned anything, then what are his odds of succeeding next time? He should be a cereal entrepreneur rather than a serial entrepreneur.

Entrepreneur B has thought about what happened, and about what she might have done differently, in very specific terms. She has held herself accountable and has thought about what she would do differently next time. She also knows that the market went bad but she recognizes that it was her responsibility to anticipate that.

Of these two entrepreneurs, which do you think would be more likely to succeed in the next venture?

Self-assurance

Starting a company is hard and a lot of what you will hear is how, statistically, you are likely to fail. If this is your first company, then you don't know what you don't know. Without self-assurance and confidence you will eat yourself from the inside out, your team will not follow you, and investors and customers will prefer to wait and see.

> *If this is your first company, then you don't know what you don't know.*

Consider these questions:

➤ In business settings, are you comfortable asking about things that come up that you don't understand—during the meeting and in front of others?

➤ Are you comfortable asking subordinates to teach you something that you don't know?

➤ Are you comfortable in virtually any setting?

➤ Do you have a sense of humor?

➤ Can you walk away from a business deal that you don't like?

➤ Can you fire someone without reservation once you've made your decision?

"Yes" is a good answer to any of these.

Humility

Humility is tied closely to self-assurance—the yin to its yang. If you are confident, it is easy to have humility. Humility is also the absence of arrogance. Humility allows you to learn through your whole life and in every situation. It allows you to admit errors and hold yourself accountable. It allows you to set realistic expectations and meet them. And it allows you to ask for help.

Consider:

➤ Are your competitors all bozos?

➤ Are you the smartest person at your company?

➤ In your industry?

If your answers to these three questions are "yes", then you might want to work on your humility.

Humility allows you to get help and thereby avoid mistakes. It also allows you to recognize your mistakes and then learn honestly from them. This, in turn, makes it possible to make mistakes without damaging your company; which allows you to move quickly, thereby risking mistakes, and learn; which is more beneficial than mistake avoidance. In other words, humility helps you to succeed and isn't just about making you a nicer person—that's a nice side-benefit though.

Sense of Urgency

There is so much to do and you can't afford to ponder too long. Better to take aim and pull the trigger. If you miss the target then assess why, adjust your aim and fire again.

A good entrepreneur pulls the trigger, gets results and then re-aims.

This sense of urgency means that when an issue arises you deal with it quickly. This should not be the same as shooting from the hip or making a purely emotional decision. It means moving in the right direction by taking *action*. You have written a long sales-letter and a short sales-letter and you can either read books about the proper length for a sales letter or simply send out 1,000 of each and see what the results are. The latter can be done immediately. A good entrepreneur pulls the trigger, gets results and then re-aims.

Having a sense of urgency means that you drive yourself and others to near-term deadlines. This as opposed to excessive planning and consensus building, which can take too much time and not really improve the probability of getting the desired result. Urgency means that when you close a meeting you are clear on what actions are to be taken, by whom and—most important to this section—when. Companies and entrepreneurs with senses of urgency attract people who want to maximize their effectiveness.

Without a sense of urgency, a company tends to drift sideways. The days are full but not much seems to get done. Pretty soon, a year has gone by, there's no product, no sales and no money.

Drive

You may go for long periods of time with little or no positive feedback. Your life will become consumed by your company if you want to be successful. Do you have the drive to make your enterprise a success? To work on or think about your opportunity nearly all the time? To keep going when you are told that it is hopeless, that you are unqualified, that there is no market or that your widget will never work?

> *Drive is a great thing if you have done your homework and are satisfied that your opportunity is both feasible and a good fit for you. That is not the same as doggedly pursuing something that really does not have a market or that requires a change in the laws of physics to become reality. Thousand-dollar satellite-phones that do not work well in buildings or cities and are the size and weight of bricks are not good bets when you have to pay for launching a satellite constellation. Perpetual motion machines are frowned on by investors and the patent office.*

If you are reading this book and interested in starting your own company, then you are probably in the 90th percentile or above in intelligence—so what? That means that there are millions of people in the US alone who are at least as smart as you are—and they are all obsessed with succeeding. I have seen many first-time entrepreneurs assume that they will be able to substitute their intelligence for drive. Perhaps they think they will set up a clever process or system and that the checks will just show up. It rarely works that way—there are just too many smart people with the same information available to them for success to be easy.

We all have different ways of maximizing our efficiencies, and the more experienced you are the less nose-to-the-grindstone time you will have to apply. Still you need to be obsessed with making your company succeed. You need to think about it on the toilet and in the car and mull over what you are going to achieve tomorrow, what went wrong today and what you can learn from it. Do you want to live like this or do you want to walk out the door at 5:00 PM and not think about work until 8:00 the next morning? The latter is just not a reasonable expectation for the first-time entrepreneur.

So, in terms of time, what does it mean to be driven? Does it mean 12 hours a day seven days per week? For people with relatively little experience, it could be close to that in the first year or so. Moreover, if your primary contribution is as an individual contributor rather than as a leader and/or manager, you will probably spend more time with your nose to the grindstone. If you are more experienced or have an opportunity that you can largely lead and/or manage, then it will take considerably less time in the office. In this latter case it is probably best not to work 90-hour workweeks. Except for very rare exceptions, too much focus-time can make you stale, unimaginative and myopic; i.e. there is a danger that you will lose the big-picture context and the ability to be resourceful on a continuous basis. So, by "driven" I mean that it will occasionally take very long days of 12 and sometimes 24 hours. But, more importantly, I mean that you can't stop thinking about your venture and how you can do better tomorrow than you did today.

> *Here is an example of drive: I know one CEO who had started several successful companies. She is probably the most determined entrepreneur I have ever seen. Evidence of this was clear in her response to the venture capitalist that would not commit to a meeting. She threatened to take her sleeping bag to their offices and camp outside their door until they met with her. She also let them know that she would call the local television news departments with this great story. She got the meeting.*

Agility

By "agility", I mean the ability to change course in an instant; the ability to embrace changes in your external environment and turn them to your advantage. In starting a company, you will make some bad decisions that you need to correct quickly. Most individual bad-decisions are not fatal on their own. The key is quickly correcting the bad decisions. Your external environment will change in ways that you don't or can't anticipate. You need to recognize those changes quickly and adapt to take them into account in a way that benefits your company.

To assess your agility, consider these questions:

➤ In previous jobs, did you do what you were told or did you adapt what you did *as* you took action and learned?

> How many jobs have you had?

> In how many places have you lived?

> Do you like traveling in countries where the people do not speak your native tongue?

> Have your ideas about the company you might start changed since you first developed them and have they responded to feedback from others?

> If you have ever been laid off or fired, were you excited with the new possibilities?

Entrepreneurial Characteristics in Action

In this section I will describe a few types of entrepreneurs and some of the pros and cons that often come with the "type". No doubt you are much more complex than any one of these types and you will almost certainly see parts of yourself in multiple descriptions. The purpose of this section is to start you thinking about what kind of entrepreneur you are. This will allow you to screen opportunities more efficiently for their fit with your preferences and your strengths. It will also help in determining what your plan with the company will be—how long you stay, in what capacity and with what corporate culture. For example, if you are an inventor, then you probably should not start an accounting consultancy. If you are an accountant, then you should probably not try to start biotechnology company.

Finally, this section is also about expectation setting. As you start to see yourself as a composite of these types, you will recognize, through this section, *Over and over again—it's team, management team, people.* some of the challenges that you might face. You will also see that every type needs other people to balance it in order to achieve success. Over and over again—it's team, management team, people.

The types of entrepreneurs we'll consider are:

> the technologist-entrepreneur

> the inventor-entrepreneur

> the marketer-entrepreneur

> the lifestyle-entrepreneur

> the phase-entrepreneur

> the manager-entrepreneur

> the leader-entrepreneur

> the traditionalist-entrepreneur

> the gold-digger-entrepreneur.

Technologist

Pure technologists like to create new technologies. They like the act of doing technology as an individual contributor. They are often introverted. If you are a technologist, then you will probably need to find people to help you with business, sales, marketing and finance. You are probably smart and can apply yourself in any of these areas but it is not your unique ability, and although it may initially be an interesting intellectual challenge, you will tire quickly of spending time in these areas. Moreover, spending time in these areas is probably not going to be where you add the most value to the company.

As a technologist, you may well find that it is best that you move on after the first one to three years of the company. As the company grows, it will become more process-oriented and your market or product may mature to the point at which technology becomes less important than operational excellence or sales and marketing. You would do well to recognize this as it occurs and do the right thing for your company's success rather than trying to make the company adapt to your comfort zone. Your dilemma is whether to stay or to move on to your next venture.

If you stay with the company, then how do you maximize the value created from your technology contributions? Or, more fundamentally, do you necessarily want to maximize the value? If you excel at technology and want to stay with the company, then you will likely have to give up some power to other people to maximize value created within the company. This frees you to focus on technology, but, depending on your preferences, you might find it unbearable to give up control and/or decision-making authority. Many technologists have chosen to restrain their companies and their value creation because they, or they and the founders, prefer the lifestyle of a small-technology company. The choice is yours but there usually is a tradeoff here.

Leaving the company and starting your "new new-thing" may be the best way for you to create lifetime value. In this scenario, you stay with the company until you can replace yourself and bring in a new management-team. You stay to foster the transition and then you go and start from scratch again with one of those great ideas that is burning inside you. This can get tricky, however.

The New New Thing: A Silicon Valley Story by Michael Lewis (W. W. Norton & Company, Inc., New York, New York, 2000) is a book that tells the story of Jim Clark, who is probably the best-known example of an entrepreneur who moves from one opportunity to the next. Great book.

Leaving a company before it can be harvested comes with some hazards. If you don't have a board seat, then the company may get into trouble without your knowing about it or being able to influence it. Depending on the changes that occur in subsequent years and the people involved as management team and investors, you could find yourself in court to try to collect what you are owed. Or worse, the company could drag you into court to try preemptively to take away your right to collect. Most of my dealings with investors and entrepreneurs have been great, but, given the large numbers of companies with which I have worked I have seen some pretty low behavior. While these shenanigans are not the norm, they are certainly not unusual either. And, as your attorney will most likely verify, a clear and iron-clad legal agreement is better than the alternative, but if someone is determined not to pay you then you will have to fight hard—regardless of how right you are in either a legal or moral sense.

> *A company that I worked with was recently acquired and the founder went to work for the acquiring company. He quickly tired of working for a large, bureaucratic company and took a closer look at the agreements he signed in anticipation of leaving to go back to his true love—starting companies. It was then that he found that there was a provision for a mandatory buy-back of his shares from the parent company if he left—at book value. At a rapidly growing, private company book value can easily be zero or negative. The net result is that if he leaves he might end up with zilch for his options. His attorney either missed this in reviewing the documents or failed to tell his client—yes, both are bad things.*

There are countless ways in which you can get screwed after you leave a company. This is where a good attorney can help—but make sure you understand what you are getting into from the start. And, as with most everything in business, the people involved make it or break it—if the people stink, don't expect the deal to smell any better.

... the people involved make it or break it—if the people stink, don't expect the deal to smell any better.

Having just said that you may get screwed by the time you can collect any money, it's time to point out that many technologists overvalue their contributions early on in companies' lives. By the time there is profit or an exit from a technology company the technology will have been only a minor part of that success. There is a lot of execution that has to happen between technology development or prototype and the time when you get some liquidity. You should expect to get heavily diluted in your ownership by the time you cash out. This is as it should be and you should expect nothing different. As will be explained below, dilution is a good thing so long as the increased value of your percentage of the company is more after the dilutive event that decreased your percentage.

Business and money are like water—they flow around obstacles, move downhill and pick the path of least resistance.

This paragraph is really important—I have seen countless technologists bury their technology by making it too expensive (overvalued) or making themselves too hard to deal with. Business and money are like water—they flow around obstacles, move downhill and pick the path of least resistance. If you won't talk to an investor or customer without a multi-page non-disclosure agreement (NDA), then they will probably find someone else. There are plenty of cool technologies and brilliant technologists. In fact, if you have a great technology-idea, you can almost bet that someone else has already thought of it. The real question is who takes the risk out of it and makes it available to customers in the right package.

> *One of the things you notice after you have seen hundreds of business plans and proposals is that many people who don't know each other hatch nearly identical ideas at the same time. This should not be too surprising since you are not the only smart person in your field and there are other people who have the same access to information as you. The differentiators are that some people do, while others talk, some people execute better and occasionally there is some luck to it.*

Many technologists love the activity of creating a technology so much that they neglect results and refuse to submit to deadlines, claiming that innovation can't be planned. And perhaps it can't, but customers won't buy effort alone either. If this is a problem for you, I recommend that you allow someone else to manage you. This will relieve you of that burden so that you can take a technology leadership role rather than a management role.

Inventor

There is often huge overlap between technologists and inventors. The differences are important, however, in determining how entrepreneurs create value and where they fit into companies. Inventors may or may not be good engineers. Technologists may be good engineers and excel at incremental innovation but not make the leaps in innovation that inventors might.

Inventors can create substantial value for companies. Innovation can create a barrier to entry by competitors and ensure high margins for the company for far into the future. However, invention is usually only a first step on a very long path to realizing a financial return.

If you are an inventor, you can create intellectual property, technology, products or companies. It is hard to make money out of creating intellectual property alone. Looked at from the perspective of a licensee, acquirer or investor, there is usually substantial remaining risk in creating a product and bringing it to market. Potential customers also have to make "make or buy" decisions. They may decide that they have the in-house expertise to invent around your patent.

Imagine that you have your patent and you get a meeting with the VP of Business Development at a major consumer-electronics company. You are savvy enough to make sure that all the right people will be at the meeting so that they can take the next step in acquiring your invention. Their CTO will be there along with several engineers and a product manager who manages the product line that would use your invention. You give your presentation and they ask a lot of questions and are clearly excited about what your technology could do to enhance their competitive position and increase their market. As soon as you leave the room at the end of the meeting, some version of the following dialogue will occur:

VP of Business Development: Well, what do you think?

Product Manager: If we can get this developed by the Super-Gizmo product launch scheduled for 2005 we might double our sales and increase our gross margin by 50%.

CTO (Looks at engineer): Can you invent around these patents?

Engineer: Yeah, I think so. We have been looking at this problem and although his solution was damn clever I think we could invent around his patents with three months' effort.

CTO (Looks at the engineers): How long would it take you to do this from scratch?

Engineer: Two and a half years to pre-production prototypes. Ten, maybe twelve man-years.

> **VP of Business Development:** *So if we acquire this invention we basically save three months development time and keep him from selling the invention to a competitor.*
> **CTO:** *That's the way it sounds to me.*
> **VP of Business Development:** *So its only real value is to keep it out of our competitors hands since even if we acquire it there is still significant risk that some problem will arise during the development process?*
> **CTO:** *That's right.*
> **Product Manager:** *We only have one competitor right now for this product and they have never licensed any technology from an outside inventor. I would love to see them blocked from this technology but it probably isn't worth much to us.*
>
> *Some weeks later: After letting the inventor sweat and not returning five of his voicemails, the VP of Business Development calls the inventor and offers the inventor 2% royalty on any Super Gizmo that they build using the invention, provided that the Super Gizmo Co. has a four-year exclusive on the invention. He gives the inventor three days to decide.*
> *No cash. No risk to Super-Gizmo Co. No guarantees that they will even use the invention.*

You may think that your patent is very broad—and it may be in a *legal* sense. However, just as you were clever enough to figure out how to do something new, there may well be others who are clever enough to solve the same customer-problem in a different way that does not infringe your intellectual property. The fact that you have not thought of something does not make it unthinkable.

Consider:

➤ If you license the technology, how are you going to anticipate all future events so that you receive the royalties you are due?

➤ How will you charge? A percentage of revenue? A flat fee per unit?

➤ What if the licensee modularizes her offerings or sells the part on which you are owed royalty at a loss so that your percent of revenue is decreased? And so on …

➤ Then, given the complexity of policing your return, will you have the resources to wage a legal battle with a large and well-capitalized licensee?

Go through the worst-case scenario at least once—attorneys are great at this and can be a big help here.

If you create a technology, then much of what was said above about the technologist applies. By developing the technology to prototype, you will have taken most of the pure-technology risk out of the equation for an acquirer. However, that acquirer still needs to figure out how to take the prototype to production—which is often considerably harder than most people imagine. The acquirer is also faced with market-risk as people might not purchase the final product in the numbers that you would like.

It bears repeating here that you should not overvalue what you have because you may end up owning 100% of zero dollars. Be cognizant of all the effort and risk that remains in taking your innovation successfully to market.

... you should not overvalue what you have because you may end up owning 100% of zero dollars.

Another consideration to cover here is that selling your invention at any stage will not be a slam-dunk and sales may not be your forte. Build it and they will not come. Are you prepared to ferret your way into big companies and convince them to buy something that is very risky and difficult to explain? Are you prepared to have most of your queries go unanswered? To have most people say "No". It is seldom that buyers will find you by passive means such as Web sites, Internet listings with brokers, trade-shows or ads in relevant publications. This usually only leads to many hucksters contacting you to dip into your pocket with no assurance of results. In other words, you are going to have to identify customers and pick up the phone to call them or find someone who can do this for you.

Marketer

Marketers and salespeople often make awesome entrepreneurs. Having insight into customer behavior and the instinct to sell effectively to those customers are arts of real benefit to a startup.

If you are a marketer you can bring a customer perspective to the company. The product or service will then be targeted at sets of customers for whom the pain is acute and clearly relieved by the product. You will be comfortable picking up the phone and getting people excited about what you are doing when it is fully developed in your mind, but only partially developed by engineering. You will then find it easier to recruit manufacturers, vendors, marketing partners and customer commitments.

You may get excited about a technology because you see the potential in it. You see the products that can be created, the customers who will buy and how you will reach them. One of the things you need to find out, however, is whether the technology can do all of the things you so clearly envision. Technology often seems a magical thing to marketers and it is easy to think that you just need to find clever people to bridge the gap between the current state of the art and your vision. People have been sent to the moon after all—how hard could it be to make this little gizmo you imagine?

The dangers here are that you recruit a technologist who tells you what you want to hear instead of what is really possible. It may be hard for you to determine the difference between a sycophant and someone with a can-do attitude. Even if you find the very best technologist, you may be perpetually disappointed that the technology does not meet the perfection of your vision. If this is a concern for you, you should find some technical people with interests in your success and no reason to BS you. Use them to ground you and help you match technology, technologist and market opportunity.

Another potential hazard is that your company might be too slow to get a product out because the product never meets the standard you have set in your own mind.

> *In one instance, a company that was run by a marketer abandoned a perfectly good product to do a "better", but technically more risky, product, which never got out the door. The initial product had customer commitments and was mere months from passing production verification tests. This product, however, was short of the one envisioned by the CEO. The product envisioned by the CEO would in fact have been better but it did not yet exist. In the best of worlds it would have taken a year or more to complete the engineering and go through the manufacturing and development phases. It turned out that this was not the best of worlds, and years later the product was still not achieving financially viable production-yields. In the end, with production and sales years behind schedule, the company ran out of money. The value of that initial product was never realized and the capital structure made it impossible to turn back.*

Lifestyle

All types of opportunities suggest lifestyle choices. However, I use the word "lifestyle" here in a way that many investors and entrepreneurs use it. While people who start companies end up with the companies impacting on their lifestyles, so-called "lifestyle entrepreneurs" are attracted to entrepreneurship because of how it affects their lives *outside* of work.

> *Classic examples are parents who want to choose their own hours, pick their children up from school or take the kids to the park at noon on a weekday. Another example is the woodworker that wants to move to the country and have a sufficiency livelihood and self-supporting hobby.*

These types of businesses aren't the ticket to riches and creating high-growth companies. They are fine businesses and they bring a lot of intangible or "soft" return on investment to the entrepreneurs that found them. These businesses can also create a lot of value for their customers and employees.

However, I would never invest in one because the entrepreneur has too many priorities ahead of maximizing the success of the company, and it is only through that maximization that an investor will see a tangible return on investment. If you are going to take this route, be aware that you will be on your own even more than most entrepreneurs.

"Away-from" versus "towards" motivation

This is an appropriate place for the obligatory paragraphs on "away-from" versus "towards" motivation. People who do things as a result of an away-from motivation are trying to avoid some negative experience, or they are doing the new thing out of fear of something else. People who are toward motivated are looking to the future that they want to create or the vision that they are pursuing. We all have some of both types of motivation depending on events, our current situation and the progress of our lives. I am overwhelmingly toward motivated but I'm certain that I could make an exception if a bear chased me.

I bring this up here because I have found that in people who start lifestyle businesses there is often some "away-from" motivation at work. They no longer want to deal with office politics at those huge companies in smoggy, high-crime cities so they "want to move out to the country and paint the mailbox blue". There is nothing at all wrong with this. The catch is that, maybe, after getting away from cubicle-hells in those smoggy cities, they will, having settled into their lifestyle businesses, miss the interactions and stimulation that attracted them to the smoggy cities in the first place.

> *On the one hand, I have seen several technology-executives and engineers get fed up with some (perceived) negative aspects of the technology-*

development treadmill. After a year or so of pounding nails, landscaping or raising kids they are dying to mix it up again with a bunch of aggressive geeks.

On the other hand, I have a friend who was an aggressive Silicon Valley marketing-and-business development executive who loved the thrill of new-product launches. She tired of the tech-treadmill and purchased a coffee shop five minutes from her house in the Rocky Mountains. She frenetically remodeled, changed the branding, added product sales, added special events and aggressively promoted the new atmosphere of the shop. I was certain that she would miss high-tech as soon as the novelty wore off and she was running, rather than aggressively building, her business. I was totally wrong. It has now been going for almost two years and she absolutely loves her new lifestyle.

An old rock-climbing buddy resolved the lifestyle issue in a unique way. He was both a homebuilder and a freelance sound and film editor. But rather than do them both part-time, he would alternate years and totally immerse himself in one or the other. He would spend a year in Los Angeles editing, networking with film people and enjoying an LA social scene. The next year he would move to the mountains surrounding Lake Tahoe and build and sell a house while he enjoyed his mountain bike, climbing and backcountry skiing. He found both lifestyles very rewarding in their own ways and in appropriate doses.

Phase

The phase-entrepreneur may be especially well adapted to adding value in one phase or a few phases of a company's development. The example most relevant to this book is the startup entrepreneur. This entrepreneur loves the small company, the fast pace, the grand vision and the absence of bureaucracy. The long hours, the lack of specialized help, the lack of resources and the lack of security don't bother this entrepreneur in the least. If you are a startup entrepreneur and your life's mission is starting companies, then recognize this early on as it will save you a lot of pain. Prepare to leave after a period of time—think about recruiting a team to realize the full potential of the company you started, which in most cases will also be the route to maximizing your financial return. Communicate to your executive team and your investors that, while you want to stay involved with the company for a long time in an advisory or board role, you plan to leave once the company reaches a certain stage.

The figure below shows a typical company-development and the relative amount of time spent in each phase. Arrows indicate phases that continue indefinitely. Hardware takes longer than software, which takes longer than services, so you can adjust to your own situation.

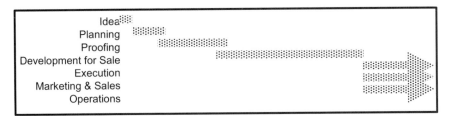

Not only do the activities of the company change over time, but also the cultural emphasis, as illustrated in the following sketch of the development of a technology-based product company and shown in the figure below it:

> *Initially there is an emphasis on innovation and a very loose environment within which people can innovate. There usually aren't many people in the company during the early phases—maybe five to fifteen. There is almost no process. There is also very little money because of few or no sales. As time goes on the technology or service is developed. This requires tracking of engineering changes, ensuring that market requirements are known and the product satisfies these requirements. That typically requires some process and some rules about how things will be done. As the product moves to manufacturing there are quality assurance processes. In moving to sales, marketing starts developing product brochures that have to be checked and submitted on deadline. Sales develops a funnel and is responsible for prospecting and sales— usually monitored at some level on a weekly basis. Pretty soon there is pressure to increase profit or decrease price to increase market share. Before you know it, engineering is trying to wring dollars, then quarters, then nickels out of the bill of materials and assembly costs.*

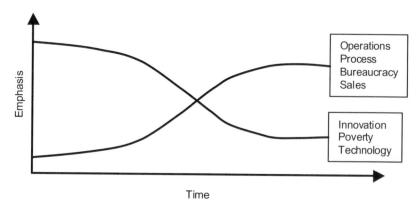

Too often startup entrepreneurs try to hang on too long and investors replace them or the other members of executive teams find it necessary to remove them. It is not pleasant, it is not good for the company and it is not good for the entrepreneur. You chose your team for a reason and you may want to work with the team members again in the future. I have seen many companies struggle through this phase and waste months to a year making this unnecessarily painful transition.

Worse off of course are the companies that never make this transition when it is necessary and let people hang on to avoid conflict. These companies become zombies—the walking dead.

Manager

"Companies do not run out of money, they run out of management." Manager-entrepreneurs excel at goal setting, managing to results and organizing people and resources efficiently. These can be very valuable qualities in an early-stage company. Managers may not need too much background in the field of their companies—so-called "domain expertise"—since they can manage people well.

An investor once commented to me that "Companies don't run out of money, they run out of management"

If you are this type of entrepreneur, you may want to look for opportunities well suited to your managerial strengths. For example, buying a business that is underperforming because of poor management or doing a rollup within a fragmented and poorly managed industry. Other good fits are process-oriented companies. For example: business-process software, ERP software, chemical-based products and advanced manufacturing.

Often managers are not effective leaders. If you just manage, then your people will just do their jobs, which is usually not enough in a startup. To really break through you need your people *The first things withheld when a company is over-managed and under-led are creativity and resourcefulness.* inspired so that they are problem solving for the company at all hours, so that they are resourceful and creative. The first things withheld when a company is over-managed and under-led are creativity and resourcefulness. So you may need to develop your leadership skills or find a co-founder that can inspire the company. Someone with good marketing- and/or sales-instincts can be a great complement to a manager.

Another thing for managers to watch for is the temptation to over-plan. While you certainly need a plan you also need to recognize that you are charting new ground and that the map is not the territory. Be ready to adapt to new ideas and changing market-conditions or better information about your competitors or customers. If you are creating something new you may find the lack of predictability frustrating. When the VP of manufacturing tells you that his budget figures are plus or minus 30% and that the schedule could increase by one quarter you need to understand that he is giving you the best information he can.

Another concern with pure managers is that they can introduce too much process and control in the early stages. This can stifle innovation and employee initiative by taking power away from employees. It also can lead to the early departure of some of the people who will be key to your success through the startup phase and give you a sustainable advantage. It is all too easy to end up with people following the process and "checking off the boxes" but not really achieving quality results. In a later chapter I will discuss the role of process within companies.

Despite the concerns we've covered here, managers succeed as startup entrepreneurs every day and there are many types of opportunities that are especially well suited to them.

There is very strong demand for good managers within young companies, but usually after they get through some of the early phases described in this book. One approach you might consider is to find companies or investors that are starting to see the need for effective management. In this case, you can use the rest of this book as a guideline for vetting which companies are a good fit for you, rather than determining which opportunity you will start from scratch. The other way in which you might use this book in joining an under-managed company is to complete the preparatory work and planning that may need to be done—either for the first time or revisited.

Leader

Leadership is extremely valuable to all companies but to startups in particular. In contrast to large companies or even companies with more than a hundred people, leaders of startups will have daily or weekly contact with everyone in their companies. They will know the teams at a more personal level than the CEO of Proctor and Gamble. Your team will see your reaction to events as you ride the startup roller coaster. If you are a leader-entrepreneur, you will have good luck and bad and you will have failures and successes. Good leaders help their companies put both into perspective.

People do these things voluntarily with good leadership; no bonus or raise is large enough to motivate them in the same way.

With good leadership, people come to work excited about making a difference to their companies. When they are in the shower or are driving home, they think about how to move their companies forward. They struggle with new concepts to find innovative solutions. These are all things that you can't *buy*. People do these things voluntarily with good leadership; no bonus or raise is large enough to motivate them in the same way.

While the most visible leaders are extroverts, this is not a requirement. There are many examples of quiet leaders and there is evidence that these types of leaders are most effective. This unconventional view is expressed more completely in James Collins' description of "Level-5 leaders" in *Good to Great*. This book is more appropriate to large companies and its coverage is broader than leadership, but any startup entrepreneur can learn much from it.

The best leaders are self-assured but have humility—they are not arrogant or narcissistic. (There are some that believe that narcissistic leaders can excel—I differ, believing that these "leaders" invariably hit brick walls, especially with senior team-members who have seen the scenario play out before.)

Leaders need to know whether they have good management-skills—many don't. In the absence of good management you will have motivated and excited employees moving in too many directions, and not communicating well; they will get discouraged with the apparent disorganization.

To reach its potential your company will need a leader. The question is whether that leader is you or someone else. If it is you then you may need to learn some new skills and develop some new habits. Depending on your experience as a leader, you may find that you can't develop quickly enough to keep up with the demands of your company.

I could go on for a long while about leadership but I really wouldn't be improving on the many excellent books that exist on the topic. I highly recommend *The Five Temptations of a CEO* by Pat Lencioni. If you read only one book on leadership this should be the one. This is a short and elegant book that really gets to the essence of what makes great leaders—and what causes others to fail as leaders.

Traditionalist

For the purposes of this section, a traditional company is one which has an existing market, product and/or service. The interrelationships among the competitors, their customers and their suppliers are often well established and change slowly. A traditional entrepreneur is one who is attracted to such companies.

If you're this type of entrepreneur, in some ways you've got it easy in that you know that the product can be made and you know that it can be sold. The new question is how you can take customers from your competitors. If your strategy is to beat them on price by doing the same thing they are doing, then you may want to think more carefully. If several competitors are charging similar prices, there is probably a reason. It may be that the development or startup costs are larger than you think or the operating costs are larger than you estimate. Recheck your assumptions—don't ever assume that multiple competitors are stupid. You can still compete purely on price but "that's a hard life my friend" and you'd better be an obsessive manager-type to maintain your operational edge.

Still, many people have won at this game and it is at least as viable as any other startup, but think ahead about how you are going to excel in a traditional industry. If you have an innovative way of producing or can angle an exclusive relationship with a company that will enable this, then you might be able to compete on price and maintain margins. For example: suppose you have identified a manufacturing process used in another industry and see how it can be applied to yours to obtain efficiencies. And suppose that you can get an exclusive relationship with the companies that possess this process.

You also might be able to use a different strategy or business model. Your competitors in a traditional industry will often react too slowly to counter your moves or be too arrogant to see the benefits of your approach. Be resourceful and find a lever with which you can roll your competitor over the cliff.

There are plenty of other ways to compete: marketing, sales, existing relationships, key accounts and so on. But this is a tough road that requires extreme tenacity and the ability to multi-task.

You may have noticed that the notion of competing comes up frequently in this section. That is because, in a traditional industry there are established players that you need to beat in order to get business. Unlike creating a new market, this is not a win-win game—every customer you get is one that you take from a competitor or keep the competitor from acquiring.

A big question you should ask yourself if you think this is your entrepreneurial type regards your willingness to try to beat competitors day after day:

➤ Can you frame the way in which you compete so that it is enjoyable?

Consider the following quotation:

> *"One simple way to find challenges is to enter a competitive situation. Hence the great appeal of all games and sports that pit one person or team against another. In many ways, competition is a quick way of developing complexity: 'He who wrestles with us,' wrote Edmund Burke, 'strengthens our nerves and sharpens our skill. Our antagonist is our helper.' The challenges of competition can be stimulating and enjoyable. But when beating the opponent takes precedence in the mind over performing as well as possible, enjoyment tends to disappear. Competition is enjoyable only when it is a means to perfect one's skills; when it becomes an end in itself, it ceases to be fun".*—Mihaly Csikszentmihalyi in *Flow: The Psychology of Optimal Experience*, pg.50.

Gold-digger

There is nothing wrong or foul about wanting to make money. I hope that you do. There are few things as satisfying and as beneficial to society as creating value so great that people will work to earn money to buy it. But most of us are motivated by money only in its measure of value created, and it is the value created, the thrill of creating a market that had never existed, that are most rewarding. Gold-diggers are entrepreneurs who don't really care about the market they are in or the product or service that they sell—they just want to make money for the sake of making money.

Conventional wisdom claims that you need to be passionate about the business you are in. The notion that passion was a prerequisite to success became so over-hyped that I came to refer to it as the "P" word for awhile. A word whose meaning had been diluted by out-of-context overuse. While the "P" word may be politically correct it does not allow for the gold-digger's success. The conventional wisdom is half-right in that you need to be passionate—but a passion for making lots of money can be very motivating for some people.

If you are a gold-digger then you are probably not going to be too much fun for most people to work for, since most people are not primarily motivated by money. As far as possible, you will need to fill out your team with people who are also primarily motivated by money. For this reason, companies that succeed by outselling the competition are probably a good fit. Then you can recruit a sales-oriented team and good salespeople had better be motivated by money.

Timing

There will be times in your life when it is better than other times to be an entrepreneur. This section will take you through some considerations about timing. Some of these issues are out of your control (e.g. economic conditions), others you can change over time (e.g. financial preparation) and others will change over time (e.g. your kids will grow up).

Can You Afford to Fail?

This is the big downer section. As entrepreneurs we tend to be optimistic and certain that we can *make* success happen. This is the section in which to be a bit morose and do the worst case-analysis. Most people who take the time to do this actually feel better about embarking on risky ventures. They know the worst that can happen and they have established limits to what they will allow to happen. Doing this puts you back in control.

This is the section in which to be a bit morose and do the worst case-analysis.

Be hard nosed about this. The next two chapters will cover opportunity screening and planning. In these chapters you will get the background to estimate what it will take for you—the person with bills—to reach positive cash-flow. In some cases this will be proving the company and then getting investment, in other cases it will mean achieving sales and profitability.

Know how much you are willing to put at risk—will that amount bankrupt you and your family? Might you lose your house? What are your job prospects if you fail and have to look for a job? Your comfort zone today may be different than your comfort zone at some point in the future.

As a starting point, at least try to write down your limits, because this will help you to qualify opportunities. As you work through the next two chapters, you will be able to compare your opportunity to your limits and see if it is a good opportunity for you at this time. Establish your limits by:

➤ setting a number on how much money you will risk

➤ defining failure

➤ defining success

> ➤ putting a time limit on how long you will pursue an opportunity without success

> ➤ listing some events that will cause you to stop.

> *For example: I will invest no more than $100,000 of my own money. I will have failed if I have not sold more than $500,000 at the end of 24 months—if I can't do that then this is not a viable business. If 3G wireless technology has not rolled out in three major US markets within two years then I will have been too early and will continue only with outside investment.*

This list will vary considerably among readers. If you are twenty-two and have no assets to lose, maybe maxing out your credit cards and signing for debt personally is not too scary. If you have two kids in college and a mortgage, even if you have considerable savings, you might decide to make sure that you keep enough saved to get your kids through college and make six months of house payments.

Does Your Support Make This the Right Time?

In most cases this means your spouse or partner, but it could mean friends or relatives without whose support you might strain an important relationship, or without whose support you might find this journey terribly difficult. If all you are hearing at home is how risky this is and that you might lose all of your savings, it will be hard to go after your opportunity with the gusto it requires.

One of the themes of this book is to set some realistic expectations about starting a company for the (would-be) entrepreneur. In talking to a partner before starting this journey in earnest, have them read this book, or highlight some passages that you think will give them some insight into this process. This is still no replacement for living it but it will put things in perspective and counter some of the startup romanticism that is rampant in magazines, newspapers and books. As a general rule people don't like it when reality does not match their expectations—it is better to set the expectations appropriately from the start.

You will have rough times, tough decisions to make and occasionally incredible stress. You will also have the joy of making something happen…

You will have rough times, tough decisions to make and occasionally incredible stress. You will also have the joy of making something happen or bringing into existence a product or service that people love so much that they will voluntarily pay for it. It's important that both you and your partner or spouse are ready for the rough stuff as well as the fun stuff.

Do Your Skills Make This the Right Time?

You will need some skills to be successful and these skills should match the needs of the company. That's pointing out the obvious but you should do some skill assessment to determine whether you are really ready to start a company. I don't mean taking a battery of tests but simply recognizing what you are good at. If you have a lot of experience, then starting a company may be a natural continuation of the skills you already use on a daily basis and may even take for granted. For example, if you are in sales, then you will probably leverage your sales and marketing skills to develop strategy, sell the product, raise money, entice vendors to work with your company and recruit top-notch people and keep them motivated.

If you are a recent graduate, then it probably makes sense to be a little more explicit and list the skills and background you will bring to the company. Just having the idea for a product or service is a very small part of the battle. Most great ideas never make it to market.

The real value is created in *doing* the business, which requires skills and some of the characteristics discussed above. Human beings can generate ideas out of nothing but chemical energy, so there is infinite capacity for idea generation on this planet. The real challenge is knowing which of the ideas are good and then bringing the people and skills to bear in evolving those ideas into something that is valuable to a customer.

Does Your Financial Preparation Make This the Right Time?

In 99.99% of the cases entrepreneurs will need some money to start their companies. In many cases, it doesn't take all that much but do you have enough? The planning stage—in which you get very specific about how much money it will take—will yield much of the information you need to answer this question. You will also need to think about your living expenses during a time when you may have little or no income.

If you don't have any financial resources, then you probably aren't ready to start your company. However, if you are prepared in all other ways, this is the perfect time to build your resources, maybe gain some additional experience and use that time for planning and vetting opportunities so that when you are ready to pull the trigger you bag your game.

Does Your Commitment Make This the Right Time?

You take the first step on any adventure when you explore, gather information, plan and dream. You take the second step when you fully commit and leave the past behind. In real terms, the second step may mean quitting your job, investing all of your savings, borrowing against the appreciation of your house, borrowing from a friend or relative or moving into lower-cost housing. This second step is when things certainly become more interesting and when they get more fun for the right type of person. You won't be able to blame your boss when things don't work out. You won't be able to advance your career through internal politics.

You will be able to see and count the fruits of your labors, creativity, leadership skills and intelligence.

You will be able to see and count the fruits of your labors, creativity, leadership skills and intelligence. You will have that special satisfaction that comes with making something happen.

You may or may not be ready to make a full commitment and there is nothing wrong with that. As with financial preparation, use the time between now and commitment to work through the rest of this book and consider numerous opportunities until you find the opportunity that you are ready to commit to fully.

Do External Conditions Make This the Right Time?

There are many things that are out of your control but which time will change. You may be waiting for an enabling technology to come to fruition so that, combining it with yours, you can create a market.

> *One example of this is the companies that would take advantage of the high bandwidth that will be offered by 3G wireless. As 3G is delayed by years from the projections of two to four years ago, some companies that had expected 3G to arrive by now are folding up. These companies and their investors would have done well to look more objectively at external conditions.*

Your opportunity may require substantial, up-front capital-costs and years of development. Such an opportunity only makes sense if investors can see a significant return on their large investment. If this can only be achieved through an IPO then it will be difficult to raise money for your company when the market for IPOs is soft.

If external conditions are not favorable for the opportunity you have in mind then:

➤ do it anyway at considerable and perhaps imprudent risk

➤ find another opportunity that better matches current conditions

➤ wait for external conditions to change. This last option is virtually impossible for most entrepreneurs since most have an extreme sense of urgency.

Myths

In this section we'll consider some of the myths that have developed about startups, and discuss how these might relate to you and your opportunity.

Myth 1: It's All About Technology

It's not. Having read many hundreds of plans and having worked in technology and venture capital, I have seen a lot of cool technologies. Technology is important but only insofar as it can become the initial nucleus for value creation within a company. The technology must lead to a product or service that people will buy. It must be manufacturable at a cost low enough for it to make sense for people to buy it. So many technologies meet a real and compelling need but are too expensive to cause customers to change their behavior.

There are and will be many technologies that never get to market because they do not meet this fundamental criterion.

The fundamental principle for private companies is that they create so much value for their customers that their customers will voluntarily give them their money in exchange for their products or services. There are and will be many technologies that never get to market because they do not meet this fundamental criterion.

Myth 2: Build It and They Will Come

They won't. You need to sell and market your product or service. Your company cannot be solely a technology company. Be prepared to do what it takes to entice customers to buy from you. This is often a trigger point for a big change in a startup, where the focus turns from development to sales and marketing. This is often where there is a lot of internal turmoil, including terminations and resignations.

Myth 3: I Have a Chicken-and-Egg Problem

This myth has many variations, but the most common is that people think they need a product before they can close sales and they need to close sales before they can get financing and they need financing before they can develop the product. It is true that, often, they may not have anything to deliver without financing. However, you can sell things that you don't have—without lying. Also, although it is a long shot these days, you can sometimes get funding without sales. Figure out what you can do to triangulate on sales, development and financing.

Myth 4: All I Need Is Money

I have heard this hundreds of times. I usually reply with one of the following questions:

> ➢ What would you do with the money if you got it? Often, this uncovers the fact that entrepreneurs don't have plans and cannot articulate value propositions. They think that, magically, they will mix money with their ideas and their brilliant minds and be successful.

> ➢ Do you have a management team? Often this uncovers that entrepreneurs cannot attract other talented people—perhaps for good reason. It also uncovers that there is no "company" to invest in and nobody to execute on the plans, even if the plans existed.

> ➢ How would investors get returns on their investments? This question can uncover that this has not been thought through or that entrepreneurs are unclear about the market and how to sell into it. They just "know it'll be big, really big." Investors are unlikely to invest in entrepreneurial telepathy.

Investors are unlikely to invest in entrepreneurial telepathy.

Summary

By reading this chapter you will have examined yourself and hopefully built up a picture of yourself and your unique abilities. The discussion of entrepreneur types was intended to help you see yourself, probably in several of them, and, through that, to alert you to some of the things you may want to consider and to look at the trajectory you might take.

The section on characteristics will have dashed any hopes you may have harbored that being a first-born child will ensure your success. But, more importantly, it will have made it clear that you yourself—rather than any accident of birth—determine your success.

In reviewing the characteristics of successful entrepreneurs, you may have found that you were strong in all of those areas or that you either need to develop in some areas or find a team member who compliments you by providing the characteristics you lack.

This reflection on yourself will be useful throughout this book as you evaluate and prepare to start your opportunity. You, the entrepreneur, will be the driving force for your company. You deserve an opportunity that you can succeed at—both financially and through the enjoyment it provides.

3. SCREEN LIKE AN INVESTOR

One of the most valuable skills I learned in getting a Ph.D. in physics was how to do back-of-the-envelope calculations instead of going into excruciating detail. This skill extends well into the investment and business world, where one seldom has enough time or information to do a detailed analysis anyway. It is especially valuable in doing what-if scenarios, such as in looking at numerous opportunities to get a quick sense of whether they are worth pursuing before you spend the time to work through the details.

You will be investing your time—a valuable chunk of your life—in this endeavor. You will be doing this to the exclusion of other ventures—to the exclusion of a steady job where someone else takes the risk and has the headaches. And you will probably be investing at least some of your own money. So, before you make all of these considerable investments in an opportunity, you should learn to think like an investor.

This chapter will give you some tools, perspective and background so that you can vet opportunities in much the same way as an investor would. Moreover, as an investor does, we will give an opportunity a first pass in a very short time. In what follows, I will list a number of things that you should think about before you invest yourself further in a given opportunity. Try to work through each of them as best you can in less than ten minutes per item on the list. If you absolutely don't know then just put a question mark or list a few things that you need to do to address the issues, and move on to the next.

Customer Pain

As an investor, you should look carefully at the customer pain that is being relieved by your product or service and whether customers know that they have these pains. In the absence of customer pain you have a considerably harder sell for your product or service— *In the absence of customer pain you have a considerably harder sell for your product or service—your customer currently has no compelling reason to buy.* your customer currently has no compelling reason to buy. Without customer pain you will not only need to educate your customers about your benefits you will also have to convince them that they really need this product. It can be done (think lava-lamp and pet rock) but you have just made your job a lot harder and your investment a lot riskier.

Consider:

➢ What is your customer's pain?

> What problem do you solve for your customers?

> What do you enable them to do that they would like to do and currently cannot?

Write one or two sentences that capture this pain.

Customer

You aren't likely to hit something you don't aim at. So, if you don't know your customers, then you aren't likely to sell to them in the absence of an infinitely large marketing-and-sales budget. Think of a few types of customer and be specific about who they are; e.g. single fathers in Boston with children between the ages of 4 and 11.

You should be able to list the requirements of each type of customer; i.e. what your product or service must provide in order that the customer will buy it. Some examples are: price, memory, warranty, speed, weight, number of pixels and so on. Also, you should have some idea how you will reach each customer and convince the customer to buy. In other words, how you will market to the customer. Some examples are: leverage membership in the American Medical Association, use an email list from your partner's consulting company, get a review in the *Anchovies-Today* trade journal.

Make a list of customers and a description no longer than one sentence for each. Then create a matrix; i.e. a table that has customers listed along the left-hand column. In the second column list the market requirements and in the third column list how you will reach these customers. You can do this also in a text format, but using a table will require you to really get at the meat and make your entries brief.

Look over your matrix and take a crack at ordering it based on who the "best" customers are. What "best" means will vary for every opportunity and this is where some intuition and domain expertise can be of great help. Some considerations: ease of reach, level of pain or need, ability to buy and size of segment.

Benefits

Whether you work with products or services, know your benefits. How will your customer benefit from your product or service. At the end of the day, customers care little about the features. If you buy floor cleaner, you care a lot about whether it will clean your floor and you probably care about whether it gives off toxic fumes but you probably couldn't care less what emulsifier was used in it.

Examples of benefits are: faster weight-loss, increased sales, lower costs, lower energy-costs, higher speed, more square footage, more comfortable and greater comprehension.

List your product or service benefits. This list doesn't have to be long, it just has to be the right list. Many entrepreneurs try to stretch the list but this only dilutes the impact of the one to five most important benefits. In many cases the benefits will not immediately come to mind but the features will. From the features you can make a two-column table in which the features are listed in the left column and the benefits associated with each feature appear in the right-hand cell next to each feature.

Consider:

➢ How do your benefits match up to the market requirements of the previous section?

➢ And, from that, which customer segments will benefit most from your product or service?

Value Proposition

Now that you know your customer and your benefits, imagine what you would say in making a sale to each of your customer types. Consider:

➢ What is the value that the customer receives?

➢ Can you put a number on it as in savings per year or length of the payback period?

➢ Can you talk about problems that you know customers know that they have?

Try to write your one- or two-paragraph pitch in terms of benefits and value to the customer. Then extract from that the one- or two-sentence value-proposition.

Competitive Risk

Regardless of what you might think at first blush, you do have competitors. If you can't find them you aren't looking hard enough. You will appear naïve to a

Regardless of what you might think at first blush, you do have competitors.

professional investor if you claim to not have any competitors.

There may not be anyone currently doing exactly what you plan to do. Nonetheless, there is probably someone meeting the same or similar need in another way. Before I bought a Palm Pilot I would scribble my schedule on an index card and stuff it in my pocket—try to match that for price, battery life and image contrast. There are also plenty of people who could become competitors if you prove to them, through *your* success, that there is a market.

You will probably be creating a product or service that allows people to do something they already do but in a significantly better way.

> *The first spreadsheet-program for personal computers allowed people to do their books on a computer, rather than by hand entry into journals, followed by manual calculations with an adding machine larger than most laptop computers.*

These are great markets by the way. You don't need to change people's behavior fundamentally or make huge assumptions about what they want to do. You do have to make sure that your way is a significant improvement in some way—by an order of magnitude or better.

So list your competitors and then group them. One group might be direct competitors that sell what you plan to sell. Another group will probably include indirect competitors—those whose product serves largely the same purpose for your customer. Yet another group will be those who could easily enter your market with the same or similar products.

Now create another table. The left-hand column should contain the classes of competitors. The second column should show the list of problems with their products. The third column should list their product benefits. You can now use this competitive matrix to compare the benefits of what you are proposing. In some cases you might wish to mix in features supporting benefits so that you can compare on a quantitative basis.

Market Risk

This is a very broad topic and includes the size of the market as well as the likelihood that it will accept your product or service. If the market already exists and is relatively static, then you can probably get pretty good numbers on its projected size for a few years hence. If the market is growing quickly, or does not yet exist, then the market data will be harder to come by and of questionable value.

You can obtain data from one of the large market-research firms such as Gartner, Forrester or IDC. However, this is usually expensive and, unless you know exactly what you are getting beforehand, you might find that it isn't terribly useful. In the first place, you can usually find the macro numbers in articles or by doing some Internet sleuthing. By the "macro numbers", I mean, for example, the dollar value of ERP software sold. Secondly, you need to make sure that the micro numbers are "sliced" in a way that you can use. If the data is segmented by application and customer set, do these applications and customers relate to your specific product or service? Thirdly, and most importantly, try to determine whether you will obtain any insights through the data—if it merely verifies the obvious or what you could compute on a napkin, then it is not of much use.

Some investors will insist on seeing this sort of data. However, many investors are as skeptical as I am of projections for emerging markets and don't put too much emphasis on them. Current market-size is another kettle of fish, however—this is dealing with objective reality rather than opinions on top of trends. You should always try to obtain the numbers for current market-size.

You should always try to obtain the numbers for current market-size.

So, now you have an estimate of the market size. It's time to sanity-check your opportunity.

Consider:

➢   If you got 1% of the market would it be a business worth pursuing?

➢   What if you got 5%?

If you need to get above 5% of the market to have a good opportunity, then you are getting into risky territory. While the market leaders often take more than 5% of the market, there are only a couple of them. Wouldn't it by nice to know that even though you intend to be the market leader, if you fall short, you will still have a viable business? Or that you will be an attractive acquisition target for one of the leaders?

> *Some markets are so obviously huge that you and any investor know that your sales will be limited by execution. I once worked on starting a company that would sell into the mobile-handset market. While we did our homework and had the market size, we pointed out in the business plan that sales would not be market constrained and left it at that without any of the percentage analysis. Investors appreciated that we didn't bother with silly projections based on percentages of such an enormous market.*

Market sizes for new applications of products or new services are very hard to get. You can commission studies by market-research firms. Some firms, e.g. Gartner, do great work—others would barely get a C in an undergraduate marketing-course. If you do decide to go to this expense, then ask to see some of their previous work—*especially* if it is outdated and you can see how accurate they were. Ask yourself these questions:

➤ If I were in the business to which the report applied, would I be able to take action based on the data?

➤ Would I believe the data and be willing to bet my company on it?

➤ Was the data supported with some reasoning and were the assumptions clearly stated?

Another way to get market data is to find markets that are similar to your proposed one and use those as the basis for an estimate of your market. Still another way is to call analysts and marketing executives that might have some intuition in your market and ask them what they would estimate. Recognize that they are just giving you an educated guess—but it's better than flying blind or using just your own, less informed, guess.

Management Team

Right now the management team may comprise you alone—hence the importance of the previous chapter in helping you to learn enough about yourself and what it takes for you to be able to "screen" yourself. Then, if you are truly prepared to take the leap, you can pick an opportunity that best matches your strengths—which is covered in more detail near the end of this chapter.

If your company is going to grow, and certainly if you will be accepting outside funding, you will need to recruit and develop a management team. The opportunity and the skill sets of the people you have will determine the functions that belong at this level. They typically include: finance, corporate development, sales, marketing, operations, manufacturing, engineering and technology.

Make a short list of the functions that are critical to revenue and success. Now try to put a few names of qualified people next to each function.

If there is no one that you know who is qualified, resist the temptation to hire a friend simply because of this. This can be disastrous.

I know of one "startup" that had a CEO who was in his sixties. Nothing wrong with that, but he hired several people for his management team whom he had either known for decades or had had as his childhood friends. The longevity of their relationship was their sole qualification. The head of marketing was a lifelong corporate-attorney and the head of research and development was a lifelong government-employee who had retired as a project manager. This was an extreme case of hiring unqualified friends and it ended badly. They started fighting and backbiting almost immediately. They looked high and low for where to put the blame for their inability to execute. Investors saw through this and wisely chose to buy stock in the Brooklyn Bridge as a lower-risk option.

Having cautioned that you should be careful in hiring friends, hiring *qualified* people that you have known or worked with for a long time is ideal. It is extremely common for the initial management-team to fire one or several of its members within the first year. In my experience, this occurs 33% to 50% of the time. This is usually a long, drawn out process that slows the forward progress of the company for weeks if not months. If you have worked with the members of your team, the risk of this happening is greatly decreased. If you have not worked with the people that you have in mind, then start spending time with them for as long as possible before you and they need to commit. This will allow you to determine their competency, their strengths and weaknesses, their goals and preferences. With this information and a shared vision, you at least have the information to create a win for them individually as well as for the company. This is probably the second best way of mitigating the risk of early management-discord.

If you don't have people in mind for the functions you need to cover, figure out how you will find them. People are *People are going to be your key to success.* going to be your key to success. If you need to hire someone whom you only know from references and a few meetings, think carefully about any friction between you that concerns you.

> *I remember at one company in which one of the executives and the CEO were constantly at each other's throats. They were both solid, A-level players but there was no way that they could work together—they were too culturally dissimilar. The CEO finally asked the executive to resign and he went on to found and run another company that he made more successful than the one from which he was forced to resign.*

Just because people are good, this does not mean that they will be effective members of *your* management team.

If you are going to get investment from sophisticated investors, then be aware that they are going to look very closely at you and your management team. Usually firstly as individuals, secondly as a team and thirdly in terms of your backgrounds. Investors know that it is hard to find people with the right personal characteristics and motivations—in a team with good interpersonal chemistry and synergies.

Your management team should be complementary. If you are a leader with limited management skills then one of your team should be a manager with startup experience. If you are an introverted technologist then find a leader who shares your vision—preferably someone you trust to be CEO of your baby. If your background is marketing and sales, find someone who excels at operations and at looking inward at the company.

Consensus is great when it happens and it will probably happen most of the time—but when it doesn't, someone needs to make the tough call...When everyone makes decisions, no one makes decisions.

In structuring your management team and talking to your team in the company-formation stages, at some point you must determine who is the boss. When you are talking about your new venture in your living room with a beer in your hand, it will be tempting to think that you are such good friends that you will always be able to get to consensus. Consensus is great when it happens and it will probably happen most of the time—but when it doesn't, someone needs to make the tough call. Moreover, after that person makes the tough call, everyone else needs to be fully supportive of the decision. When everyone makes decisions, no one makes decisions.

So, after all this thinking about functions, individuals and interpersonal relationships, do you have a team or not? How many people remain on your list? Next to the list of people, list the top three to ten strengths of each of those people. Also list areas in which they are especially weak or that concern you.

Consider:

➢ Is the team complementary?

➢ Will the mix of Sally's sarcasm and Joe's sensitivity be the cause of World War III?

➢ Among your team, would you have the top-ten characteristics of the previous chapter?

➢ Is your team ready to start when you are?

➢ If you are investing, are they also willing to invest or take low salaries until profitability is reached?

Manufacturing

This section obviously is relevant only to companies that make things, rather than to retailers, brokers or service companies. Even though manufacturing may be far down the road—as long as several years for some startups—it should be considered as part of your opportunity vetting.

In a typical trajectory there is early technology-development that then results in a crude experiment or lab prototype that works only occasionally. The tendency then is to think "I've proven that it works—how hard could it be to make them by the millions?" The next step is typically the making of some hand-built prototypes that work nearly all of the time and are used in demonstrations to customers and investors and sold on a limited basis. The tendency then is to think "I just need to give this prototype to manufacturing and we ought to be able to ship in volume within six months—after all, all of the hard work is done." The next step is all too often a huge delay in getting the product ready for market. This happens for two broad reasons:

➢ the company cannot adapt to the cultural and organizational demands of manufacturing

➢ the widget turns out to be really difficult to make at a low-enough cost to meet market demands.

Let's deal first with the organizational issues. Up through the prototype stages, the company will not have needed much process or management. There was probably a "just do it" attitude, which is extremely valuable to a startup. As the company approaches the more process-oriented task of manufacturing, you need to begin to manage and coordinate groups of people, vendors, assemblers and testing companies.

You will need to specify very clearly what you are making. You will have to have drawings and version control so that you can have tooling made for production or to pass on to the *... you can't afford to iterate too many times when each iterative cycle is both costly and takes months.* fabrication house. When everything is done in-house or in small quantities, it is more efficient just to iteratively refine the hardware. But when you are about to invest many months and hundreds of thousands or millions of dollars, you can't afford to iterate too many times when each iterative cycle is both costly and takes months. So now you have to have documentation for everything that goes to manufacturing and you need to control the documents—this is usually a big change within a company that has an early-stage product.

The other organizational issue that might arise is that you might not have the right people to get you effectively to manufacturing: the people who may not be as creative as the technologists and marketing visionaries but who have the management skills and experience to plan and implement processes. You will learn to love these people when you see what a good manager can do.

It's important to keep your balance during this transition. I have seen some very good companies anticipate this needed change. That was good. But then they fouled it up by swinging too far in the direction of control and process throughout the company. Those companies hired operations or manufacturing people who tried to apply rigorous process across the company and then "enforce" those rigorous processes. The net result was that some of the most effective and innovative people left and the company was paralyzed, caught up in the activity of shuffling papers around rather than getting things done (activity instead of results). Then, because the manufacturing managers did not have the problem-solving skills to work through the process issues, the company lost over two years in getting to market.

The message, again, is hire someone or ally with a company that can help you with these details and thousands more.

When trying to estimate the difficulty of making your widget, try to find people with similar manufacturing-issues and talk to them. You aren't going to find the most important information in books, so you will have to get it from people in similar fields by allying with them, networking with them and hiring them. Making ten or a hundred of something is very different than making tens or hundreds of thousands *per month*. And subsidizing low yields with venture capital can go on only so long. If there is process, it needs to be nailed down and documented. You need quality-assurance processes and people. You need to pack and ship the stuff. Financially, you need to fund inventory or get your vendors to do so. You need to plan for returns in terms of process as well as adjusting your financial projections. You need to focus relentlessly on your bill of material costs and shave pennies, dimes and dollars. You need to have a warranty policy. You need to do production-verification testing. The message, again, is hire someone or ally with a company that can help you with these details and thousands more.

In thinking through your opportunities, list the risks to manufacturing and ways to deal with each of them. Again, this is an area in which you can learn much by talking to people because your assumptions may not be correct.

I remember a company that had a Taiwanese manufacturing-partner for assembly. They had found a material that they needed in Japan. A reasonable person could be forgiven for assuming that they would ship the material to Taiwan and the Taiwanese assembler would include the material in their assembly process. In talking to someone who had dealt with this issue at another company, we discovered that the Taiwanese company would not qualify the Japanese vendor and that we would have to find another source for the material. This cost the company months, but if we had never asked the person with the right experience, it could have been a fatal setback for the company.

A big question with which many technology companies struggle is whether to outsource the manufacturing. In theory this sounds great. If you can make it work, then you don't have to deal with quite as severe a cultural shift. You do not need to recruit as many operations people. You can focus on some core technical- and/or marketing-competencies.

However, initially you will not have much clout with manufacturers. This has two drawbacks:

➢ it is then difficult to line up multiple manufacturing-partners; i.e. to hedge your risk

➢ it is difficult to get mind share within the manufacturing company when you are not a significant source of revenue for them.

As a result you can end up captive to a manufacturing company that is not as committed as you would like—or as you would need— it to be. If you have just one partner and they are not performing, you have little negotiating leverage. No matter what, it is unlikely that your manufacturing partner will ever be as committed to your success as you are.

No matter what, it is unlikely that your manufacturing partner will ever be as committed to your success as you are.

A middle path to take is to do low-volume manufacturing- and process-development in-house and outsource volume manufacturing. You become your own backup plan of last resort. It also usually makes sense to start with two partners and split the volume between them. When you reach a volume at which you have realized most economies of scale, then you recruit third, and sometimes fourth, sources. This means that if one of them burns down or becomes uncooperative, you can shift the volume to the other manufacturers with little or no disruption in supply to your customers.

Consider these questions:

➢ Who will make the widget?

➢ What are the key components?

➢ What special process will need to be developed to be successful?

➢ Is there existing infrastructure somewhere for making this or will you have to invest in it yourself?

➢ Who will carry inventory?

➢ Are there any import/export issues?

➢ Are shipping costs excessive?

➢ Can you envision a manufacturing process that results in the highest yields and the lowest cost in damaged goods in process?

➢ Are there any environmental issues associated with the chemicals and materials you will use?

These questions should get your mind working. However, to put some structure on this, grab a pencil and sketch a manufacturing process with all of the necessary steps. Show inputs and outputs so that you can identify sources or determine where they are lacking.

Regulatory and "Approval" Risk

Consider:

➢ Is there any regulatory risk?

➢ Do you need a government body or other organization to test and bless your product, manufacturing process, service, or material-handling capabilities?

➢ If you are exporting, do other countries require approvals?

➢ Will retailers or other customers require certain approvals?

When someone at a regulatory organization tells you that everything that you need to know is on the Web site or in publication 444-x.6, don't believe it.

If the answers to any of these questions is "Yes", then you need to anticipate delays and plan to meet the requirements of the organizations requiring approvals. This is another area in which you will benefit from getting experienced help by hiring a company to take you through it or a consultant who is familiar with the process. There will be so many subtle things to know regarding how to jump through these hoops that cannot be found in a book or on a Web site. When someone at a regulatory organization tells you that everything that you need to know is on the Web site or in publication 444-x.6, don't believe it. That Web site may not tell you that if you staple the pink copy to the yellow copy at the top, left corner it will be returned to you (3 months later) so that you can staple it at the top, right corner and resubmit it. Obviously I am making this up but we all have our horror stories about organizations that don't need to provide a product or service for which people will *voluntarily* pay—think post office or planning department.

The quick way to get some idea of the approvals you might need is to simply look on the labels and stickers of similar or competing products.

Technical Risk

Technical risk is one of the two scariest risks in starting a company—the other is market risk. This is because there may be some fundamental reason

You have to put the technology to use in a real product to test this.

why the technology won't work in the way you anticipate and there is just no way to know without jumping in and meeting the risk head-on. You can go only so far with research and planning, and with equations running around in your head. You have to put the technology to use in a real product to test this. While physics and engineering are well-developed fields and the basic laws and theories are well known—there are always new ideas and ways of doing things, else they couldn't give away one of those Nobel prizes every year.

Many real-world products and technologies have aspects to them that are just too difficult to model. Perhaps it will turn out that the secret goo you're thinking of cannot be processed in a way that removes the goo-affinity ion and, as a result, the goo turns purple when exposed to air. In many cases that you could model, neither you nor anyone else should be completely comfortable until the technology has been tested.

> *I remember that for years in the early work with displays and spatial light modulators, ions would move across the liquid crystal filling and permanent patterns would appear in the image. At the time, no one seemed to be able to figure out what really caused this, although there were certainly plenty of theories. At the time, the best companies had to figure out processes and techniques that eliminated the problem without even understanding the underlying cause. Not very satisfying from a technical perspective but exactly what needed to be done at the time.*

If you have a technology background, then seek out people who will tell you if your technology won't work. There are plenty of smart people out there who will happily find every possible reason why it will not work or express what would concern them about it. University researchers are excellent sources for this because they like the intellectual challenge and exposure to novel technology. They are also not as likely to steal your idea as some others might be.

Compile a list of all the risky technical challenges—limit it to ten items for the purposes of this section. For every item in your list, describe how you can quickly and inexpensively prove that the technology will *not* work because of that risk. If there turns out to be a fundamental problem, it is better to find this out early and change courses or change opportunity. Then also describe briefly how you might quickly and inexpensively prove that that risk is *not* a limitation. Order this list from most to least risky. That is the preferred order in which you should test your technology.

Financial Risk

In the simplest terms, this is the risk that you will run out of money. This can happen for many reasons. The most obvious is that you can't raise enough money fast enough. You could also be planning to finance this opportunity yourself and could have underestimated expenses or the sales ramp. You could find that the vendor who was going to finance your inventory has gone out of business and no other vendors are willing to finance inventory.

Assess what your top one to three financial risks are and what your backup plan is in case they occur. Write this down.

Financial Needs

To get a rough estimate of your financial needs you can start by looking at what similar companies have spent on startup. If a similar company received venture capital, then you can find out how much it raised to get to various stages of development. If it has not been funded with venture capital, then you can try calling the CEOs of non-competitive companies that are similar. While you may not get an exact number, you can probably get some ballpark numbers—answers such as: less than a million dollars, between three and four million dollars, in the low hundreds of thousands. If *your* estimate is far different from what your research indicates then what are you doing differently that explains the difference?

The other way to get a rough number is to do some back-of-the-envelope planning. Consider these questions:

➤ How many people will you need when and what will they cost?

➤ What is your infrastructure cost (rent, furniture, etc.)?

➤ What major equipment will you need and when?

➢ What are the means and costs of marketing?

➢ How far out are sales?

Once you have your number, double it. When doing a rough calculation you will almost certainly leave things out, while you are unlikely to include anything that is unnecessary. Remember that this is a sanity check and you will be refining these numbers later.

Leaving Your Current Employer

For the opportunity that you are considering, will you be violating any agreements that you have with your current or past employers? Some of these agreements may keep you from competing with the company in the area of this opportunity. They might restrict you from recruiting some of your management team or contacting key-customers. These restrictions could be direct, for example if you are trying to hire someone with whom you currently work or to contact a current customer. Or, the restrictions might pass through from another agreement; for example you have an agreement with your employer that requires you to honor your customers' non-disclosure agreements.

Consider these questions:

➢ If your opportunity depends on technology, is that technology clearly owned by you?

➢ Did you develop that technology purely on your own time?

➢ What does your agreement with your employer say? If there is any ambiguity, then have an attorney double-check your agreements with your employer.

➢ How can you and your employer benefit from your departure?

➢ Could your employer become an investor, vendor or customer?

➢ You have the relationship: how can you use it and leave your current employer on good terms?

Pricing

Pricing is more art than science. You are trying to maximize profit and therefore the tradeoff between price and *Pricing is more art than science.* volume that will yield the greatest overall profit to the company. There is no magic formula for this and you will probably have to experiment with coupons, discounts and other promotions in order to fine-tune pricing. However, if there is a competing product or service that meets the same customer-need, a good starting point is to use your competitors' pricing as a guide. If your secret sauce is better than your competitor's, then you have to decide whether you should charge more for it or charge nearly the same price and use the better value-proposition to build market share.

The other ballpark number you need is the amount for which you *must* sell it in order to make a profit. This is best done by working through the financial spreadsheets. However, to get a rough estimate, start with your bill of materials cost and figure that your breakeven price to the end user would be between three and six times your bill of materials costs, depending on the margin-stacking through your channels.

So, out of this section you have three ballpark numbers:

➢ What your competitors charge or what it costs to do the same thing now. Call that "A".

➢ What you must charge to make a profit. Call that "B".

➢ What you think you can price at; i.e. what the market will bear. Call that "C".

If it is true that B<C<A, then, within these approximations, your pricing will allow you to sell and make a profit. If C>A then you need to think carefully about how you will justify this higher price to your customers. If you have an entrenched competitor then you need to change customer perceptions and behavior, which is especially unattractive if they have to pay more as well.

Bill of Materials Costs

In simple cases, this is just a matter of having a design and making a lot of phone calls to estimate cost at various production-volumes. So, if you have a design, the exercise is clear: list the bill of materials (BoM) in a spreadsheet, make some phone calls and list the prices next to the items. Be careful not to overlook seemingly inconsequential items.

> *Here is a hardware example. It is tempting to omit the price of connectors and cables, deeming them minor perturbations on your bill of materials, but you will often find that they are among the most expensive components. This is where experience is a big help—so that you know what the gotchas are and don't become a prisoner of your assumptions.*

If you don't have a design, which is often the case for an "idea-stage" opportunity, you need to find alternative ways of estimating cost. This is where an experienced engineer who has taken a similar product to production can be a great help. You may not know exactly the components you will use but you can probably get within a factor of two with your own experience or that of a good engineer.

You will also want to compare your estimated costs with either the BoM costs or prices of products of similar complexity. It may be hard for you to get cost numbers for direct comparison, so you will usually have to work from retail or wholesale price. This is mostly a sanity check that will tell you if you are off by an order of magnitude.

There are some estimation programs that do not require very specific design information to work out an estimate. They tend to work best for very large projects and mature technologies. The reason why they work best on large projects is that they are based on statistical averages, and the larger your project (think airplane), the more likely it is to behave in an average way. The smaller your project (think optical switch), the more likely it is to be exceptional and for the models to fail.

Doing these back-of-the-envelope exercises can save you a lot of time and money.

> *I helped start a company that had an interesting technology for searching for images in large databases. The technology looked as though it would work and would be far faster than existing approaches. We did some back-of-the-envelope calculations and found that it would cost between fifty cents and a dollar to do a single search—this estimate took about ten minutes. Clearly that was not a viable technology-solution for advertising-supported search-engines (banner ads sell for a fraction of a penny). In other words the bill of materials costs, added to facilities fixed-costs, was greater than the price that could be charged. As a result of this back-of-the-envelope exercise we "re-invented" the technology so that, although the quality of the searches would be lower, the price would be lower by two or three orders of magnitude.*

The result of this section, combined with that of the section on pricing, will enable you to determine whether you can make your widget or provide your service at a competitive price. There are many very cool technologies that never find their way into the general market because they can't be made inexpensively enough.

Vertical vs. Horizontal Markets

While horizontal markets are where the potential volume is, it may be hard to break into these markets if your product or service is not yet widely accepted.

In these early vertical markets, customers may put up with some usability shortcomings that would not be permissible in a broader market.

A common strategy is to start in vertical markets, where the application of the technology is narrow and compelling. In these early vertical markets, customers may put up with some usability shortcomings that would not be permissible in a broader market. They will do this because the benefits are so compelling.

> *Early supercomputers were incredibly complex to program compared to today's personal computers and workstations. But if you wanted to model where salt-domes and oil deposits were located, there was just no other way to do this a few decades ago. Moreover, by using these supercomputers to model before drilling, the exploration companies saved far more than it cost them to do the modeling. This was a great vertical market where the hassles and expense were overwhelmed by the benefits to the customer. But, to reach the horizontal markets, computers had to reach much lower price per performance and much greater ease-of-use before engineers could generally use workstations and PCs.*

For the same reason that vertical markets are willing to put up with complexity and product flaws, they are also usually willing to pay a higher price than would a general consumer. By starting in vertical markets, you can buy yourself time to work out manufacturing processes and operational inefficiencies.

Vertical markets buy you time and experience to refine your product for the horizontal market.

Vertical markets buy you time and experience to refine your product for the horizontal market. No matter how many focus groups and market studies you do, there is nothing like real experience with real customers spending real money. Moreover, by having some product in use over a period of time, you will get data that is usually unobtainable through relatively short-term market-studies.

Vertical markets often also have some marketing, sales and distribution efficiencies. To reach customers in a horizontal market, you may need to buy television advertising and develop extensive retail-channels. But for a vertical market you may need just a sales force that sells directly to the customer. You may be able to ship directly from your warehouse or assembly area to the customer. In most cases, vertical markets are business-to-business markets, so you may be able to leverage a key relationship with a large company into thousands of unit sales rather than needing to sell to each of those thousands of end-users.

Consider these questions:

➢ What is your rollout strategy?

➢ Do you plan to start in vertical markets at first? Which ones?

➢ If you are going to try to go directly into a horizontal market, are you prepared for the operational risks?

➢ How will you scale quickly without taking intermediate steps?

This is more a food-for-thought section than an exercise. Vertical markets may not have the size or the sex-appeal of horizontal markets, but using them can be a lower-risk way to build a great company.

Unfair Advantage

This term is a bit of a misnomer. Unless you are into gunplay or blackmail, most any advantage you have is perfectly "fair". Still the term is common and it typically means the following, either separately or in combination:

➢ Hard or impossible for competitors to copy or work around. This could be technology, relationships, process or many other things.

➢ Greatly surpasses existing ways of serving a need for customers. Think in terms of orders of magnitude: 10X improvement in productivity, 10X increase in performance, 10X faster, 10% of the cost or 10% of the downtime.

One of the reasons that unfair advantage is important is that the hurdle to making people change their behavior is high. And no matter what your opportunity is (other than buying an existing business), your customers will have to change their behavior. They will have to start buying from you instead of their current vendor. Or they will have to start buying a new product or service, change the ways that they currently do something or start doing something altogether new.

Another reason why unfair advantage is important is that it implies better-than-average future earnings. With an unfair advantage you can maintain higher margins and/or grow market share and sales at a high rate. Both the high margins and high growth-rates are critical to maintaining competitive advantage and maximizing the company's valuation. Increased earnings or increased valuation increase your and any investors' rate of return.

Consider the following:

➤ Describe your unfair advantage or where you think you can develop one.

➤ Can you quantify, in terms relevant to your customer, the magnitude of this unfair advantage?

➤ What will it take to know this is an unfair advantage; i.e. test-market results or proof of principle?

Natural Size

Most businesses have a natural size that is driven by up-front costs such as development or capital costs, or a natural size that is driven by

Other companies have a natural size because of their ability, or lack of ability, to scale.

the size of the market that can be reached economically or by marketing costs. Other companies have a natural size because of their ability, or lack of ability, to scale. Natural size, then, is driven by:

➤ development costs

➤ capital costs

➤ market size

➤ marketing costs

➤ scalability.

For opportunities in which the technology or development risk is considerable, the costs will be high. You will usually need to have an opportunity size that can pay back this development cost quickly and provide a good rate of return for investors. In other words, the market needs to be large and the rate of growth high. While you can bridge to the larger market through a vertical-market strategy that can sustain growth, the natural size will often require you to move past the vertical markets to larger, horizontal markets within one to three years of first sales.

The necessary capital-investment also determines what size the company needs to be to make sense.

> *If you want to be a fiber-optic carrier, then you have to be big. If you can't provide enough capacity and enough geographical diversity in that coverage, then there just isn't a compelling value-proposition for the customer. Likewise, satellite-TV and cable companies*

need to be large because of the infrastructure costs they incur. Another great example is semiconductor fabrication.

There are some companies that need to be small because of the market size for their product or service. There are many software and hardware products that serve very narrow, niche markets.

Panoramic-camera companies that produce ultrahigh-resolution images are good examples of this category. The market for this high resolution is very limited and hard to reach. Because there is a small market, the development costs must be kept low since they can't be amortized over large unit sales. If the development costs are low, then production costs are high because it takes money and time to wring cost out of a product and develop more advanced manufacturing systems. This forces the unit costs and unit prices to be high, which is totally consistent with a compelling niche-market. Moreover, because of the development and component costs, the product is very expensive. At roughly $5,000 to $10,000 per unit there just isn't a very large market, and a high volume within this market would result in a few hundred sales per year. A phenomenal success with this product would be to sell thousands per year. So this could be a multi-million-dollar business and provide a great income to the people that work for that company. Even though the sales are relatively small, it could also provide a great rate of return to the founders because little capital was needed to start it. Businesses whose scale is naturally small can be excellent opportunities if approached with their natural size in mind.

The advantage to this type of business is that you will not have to become as obsessed with operations as you will in a larger company. You will be able to know everyone in the company and be involved in all aspects. The disadvantage is that you may not be able to fully leverage your leadership skills, if that is your bent. Or you may find it boring after a while because, after the initial development and initial ramp in sales, the sales level off, as do the changes.

The classic example of a company that does not scale well is a service company. At best, the brand scales but the added value does not. Some service companies can get enough leverage from their brand and marketing to go big, but they are the exceptions. Successful examples of this type of company are KPMG and Price Waterhouse. They have developed well-known and respected brands and have many consultants over which to distribute their marketing costs. Still, if you look at the price to sales ratios of even successful service companies, they tend to be low compared to successful technology companies.

Most service companies do not scale well due to their lack of operating leverage. Of every dollar that comes in, a nearly fixed percentage has to go back out as costs. In service companies these are primarily labor costs, as shown in the figure below.

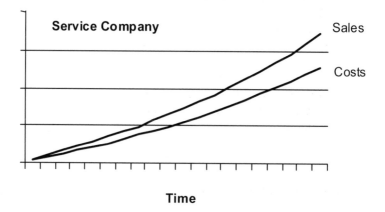

At the other end of the operating-leverage spectrum, software companies and some Internet companies scale very well. Hardware companies with good technology can also do well, though less so than software and Internet companies.

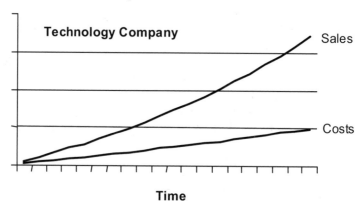

Let's take software as an example. After the product is fully developed, providing it to the customer is just a matter of printing manuals and compact disks—maybe a few dollars out of the hundreds or thousands of dollars that the consumer ultimately pays. In this case the percentage that goes out for every dollar that comes in as sales decreases with increased sales.

After all this talk about natural size, you should be wondering what happens if you get it wrong. Let's look at two examples:

BigWords.com sells college textbooks. They had considerable buzz during the Internet bubble— remember the orange coveralls. They also went through $70 million and a subsequent bankruptcy. One of the founders bought the company out of bankruptcy court for $50,000 and they are doing just fine now. The natural size of the business did not justify 250 employees and a $70 million investment.

EHobbies had $25 million in the bank, 175 employees, a 50,000 square-foot warehouse and a TV studio. They are now down to 7 employees and doing fine.

Of course, the natural size of the company should make sense for you. If you have a great idea for bringing optical fibers to homes all over Africa do *you* really want to build such a company? This has to be a huge company with thousands of employees and the company will be raising money for many years before it is profitable. Do you like raising money? If that is not what you want to do, then you may be able to find an alternative way of making money off your great idea and letting others build the grand company to further exploit it.

For each opportunity that you are considering, write a paragraph describing the size of the company at three and five years into the future. Size could include: number of employees, sales, number of locations and number of countries with offices. Then write a list of what you like about that vision and those aspects about which you have reservations. Finally, write a few bullet points on how you can either deal with your reservations, should they become problems, or structure your business so that you make a transition to something else before your reservations can even become issues.

Value Creation

Profitability and value creation are certainly linked but—depending on the type of opportunity—you might create one in greater portions than the other. Depending on the structure of the company, your plans for the future and whether you have outside investors, you might be able to take profits out of the company as they are created. While you can buy groceries, cars and houses with that money, the valuation of your company may not be increasing during that time. Value or valuation is what people will pay for in acquiring all or part of your company through an acquisition, merger or public offering.

Value or valuation is what people will pay for in acquiring all or part of your company through an acquisition, merger or public offering.

How you create long-term value is of particular concern if you are starting a traditional company or a service company. The owners of many such companies leave them with little value outside the hard assets and receivables. It is worth examining opportunities now for their potential for value creation.

The things that people will pay for are the same things that will be of value to your company as it continues operations—with or without you. They result in growth, market share, high gross-margin and competitive advantage. In simplest terms, valuation is the market's estimate of the present value of your future cash-flows. So what will contribute to this and what should you be looking for in an opportunity?

➢ **Management team:** This usually has the greatest impact on the continued success of the company and the return on investment. Without a good management team the potential value in most of the other items in this list will never be realized.

➢ **Intellectual property:** Whether patented or not, and which may include manufacturing processes, trade secrets or even proprietary methods.

➢ **Proprietary relationships:** If you have exclusive relationships with powerful distribution or manufacturing partners, these will have value in maintaining your competitive position.

➢ **Customers:** If you have customers who are generating profits for your company, they are worth something. Their value decreases considerably, however, if there is very high churn. For example, Web-development companies have little value in their customers because they work with a given customer for six months to a year and then the customer disappears or the maintenance-level relationship yields only a trickle of income.

➤ **Employees:** People's value partly depends on how tight the employment market is, but having a group of people who know what they are doing, work as a team and are efficient has value.

➤ **Growth rate:** As potential acquirers look at your company, they will pay more for a higher growth rate since it implies higher future-returns.

➤ **Sales:** Sales may have a value independent of the profit they generate. This is so especially in cases in which acquirers believe that, through some efficiencies, they can make those sales profitable or more profitable.

➤ **Strategic value:** This is the value that results from the whole being greater than the sum of its parts. For example, if an acquirer can cut your costs significantly by using his proprietary manufacturing capability; or if an acquirer can use her sales force to sell the product you make and thereby lower the cost of sales; or if you have some intellectual property that will increase the acquirer's margins. Or, last but not least, a competitor might put a value on taking you out of the marketplace as an independent entity.

One of the best books ever written on how companies are really valued is *The Gorilla Game: An Investor's Guide to Picking Winners in High Technology* by Geoffrey Moore, Paul Johnson and Tom Kippola (HarperCollins, New York, New York, 1998). It doesn't give you any formulas, as some of the more technical books on valuation do, but it lays down the basic philosophy and theory in a way unlike I have seen elsewhere. Although less quantitative than some books, it may nonetheless be more practical. In a later chapter we discuss some methods for estimating valuation.

Exit Strategy

Usually exit strategy pertains to the event that the company will go through that will allow investors to sell their equity. However, exit strategy can also mean *your* exit strategy—how you plan to get a return—not simply in "value" but in cash. You don't have to have an exit strategy if you plan on running the company at a profit for an extended period of time. Your exit may be to lock up the doors and walk away or die, whichever comes first. However, while some investors might be content with a share of profits, venture capitalists will insist on an event that creates a market for their shares—either an acquisition or an initial public offering (IPO).

During the bubble there were investors who would screen out opportunities that did not show an IPO as their exit strategy. However,

IPOs were rare during the bubble and are extremely rare now. Lately there have been only a few technology IPOs per quarter. This can be compared to the 400,000 or so businesses started in the US every year.

A major component of any exit strategy is how you can best position your company for an acquisition at top dollar. Usually, you will get top dollar from a strategic acquirer because, through acquiring your company, he will get greater value than someone who just purchases the company to run it as it is. In the eyes of the acquirer, the combined entity will have higher future cash-flow than would be the case if both companies continued in operating independently.

List a few ways that you can make your company more valuable to an acquirer over time. If you are doing enterprise software, perhaps you could engineer it to integrate seamlessly with Oracle products so that Oracle could simply acquire you. And you might also do the same for SAP so that not only do you have multiple potential acquirers but you will also have one company wanting to acquire to the *exclusion* of their competitor. And the best of all worlds occurs when you can actually get several companies to compete to acquire your company—this will drive the price as high as it can go.

Business Model

The business model is how you make money. Sometimes this is so obvious that it is hardly worth thinking about too much. After all, most businesses make stuff and sell it, or they buy stuff and resell it at a higher price.

Maybe you have or should have a less traditional business-model. Consider the following examples:

➢ Sell printers at a loss and make money on the ink cartridges (Hewlett Packard).

➢ Sell your game player at a loss and make money on the game cartridges (Sony).

➢ Give away downloadable software "players" whose marginal cost is zero so that everyone has one. Then sell the software needed to create content for the players (Adobe).

➢ Develop product designs and sell them near cost to product companies so that they can create a market and purchase your microdisplay component (Zight).

➢ Have people bid for a service that may or may not exist at your bid price. Let sellers sell perishable inventory near the last minute to the highest bidders. (Priceline.com)

Give this some thought for ten minutes or so and jot down the business models you might pursue.

Return on Investment (ROI)

You are taking risk and investing time and money in this venture. You should ask yourself whether you can get adequate return on your investment.

Assuming that you are at the pre-startup stage as you read this, a reasonable annual rate of return on your investment would be 75% or so. In terms of multiples you can use the following table:

Year	Cumulative Multiple
1	1.8
2	3.0
3	5.4
4	9.4
5	16

Note: To compute the multiple in some future year you can take the annual return, which we'll call "AR". Add one to it to get (1+AR), and raise that to a power equal to the future year in which you are interested; i.e. $(1+AR)^Y$, where "Y" is the number of years.

Alternatively, multiply (1+AR) by itself Y times. So for three years and a 65% return, the multiple would be $(1+0.65)*(1+0.65)*(1+0.65)=4.49$.

To do it justice, this evaluation really needs to wait until a later section in which you will dissect in detail the financial aspects of the opportunity. However, just to sanity check your opportunity, estimate your sales in year five as 3-5% of the market, multiply this by two to get a valuation. Most times the price-to-sales ratio of the S&P 500 is close to two. You might do better if you have a high growth-rate or worse in a private sale—remember this is very rough. Now, how much money and lost wages will you need to put into the company to get it rolling? You really need a budget to do this but you can probably guess well enough for this estimate. How much will you be able to take out of the company in profits prior to exit? Finally, how much of the company will you own when some liquidity (exit strategy) is realized? (You may have to sell some to investors and you will need some to attract and motivate top talent.)

To estimate the ROI, multiply the percent ownership by the valuation plus the cumulative profits that will be distributed over the first three years, and divide by the investment you will need to make. If this is less than five, then you may have a dog. If your intuition tells you that it should work, then maybe you don't have the right business-model or market—nonetheless this should ring an alarm bell. If it is better than five, then you still aren't out of the woods but a finer calculation will have to wait until you have done some detailed planning. (Since this is just an estimate, I have left many of the fine points out of this calculation.)

Return on investment is the ultimate arbiter of the value you have created…

Needless to say, return on investment is closely linked to creating value. If the return is not commensurate with the risk you are taking, then you aren't adding enough value, don't have a large enough market or don't have high enough growth. Return on investment is the ultimate arbiter of the value you have created and this is why this simple calculation is so important in deciding whether this business is worth doing.

There are other returns beyond money that you may wish to consider. However, if you think you are doing something of value to others, then a numerical calculation of ROI should be valid. People will pay for what they value.

J-curve or Pie-slicing

What is a J-curve market and how is it different from others? The simplest way to see it is to use the following figure. The lower line shows a market growing at a rate of 3% per year; i.e. at approximately the rate of inflation. The higher curve, the one that looks like a "J", shows market growth for an annual growth-rate of 50%. Of which market would you like to have 5% in year one?

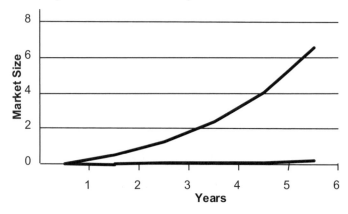

Note: Steeper "J-curves" would look more like the so-called "hockey stick," which refers to a similar phenomenon. In these markets, the early growth may come in relatively small, vertical markets until something happens to "cross the chasm" and the large, horizontal markets open up. The growth rate then shoots through the roof. The term "hockey stick" growth is common in startup and venture-capital circles and "J-curve" is nearly as common. "Crossing the chasm" is a phrase that was coined by and is the title of one of several excellent books by Geoffrey Moore.

Think back to the early days of cell phones. There was certainly competition but the market was growing so quickly that companies could focus on innovation and enabling the market, rather than on beating their competitors into the ground or extracting every penny from their vendors. The participants wanted the pie to grow as much or more than they wanted to take pie away from vendors and competitors.

The advantage of fixed-pie businesses is that you know there is a market.

However, some businesses are inherently zero-sum games, in which what you gain is someone else's loss, for example:

If you develop a new material that substitutes for paper, does not yellow and is a tenth of the cost to manufacture, then you have quite a product. However, every sheet of this paper you sell will be at the expense of traditional-paper companies.

If you open a chain of tire stores in your town, every tire you sell will be one that your competitor does not.

In J-curve markets you are faced with an ever-increasing pie and you can do well even if the relative size of your pie does not increase. In fixed-pie markets you have a certain-sized pie and you are fighting for the size of your slice.

The advantage of fixed-pie businesses is that you know there is a market. There is no question that people will buy a material that scatters light well and on which you can write, type or print; i.e. a replacement for paper.

The disadvantage is that you have to get people to change their behaviors. You have to take business away from entrenched competitors with recognized brand names, established distribution-

The advantage of the J-curve businesses is that you can ride the wave to a high upside.

channels, good cash-positions that may allow them to buy the market from you by lowering their price, and long-established relationships with customers, vendors, partners, the press and analysts.

The advantage of the J-curve businesses is that you can ride the wave to a high upside. In other words, if you had 10% of the cell-phone handset market in 1980, it would not have been a big deal. Today, however, that would represent around $50 million in sales. At the inception of such a market, everyone is trying to establish relationships and nobody has a brand in that product category. Companies often, however, have brand and relationships that they carry over from established business areas.

> *Extending the cell-phone handset example, Nokia, Motorola and Ericsson were major brands in other areas before cell phones existed.*

The disadvantage of a J-curve business is that, by definition, the current market-size is negligible. In other words, no one has yet proved market acceptance for the product. So-called "new-category products" are classic examples of products with these J-curve markets.

> *While Palm and Handspring are now relatively widely accepted, there were nearly two decades of failures in pen computing by new (GO Computer) and established (Apple Computer) companies before market acceptance took off.*

The J-curve businesses have a higher probability of total failure but also of phenomenal growth-rates and therefore, rates of return to investors. Almost universally, bigger-pie or J-curve markets are preferred by investors—especially if you can demonstrate *some* demand to mitigate the risk of loss.

Fit

By reading this chapter, you will have gained some insight into what is an attractive opportunity and what to expect in pursuing different types of opportunities. Hopefully, through the examples and discussion, you will also have gained some insight into the pros and cons of various types of opportunities with respect to yourself.

Consider these questions:

➢ After thinking through your opportunity and seeing both the upside and the risk more clearly, is it more attractive or less so?

➢ Having thought carefully about your own characteristic strengths, do they match the opportunity you are considering?

➤ You may have an opportunity that would be great for someone but may be a poor fit for you.

➤ Supposing that you have a good idea of what you want in one, three and five years, for how long will the opportunity you are considering fulfill that?

Summary

In this chapter, you have looked at your opportunity from many different angles and have read about what to expect. You have also read of the downstream ramifications of certain paths and types of opportunity.

It would be wonderful if I could claim that I had devised a special formula or algorithm that would prove whether you had a good opportunity on your hands. Unfortunately I can't. Moreover, I would be suspicious of anyone who claimed that they had.

Even though you might have a cool product or a technology that is far superior to any other, that doesn't mean you have a business.

> *I would love to have those cool windows in my house that I can switch off and on and that adjust their transmission based on internal temperature and solar irradiance—but I would only pay a couple thousand dollars extra for a house that had them, which is far less than what it would cost to provide them.*

By now you should have a sense of which of the opportunities among those under consideration are the more likely to succeed. You will also probably have found that there are some areas about which you just aren't sure and about which you either need to do some research or think more carefully; this is the subject of the next chapter.

If all the opportunities that you were considering now leave a lump in your throat when you think of investing your own money and time in them, then it is probably best to think up some others. You have little or nothing invested, so you don't even have to contend with a sunk-cost trap. Come up with another idea or find other people that have ideas and do something with them. Ideas are free and infinite—the number you come up with is limited only by you. If you are reading this book, then I suspect that you come up with far more ideas than you can *do*.

4. PLANNING

Planning takes time and effort and at the end of your planning phase you may decide that your opportunity is too risky or doesn't have the return that you expected. Hence the importance of the preceding chapters, which allowed you to do some vetting before expending much effort. If an opportunity has survived your quick vetting of the last chapter, then working on a plan is less likely to be a waste of time.

Why Planning?

This chapter's title is "Planning", rather than "How to Write a Business Plan", because it is the planning—not the physical document—that is important. Depending on your audience, your plan may be as simple as some draft "Notes to Self" or as complicated as a full-blown operational plan that lays out the first years of the company in excruciating detail.

... it is the planning—not the physical document—that is important.

There are certainly many businesses that were started with little or no planning, and that succeeded. So you may be wondering why you should even bother with a plan. There are several reasons to write a business plan:

➢ To make sure that you have a consistent and complete picture of what you are getting into and how you will succeed.

➢ To communicate internally, with customers and with vendors, about what your company is doing and why it will succeed.

➢ To inform investors why they should use their money to purchase a part of your company rather than to buy a certificate of deposit.

The most important reason is probably the first. The simple exercise of writing about your opportunity and how to turn it into a successful business will force you to find clarity and consistency in your thoughts. There is something about writing, as opposed to just thinking or talking, that makes the holes and lack of consistency more apparent. At the end of this planning phase, you will almost certainly have found some holes in your assumptions or information. That is not a reason to stop, but it does tell you where some of the land mines are and, if you choose to keep going, you need to remove the mines or navigate around them.

The simple exercise of writing about your opportunity and how to turn it into a successful business will force you to find clarity and consistency in your thoughts.

The plan is also a communication tool: a medium for communicating about your business to various stakeholders or potential stakeholders. It can be used to put your team on the same page, to convince customers to commit early, to convince vendors to take some risk and to entice busy service-providers such as lawyers, accountants and bankers. The more people believe in you and your business, the more they will help you.

One of the lessons learned during the bubble was that too many companies thought they were in the business of raising money rather than making money.

The primary reason that most people write a business plan is to obtain financing. If you need financing, this is a great use of your business plan. But, as I have said before, there is far more to a business than raising money. One of the lessons learned during the bubble was that too many companies thought they were in the business of raising money rather than making money.

The type of plan that you write for any of the three reasons should be nearly the same. As suggested in the previous chapter, while you write the plan it is worthwhile to think as a time-pressed investor would. Know the key points and make them quickly. Assume that your audience is both smart and sophisticated—don't tell them the history of the Internet or explain what return on investment means.

In the plan you should strive for clarity—most businesses are surprisingly simple when you finally know what is signal and what is noise. This is usually harder than it sounds. Resist the temptation to use a lot of marketing fluff—especially if the plan is for investors.

> *I remember one plan from several years ago that referred to an "absolutely unfathomable opportunity".*
>
> *Some words have been so over-used in business plans as to lose all meaning. There are two particular examples: the "R" word (revolutionary) and the "P" word (passion).*

The other hard part about writing a clear plan is that clarity implies that shorter is better. A good, non-operating, plan can be in the range of six to fifteen pages. Twenty pages is usually acceptable, but if you start to exceed that length, you should question whether you could make your points more clearly. Some people mistakenly believe that by giving someone a sixty-page document with appendices they will have shown that they have done their homework. What this usually shows instead is that they don't know what is really important or have not taken the trouble to figure that out. An operating plan is a different beast and can be quite long, because its whole purpose is to dive into painful details and to be used on a frequent basis—say weekly or monthly.

Be a business plan athlete. Notice how exceptional athletes make their sport look easy. If you or I tried what they make look effortless we would end up in hospital if not dead. This is because they do the preparation and training. They train out all unnecessary movement. They stay fully focused on their athletic activity during the event. Likewise, you should do the work on your plan so that it looks to your reader as though it was the easiest, most natural thing you could have done. You should have filtered out the clutter and irrelevance.

A key part of planning is working *A monkey can sell dollar* through the financials. A monkey can *bills for a quarter.* sell dollar bills for a quarter. You need to make sure that you are not doing the equivalent. The only way to do this is to work through the numbers. You can do some back-of-the-envelope-calculations, but this is the stage at which you need to dive into some detail. The best tool for this is, of course, a spreadsheet program. The financials should be done from the ground up, as this will force you to go through a lot of thinking about your assumptions and will shine light on both opportunities and weakness. It will give you intuition about that to which your business is sensitive; e.g. sales per salesperson, customer retention and so on—it's different for every business.

Finally, the financial spreadsheets become your dashboard as you operate the company. When you are deviating from schedule, projected sales or budgets there is nowhere to hide in the spreadsheets. And through the spreadsheets you know immediately what the impact will be on your company. The spreadsheets will also help you to figure out how to adapt to these deviations—to be a successful deviant. You can use top-down numbers to sanity-check your spreadsheets and the projections therein.

Something needs to be said about the purported short cuts that are for sale. There are some excellent books on writing business plans, but I think you will find that most of what they say is just common sense. Note that these books are often written for traditional and existing companies rather than startups with new products. I have not yet seen any software for writing a business plan that actually makes your task easier *and* results in an acceptable product. It is like cutting your own hair—people may be too polite to say anything, but they will notice if you have used this software. On the other hand I think you benefit significantly from the many outlines and sample business-plans you will find online for free.

You have already laid a lot of the groundwork for the plan by working through the previous chapters. By taking an investor perspective, you have acquired the basic information in many cases and know where the holes are in others. The plan will take the ballpark information from the previous chapter and put it into a coherent whole.

In writing the business plan, whether for investors or internal use or just to clear your thinking, be honest about what you don't know but need to find out. Any investor whom you might want will see the deficiencies, so you might as well come clean and demonstrate that you know what is important and that you have a path to clearing up the deficiency. If the plan is to be used internally to orient people within the company and communicate the company direction, your team will know where the weaknesses are and you will damage your credibility by not communicating them clearly and directly. If your plan is to increase your clarity of thought, being clear about deficiencies will help you figure out where to focus when starting up—which is covered in the following chapter.

In writing the business plan, whether for investors or internal use or just to clear your thinking, be honest about what you don't know but need to find out.

If You Get Stuck

You might find that you keep planning to plan but never get through it. Or you can get quite far into it but then you lose clarity and perspective. Or you might find that you can't seem to stop the iterative processes—that you seem to be getting further from a cogent strategy rather than closer to one.

There are three primary attack-points for getting started—if you are getting stuck in one direction then try another that is more your style:

➤ Outline

➤ Spreadsheets

➤ Presentation.

Outline

If you start writing with an outline, you are less likely to get stuck in the details of any one section. The outline is a list of the core themes that you want to cover and the key points that you want to make. Either as you are making this list or after you have made it, you can begin to organize the points into groupings that are interdependent or that thread the same theme. Write this as "Notes to self", without concern for grammar, spelling or completeness. It is enough if *you* know what you mean in the outline. An excellent, low-tech tool for doing outlines is outline-view in Microsoft Word. It allows you to drag text and headings up and down and therefore makes it easy to form sensible groupings and hierarchies.

Spreadsheets

The results of your spreadsheets will take up one to three pages in your plan because all that you will show is the summaries. But the spreadsheets can really help you to refine your thinking and complete your due-diligence. When you start trying to assemble sales projections you will have to face your assumptions and what you think you know. Ask:

➢ How many sales can a salesperson close per month?

➢ What is a typical time needed to close a sale?

➢ How many prospects can be generated per month?

➢ Are there seasonal fluctuations?

Through the spreadsheets you will build models that you can test. The thoughts that go behind the assumptions and the interrelationships between the variables become the material of the business plan.

The danger with the spreadsheets is that they may take you into such detail that you lose the broader perspective.

Presentation

If you find yourself diving into excruciating detail and losing your point then taking a shot at a presentation may help you to clarify your thinking. By virtue of its brevity and bullet-point information, it will force you to make decisions about what is important to communicate and what the fundamentals of your business are.

Private Placement Memoranda

If you have looked at enough plans and startup documents or searched the Web to find them, you will have come across the private placement memorandum (PPM). Most PPMs are really horrible vehicles for communicating the company vision, product, plans and financial projections. One of their primary purposes is to discuss risks openly—especially for "unsophisticated" investors. ("Sophisticated" and "accredited" have Securities and Exchange Commission (SEC) definitions different from those you will find in Webster's dictionary.)

A plan that is not forward looking and specific is worthless to any audience trying to evaluate a startup company.

There are clear reasons why PPMs end up being non-specific and content-free. Firstly, they are often written or edited by attorneys who are risk-averse and who take out as much specific or forward-looking information as possible. A plan that is not forward looking and specific is worthless to any audience trying to evaluate a startup company. Secondly, they are often heavily edited or written by investment bankers or broker-dealers who don't understand the business. (There are some I-bankers, brokers and attorneys who are superb at writing real business-plans but they are exceptions.) The bottom line is that PPMs are, typically, examples of what not to do in writing a plan.

You could cripple your future prospects if you solicit investment improperly.

Having been given that caution about using PPMs as communication tools, you may nevertheless be required to create a PPM, depending on whom you will be soliciting as investors and how you plan to approach them. This follows from Securities and Exchange Commission regulations with which you should become familiar before taking money from anyone. You could cripple your future prospects if you solicit investment improperly. There will be more about this in the chapter on financing.

To conclude this section: do not assume that you need a private placement memorandum or that the style typical to PPMs is necessarily good business-communication.

Outline

There are many places to find outlines for business plans or lists of questions that should be answered by business plans, but you can easily end up sacrificing clarity by strictly following someone else's outline. I have seen business plans for technology startups that were clearly based on formats for traditional businesses such as restaurants and auto-repair shops. This strategy doesn't work.

The following example contents are from business plans for winning companies that have succeeded and/or raised funding. Keep in mind that it was not the organization of the plan that led to the businesses' successes. (They have been edited to maintain confidentiality.)

Contents Example 1:
Executive Summary
Markets
Sales and Business Development
Market Requirements and Competition
Technology
Industry References
Products
Achievements, Milestones, Risks
Operations
Management
The Board of Directors

Financials
Offering

Contents Example 2:
Executive Summary
Markets and Market Developments
    Markets: Supply and Demand Management
    How Customers Benefit from [XYZ's] Solution
    Market Development
    Current Market Development Projects
    Market Development Partnerships
    Existing Customer
    Expansion Market
    Market Development Plan
    Future Potential Uses
Products
    [XYZ] Solution
    Product Descriptions
    Supporting the Value Proposition
    Product Evolution Strategy
    Future Product Implementation
    Product Road Map
    Intellectual Assets
Sales
    Sales and Marketing Approach and Forecasts
    Channel Development
Competition
    Competitive Positioning
    Competitive Response
Management and Operations
    Management Team
    Board of Directors
    Operations Development
Finance
    Capitalization Table
    Financial Projections Summary
    Risk Factors

Elevator Pitch

You'll understand why the "elevator pitch" is so named if you consider a scenario in which you corner an investor in an elevator and need to interest him in your company before the doors open on the tenth floor. (Pushing the emergency button is considered poor form.) Whether you are seeking investment or not, you should be able to describe your company and make its vision compelling in one paragraph or less. You will use this in your business plan, to orient employees, and in talking to vendors, strategic allies and customers.

... you should be able to describe your company and make its vision compelling in one paragraph or less.

You need to be selective in formulating your elevator pitch and hit only the high points. You are not trying to close a deal with that one paragraph, you are just trying to communicate essentials and, in the case of a business plan, make it compelling for the reader to carry on.

The elevator pitch should, at minimum, concisely state your product or service and the reasons why people will buy it. Other things that could be included are the ease of marketing, the sales you already have, status of your product or service and the timing with some trend such as the rollout of 3G or the invention of television. If your management team is strong, then this information should be in there as well.

Executive Summary

This will be the most important section of your business plan. In most cases this is all that will be read. In those cases in which someone reads the whole plan, this will usually happen because the executive summary was compelling. In the summary the reader is expected to give the writer the benefit of the doubt and expect assertions to be backed up in the body of the business plan. The summary also gives the reader the big picture before they dive into the details of the business plan's body. This big picture allows the reader to put the details into the context of the whole.

The summary should cover at least:

➢ company vision

➢ what you do or make

➢ who your customer is

➢ why the customer needs your product

➢ what the market is

➢ how you will reach your market

➢ expected sales or profits out to year three or five

➢ the status of the company, product, relationships and team

➢ the stage of the company

➢ a management-team summary.

Make sure that your summary is very clear. It should be one or two pages—no more. Not only does this make it readable, but it also tells the reader that you can communicate well, that you have clarity and that you can stay focused. While you should try to catch all spelling errors, it is unlikely that you will do so—I would be surprised if there weren't a few in this book. On the other hand, some plans are so poorly written that the writer is clearly stupid, careless, lazy, crazy or some combination of these. As in any writing, don't try to impress the reader with your vocabulary or use uncommon words inappropriately. Finally, avoid buzzwords.

> ***Myth:*** *Buzzwords show that I have the inside track on this industry.*
>
> ***Reality:*** *Buzzwords can show a lack of precision in your thinking, as in "We're really taking advantage of lessons learned from gap-analysis of the edge-of-the-cloud space." They also can show that you don't know how to communicate clearly, which will be essential in talking to customers and vendors. Finally, they suggest that you might be trying to impress rather than to communicate or that you might be too lazy to find a way to communicate to an audience beyond your immediate peers. Have a spouse, partner or a family member unfamiliar with your business read your summary and point out where you are using buzzwords—you might not see it yourself.*

Your executive summary should address the following:

- ❑ **Opening paragraph:** In your first paragraph describe the product or service and vision for company. This should be very similar or identical to the elevator pitch.

- ❑ **Establish customer need:** Discuss the level of customer pain that your product or service will alleviate. Describe how your customers are getting by now without your product or service.

- ❑ **Customer:** Describe your customers and relate that to how you will sell and market to them. Also relate the customer description to their needs.

- ❑ **Market size:** Try to come up with a number for the market size. If you have a new-category product you may need to make a plausible estimate that you support elsewhere in the plan.

- ❑ **Market acceptance:** Discuss why people will buy your product and when. If no such product currently exists, then discuss strategies for creating acceptance.

- ❑ **Sales projections:** Summarize the numbers that you derived from your financial projections. Make sure they are realistic—you can lose a lot of credibility by over-estimating.

- ❑ **Sales:** If you have sales, then talk about them. If you do not have sales, then describe how you will get them.

- ❑ **Status of product or service:** Discuss the stage of your product or service, the risks that have been removed and the advantages that have been demonstrated.

- ❑ **Unfair advantage:** Describe what your product or company has that is either impossible or very difficult for others to replicate.

- ❑ **Competition:** State who your competitors are, how you stack up against them and how you will win against them.

- ❑ **Financial needs:** State when you will need money, how much you will need, where it will come from and the results you will achieve with it.

- ❑ **Management:** Discuss the people you need on your management team immediately and those whom you have already recruited.

- ❑ **Gross margins:** State and support your expected gross-margins if you can.

- ❑ **Business model:** Tell the reader how you will make money from your product or service.

- ❑ **Price:** State the price of your product or service along with a comparison to competition. Relate price to value to the customer if possible.

- ❑ **Operations:** Give highlights on innovative ways of executing your business and draw attention to their advantages.

- ❑ **Key milestones:** Show that you know what you need to get done—and when—in order to succeed. If you are asking for money, show what you will do to increase the value of the company with the investment you receive.

Show that you know what you need to get done—and when—in order to succeed.

- ❑ **Leverage:** Discuss the innovative parts of your business, product or service that allow great returns for low resource-utilization.

- ❑ **Commitment:** If you or other founders have invested time and money in the company, make that clear and specific.

Product or Service Description

Describe your product or service and its key or unique features. Relate the features to customer benefits. If you have pictures or drawings of your product, then by all means include some but don't overdo it. Address the competitors' products or services with respect to features and benefits.

This is a good place to flesh out the specifications for the product: size, weight, power consumption, memory requirements, security, storage, interfaces, approvals etc.

Product or Service Interrelationships and Dependencies

If your product or service interrelates with others, then provide a diagram to show how. If you have a software platform, show how other software or modules relate to it. If your product interfaces with other products, then show the connection in a block diagram and note the specific interface between the blocks (e.g. RS232, USB and so on). If your service integrates certain ERP software packages and provides financial reporting, show how it ties this together. In many cases, it makes sense to include the customer or end-user in the block diagram so that the reader can easily see how your product or service fits into a user's life or business.

Diagrams help the reader put your product or service in context and see how the world needs it. They also show the dependencies. Address the question of whether there is a dependence on the existence of other interfaces, and if so, whether they already exist. If you are dependent on a standards body to create them or approve them, address this. By including the user in your diagram it may point to certain changes required in the user's current behavior. Consider whether your product or service depends on the creation, or continued existence, of other products to which it connects.

Discuss briefly the interfaces and interdependencies, giving special attention to the risks inherent in dependence on anything outside your own control.

Status of Product or Service

Tell the reader the status of your product or service—the step(s) completed and the next major step.

The following is an example of a typical progression for hardware. This progression could be easily adapted to software, Internet or service companies:

1. Idea
2. Description
3. Technology proof
4. Specification
5. Product proof
6. Prototype product
7. Evaluation product
8. Market-test prototypes
9. Alpha-test
10. Beta-test
11. Design for production
12. Pre-production prototypes
13. Tooling
14. Production verification
15. First sales.

Technology

Perhaps you have a technology that you want to license to others for productization, or include in a future line of products that your company will develop or on which your products or services depend.

Describe the technology and its benefits to your company. You will tend to focus here on the benefits to your company rather than those to the customer. This is because the customer will rarely see your technology and will experience the benefits only through use of your product or service. If you are licensing, then the customer will benefit directly from the technology.

You need to find a way to describe your technology so that a smart businessperson who does not have a science or engineering background can understand it.

When describing the technology, it is fine to assume your readers are smart, but not that they have the same education or background as your technologist. You need to find a way to describe your technology so that a smart businessperson who does not have a science or engineering background can understand it. This is often an excellent place to use figures to explain some physical mechanism or logical flow.

The benefits to your company may be many, but here are some common ones: increased efficiency, lower manufacturing costs, lower cost of providing service, better features enabled, leverage underutilized infrastructure, enable new products and markets, etc.

You may want to also describe your technology in an appendix for people with sophisticated technology backgrounds. Here it is best to assume that your audience is well versed in the subject and to avoid educating the reader too much. Keep it brief and to the point. In writing the appendix you can assume that the reader has a background similar to your technologist.

Product and Technology Roadmaps

While product and technology roadmaps should be market-driven, there is usually a natural progression and timing to such roadmaps. One stage depends on another regardless of what demand you might be able to generate immediately.

If there is a product or service roadmap, then include this as well. If you are just starting out, then you will probably, and should, focus on one or just a few products at once. However, show how you will take some core capability within the company, a set of customers, vendors or manufacturers, and leverage that for follow-on products, or product extensions, taking advantage of value already created to give those new products a boost in some way. The product roadmap will have at least a coarse timeline—maybe in quarter or half years over the first three years and then with resolution no better than one year as you move still further into the future. The text around the timeline diagram should discuss the progression that you anticipate; i.e. the rationale for that particular roadmap and again with emphasis on the leverage and the timing into the market place. This roadmap should of course be consistent with the company vision and the financial realities as projected elsewhere in the plan.

Unfair Advantage

This was explained in some detail in the previous chapter. However, for review: explain why your product or service is unique and whether it is patented or patentable. Also, state whether it can be kept as a trade secret or copyrighted. Explain how the unique aspects give you an edge in the marketplace by lowering cost, increasing customer satisfaction, filling unmet customer-need or increasing manufacturability. Explain how this uniqueness creates a barrier to market entry for your competitors.

If your product depends on a proprietary relationship or licensing agreement, then discuss that briefly here as well. If you have a unique process, whether for service or product, then include it here.

Now is the time to refine your estimates of the last chapter and talk about what you can do with the unfair advantage. You may want to increase its value in some way, either by extending the concept, process or invention or by exploiting these differently. Lay out a strategy for how you will use this unfair advantage outside of sales of the first product or service.

Substantiate here why this is an unfair advantage. For example, perform some due-diligence on other ways of solving the problem. Decide on these questions:

➢ Is yours really better?

➢ What about existing patents that have never been developed into products or services?

➢ Are any of them actually better than your approach?

Customer Need

… if you can identify customer pain and create an urgent and compelling need—so much the better.

Use the data from the previous section but take it a little further by doing some research on your customers. Talk to some of your customers and get some data. If you are selling to businesses, then interview them about the product and find out what they really want and what their objections are, and, if possible, get a letter of intent that states under what conditions they would purchase—there will be more about this in the next chapter.

As stated before, if you can identify customer pain and create an urgent and compelling need—so much the better.

Identify Customers

List and describe your customers. Explain why they need your product and, if at all possible, describe a pain that your customers feel that your product or service will alleviate.

In identifying your customers, also identify those characteristics that make them fit the product, as well as those that make it easy to market the product to them. In other words, tie your identified customers to both your product and your marketing tactics.

Customer Behavior

Describe your customers' current behavior and what you are competing with to change that behavior.

If you have invented the television and you think that its primary use is entertainment, point out that people listen to the phonograph and radio for home entertainment and go out to the cinema for video entertainment. Explain how the television will bring the cinema experience into the home and displace much of the radio entertainment.

If you have a new-category product or service, which might not force current behavior to change, then explain why people will change their behavior to buy from you and why they will see a need at all.

Customer Churn

You should have a strategy for keeping customers. There are several reasons for this. One is that keeping customers increases the value of your company. If you can sell some of your customers as part of your business, then it will increase its value to an acquirer. Keeping customers will also significantly lower your sales costs.

Companies with high churn are tough businesses.

Take the example of Web-development firms: client engagement typically runs three or six months and then, for years, the customer does not have significant need. Web-development firms have to find new customers continuously. It is difficult for them to plan their hiring because they often have huge variations in utilization. Their costs of sales are high, and they are especially sensitive to changes in the external environment.

To lower churn, you can develop a strategy for up-selling products and services to existing customers. Another option is to create a switching cost.

For example, if your component is designed into a product, it is usually time-consuming and expensive for your customers to change their designs to use competitors' components.
Or, if you are a printer and have all of your customer's designs and forms on file, it is then costly for your customers to switch to another printer. It is easier for the customers to continue to order from your company because they need not provide you with

*anything but a description or item number—probably
one that they have used several times in the past.*

Try to estimate how long you will typically keep a customer and
what you will do to keep them as long as possible. These considerations
will be used later in developing a revenue model for the company.

Market Acceptance

*The difficulties of changing
customer behavior should not
be underestimated.*

The difficulties of changing
customer behavior should not be
underestimated. Explain what has to
occur for the market to purchase from
your company. People have established ways of doing things, established
routines and established relationships. If your product or service is really
far better than what they are doing, then you might need only to get them
to change their behaviors once for them to change them forever.

This is the place to tell the reader what behavior needs to change and
how you will make that happen. In the next chapter we will go into some
of the details of how you can improve your confidence of market
acceptance without having completely developed your produce or
service.

Market Size

In the last chapter you developed a good estimate of the market size
and double-checked that this opportunity was a worthy candidate for
your efforts. Ideally, you will also be able to segment the data by
customer type, which then will help you to determine where your
marketing focus should be and how you will reach your customers.

If there are a number of market-segments that you can address, then
how do you choose which one to three to start with? This decision will
be based on a combination of factors: the size of the segment, how you
will reach it, how compelling the benefits are to that segment, how
readily that segment will adopt and the costs of marketing to that
segment. Thus, market segmentation numbers can be very useful in this
planning phase as you decide what not to do—at least at the start.

Exit Strategy

This is the place to include some more detail of exit strategy, which
was introduced in the previous chapter. If your exit is through an
acquisition, then describe the types of acquirers that might purchase and

their motivations for doing so. Then, for each type of acquirer, list by name the companies that fall into that type.

Whether you have a public-offering or acquisition strategy, tell when you think you could accomplish such an exit and when you plan to do so. Explain why that would be good timing for an exit. This timing might depend on the maturity of the company, product or service. Or it might depend on external developments: perhaps the building of a semiconductor plant by a partner or the release of an enabling product.

> *There are huge variations in valuation depending on the external environment. The mean price to sales multiple for software company acquisitions in 2000 was 9X but his had dropped to 3X by 2001.*

If your exit plan is through an IPO, then discuss what happens if the IPO can't be accomplished in the time frame that you envision. IPOs are fundraising events first and liquidity events second. Would your company be in trouble if it did not raise any money in the public markets?

IPOs are fundraising events first and liquidity events second.

You may need also to draw a distinction between your exit as an individual and that of any other shareholders. Your investors may literally exit at an acquisition or IPO by selling their shares at the end of any lock-up period. You, on the other hand, might achieve some liquidity for your shares but may not truly leave the company. In fact, if it is an acquisition, you might have earn outs that will motivate you to stay, or an agreement that requires you to stay.

Distribution

Whatever you are selling, explain how you are going to get it to your customers. If your product will be sold retail, say who your distributors will be and how distribution will work. Discuss how returns will be handled and how inventory will be financed. If your distributors will do anything to help in promoting your product, explain how that will occur. A flow chart explaining this is usually the easiest way for readers to see what you have in mind here.

If you will use a fulfillment partner, list the actual companies that might do this for you, their payment terms and who finances inventory. If your product is electronic; i.e. a bunch of bits, discuss how customers will access it. Will they download it, receive a CD or use it online?

Describe the infrastructure you will need to support your distribution. You might need a service organization to integrate your financial or ERP software with others' software. Or you might need to have enough servers and bandwidth to deliver media or software.

Business Development

Describe the business relationships—such as joint ventures, partnerships, subsidiaries, cross-holdings and alliances—that will help your company succeed. If you are still purely in a planning stage, then list the types of companies, the names of companies and the types of relationships you would develop with them. Also, it usually makes sense to state why the relationship is advantageous to both parties.

Resist the temptation to say you are "working with" companies, when all you have done is exchange voicemails. When you are found out, your credibility will suffer.

If you have started talking to people, then tell the reader where you are in those discussions: the exploratory, term-sheet, letter-of-intent or agreement stage. Resist the temptation to say you are "working with" companies, when all you have done is exchange voicemails. When you are found out, your credibility will suffer.

Board Membership

If you have a board of directors or advisory board, then provide a one-paragraph bio on each member and state in what way each member is adding value to your company. That you like or trust someone is not sufficient qualification— it is a damn good start though. You might also discuss how you use your board. Do you have quarterly meetings or do you simply call your board members on the phone on an as-needed basis? If you plan on forming a board, then describe its purpose and what roles you wish to fill on that board.

There are different opinions about boards. Mine is that boards should be comprised of people who can add real value to your company as a result of their clear thinking, wisdom and insights. I do not fancy boards that have well-known athletes or actors—unless entertainment is your business. To me this says that you are thinking more about status than results and spending time on things that do not add value to your company.

Another opinion on celebrity boards is that they can help you attract other board-members who want to associate with celebrities, or that they can help you open doors to or raise money from people for the same reason. To me this seems to be a house of cards, where people are motivated to join your board to associate with celebrities instead of the satisfaction of helping create a great company.

History

If there is a history of the company, then it should be in the plan. It should be brief and supportive of the *future* direction of the company or should provide confidence that you can reach future objectives because you have delivered in the past. It should not become educational or a personal-interest story unless the plan will be exclusively for internal use. Most readers will be most interested in your future prospects. Remember that valuation is the present value of future cash-flows. The past is instructive but is done—the dividends from past profits have already been distributed and do not necessarily have bearing on the present or future.

The past is instructive but is done—the dividends from past profits have already been distributed and do not necessarily have bearing on the present or future.

Company Structure

If you have already formed your company, then state the current structure. Also, if certain events would cause you to change structure, let your reader know what changes you would make and why.

Choosing your company structure properly can save you considerable money or make more capital available to the company. Choosing a Limited Liability Company (LLC) may eliminate double taxation of the C-corp but it might cost you later in a merger or acquisition or you may need to change to a Delaware C-corp for venture capital financing. This is an important and technical topic with too many nuances to be covered well in a section of this book. For now, it is enough to say that it is worth taking the time to learn about this and that I think most entrepreneurs who do not need venture capital should take a close look at LLCs as a start.

Choosing the right structure will also require you to look into the future and make a good guess as to how events will unfold. Consider whether you will need financing, how you will raise it, when you might sell, whether you might merge, whether you might IPO, where you will do business and where you will have a place of business. This short list is just the beginning of what you might need to consider. A good attorney can be invaluable in this area and quickly help you find a good structure and explain the risks. A bad attorney will use this decision-making quagmire as an excuse to drive around the block for days with the meter running.

Competitors

In the previous chapter you created a competitive matrix. Starting with that, you should do some more extensive research and include it in table form here. For your most worrisome competitors, you can explain in more detail how you will block them, confront them and/or beat them.

This is another area in which talking to people will provide you with far more information than you will obtain from Web sites and other passive sources. The best people to talk to are users of your competitors' products—and sometimes your competitors themselves. So long as you are not pumping people for confidential information, they will often be

Good entrepreneurs know that today's competitor is tomorrow's acquirer or strategic alliance.

upfront with you about market conditions or challenges they have faced. Good entrepreneurs know that today's competitor is tomorrow's acquirer or strategic alliance.

I remember calling the CEO of a company competing with one I was working with. I told him very roughly what we were planning to do and asked whether he saw any potential synergies or whether he thought we were directly competitive. He surprised me when he told me that they were getting out of the competitive business to focus on another. He was extremely open about the struggles they had encountered and why they were changing focus. They still thought that our market was a good one but they needed to apply their resources where they could get the greatest return and that turned out to be in another area.

Business Model

It is surprising how often this is overlooked. In some cases the entrepreneur takes for granted that the business model is obvious, and in other cases it has truly been overlooked.

This was especially true in the bubble era:
Entrepreneur: *We are going to use our first mover advantage and major buzz to garner mega-eyeballs.*
Investor: *How will you make money?*
Entrepreneur: *We will have millions of eyeballs.*
Investor: *How will you make money?*
Entrepreneur: *Based on the GUFY analysis and price to eyeballs ratio from White Shoes Investment Banking the company will be worth a billion dollars.*

> *Investor: How will you make money?*
>
> *Entrepreneur: We could sell banner ads ...yeah, banner ads.*
>
> *Investor: Banners ads sell for a few dollars per thousand and a large percentage of space goes unsold, will you have enough viewers and be able to sell enough banner space to make a profit and pay operating expenses?*
>
> *Entrepreneur: You just don't get it, do you?*

Starting from the models you considered in the last chapter, you can now take the time to fill in the details. You can look for other companies, perhaps in other industries, with similar business-models. If they are non-competitive, you can call to find out how well they work, or you can talk to their customers to learn more about their models. Sometimes you can find even more quantitative information in press releases, SEC filings and magazine interviews.

To spark your thinking, do some research on Dolby, Adobe, Priceline, Hewlett Packard (printers), Microsoft or eBay. They have all done some clever things with their business models.

Management Team

Make the bios brief and relevant to the roles individuals will fill within the company. Avoid the "I am a lifelong entrepreneur" story—for anyone who has read through many business plans

When I see too much emphasis on education in a resume or bio, alarm bells go off in my head.

this story is pretty stale and irrelevant. Unless your "opportunity" is a lemonade stand or a paper route, your experience as an eight-year-old beverage- or media-mogul isn't relevant. Since Scott Adams started his Dilbert series, the human race has evolved its BS-detection sensory organs—don't test them with your bio.

The following are some things you should include if you have them:

➢ startup experience

➢ executive experience

➢ domain expertise

➢ existing relationships: customers, allies, vendors, manufacturers

➢ past successes—try to quantify wherever possible

➢ sales or marketing experience

➢ education.

Education should be included although I think it is overrated in terms of its contribution to success. When I see too much emphasis on education in a resume or bio, alarm bells go off in my head. I worry that the person is not results oriented, is too status oriented or is arrogant and will be difficult to work with.

Use the same criteria as you used for mentioning educational details to decide whether to include details of awards: mention awards that are *relevant and results-oriented*. Your 4th-grade medal for perfect attendance at school does not count for much. A list of fluff awards is a poor reflection on the "brand of you"—it shows one of two things: either you don't know that they are fluff awards or you knowingly went out of your way to "earn" fluff awards.

It probably doesn't need to be said, but leave out of your bio things that don't have anything to do with drive or ability.

> *I once saw a resume in which the person listed as one of her achievements her high score on a color-vision assessment. Again this told me more about the person and her view of herself than it told me about her color vision. And certainly more than it told me about her abilities as an entrepreneur. (I am colorblind so I suppose this could be sour grapes!)*

If your team has worked together before, let the reader know this. This is important because it means that you already know how to work together and there is likely to be less management-team discord than if you hadn't. If you have not worked together, then talk about any prior relationship you may have had with other members. Make it clear that you did not run into each other while dumpster-diving behind the local Krispy Kreme.

Hopefully, you will have chosen your team members for their value as a group in addition to their individual capacities to contribute. If possible, write a paragraph or two on why this *team* is great, how the individuals compliment each other or how they work together to be successful. This can put the team in context as well as make clear the benefit of the team to the company and its success.

If there are holes in your management team, then describe the holes in terms of the roles to be filled. Provide context by showing how those unfilled roles will dovetail with the existing team. Tell the reader when these roles need to be filled lest they hold back the company's progress and tie those hires to company events or milestones.

Sales

If you have sales, then state what they are. Or, better yet, plot them over time so that the reader can see both sales and sales growth. If you don't have sales, then plot or state your projected sales. If you have, or will have, multiple revenue-sources then break them out individually for the reader.

The exercise of breaking out the sales for individual products and services or even by market is also a tool for you. It will help you see whether some of the current revenue-sources should be phased out or used in another way.

> *For example: if you are an Internet company, then you have the potential to sell banner ads. However, if you look at the going rate for ads and the number that go unsold, you might find that these ads would contribute only 1% of the sales compared to your core revenue-generators. It might then make sense to rid yourself of that distraction so that you can increase revenues in your core areas. That is not the same as leaving money on the table. Money on the table is money that requires no effort. However, most things in business do require effort that could be expended in any number of ways.*

Talk about your sales strategy and how you will execute it. Address these questions:
➤ If you will have salespeople, then how will they sell and to whom within your customer's business?

➤ How will you pay your salespeople?

➤ What experience will a typical sales-hire have?

This is a great time to think through the sales funnel:
➤ What efforts will be used to generate suspects?

➤ How will you qualify them to turn them into prospects?

➤ Once the prospects are identified, then what are the steps that lead to a close?

Try to be specific about your qualification criteria. This is critical for small companies with limited resources. It will be extremely difficult not to pursue what looks like a potential sale. If you have well-considered qualification-criteria, it is easier to focus your efforts where they will yield the highest returns.

Once you have your sales funnel and qualification criteria thought through, this should give way to an estimate of the time it will take to close a typical sale. It will also give you insight into how many sales the average salesperson might be able to close. These numbers can then be used to refine your compensation plan for salespeople. They are also crucial in doing your sales-projection spreadsheets.

Operations

"Operations" is about how the company will be run on a day to day basis. It's about how the product or service will be produced and how the customer will receive it. It's about where you will make your product and from whom you will buy material and parts.

Operations is a very broad topic but is so different for every company that it would be fruitless to try to cover it in too much detail. Instead, consider the following list to get the wheels turning in your head:

- **Shipping:** How will the product get to the customer?

- **Inventory:** What are the physical inventory needs, who will finance it and who will store it?

- **Vendors:** Who are the vendors that you simply must have? Do you have second sources for what they sell?

- **Facilities:** Where will your business be done? How much space do you need? Can you lease or finance?

- **Systems:** What systems do you have, or will you put in place to manage your business? Do they depend on software systems that must be implemented and integrated? When will this happen and what is the justification?

- **Logistics:** Where are the parts and how will you manage their flow to minimize disruptions and costs?

- **Returns:** How will you handle returns and what rate of return do you expect?

- **Manpower:** Will manpower needs increase smoothly or will they be highly variable? If highly variable, how do you avoid underutilization?

- **Supply:** Anticipate the possibility of demand spikes. What would be critical to meeting any unexpected demand-spikes?

- **Geography:** Where are your facilities, vendors and distributors located? What is the rationale for this distribution of stakeholders? Why is it advantageous?

❑ **Globalization:** Will you sell to non-domestic customers? Where? Will you have a presence in their countries?

A useful model for thinking about operations involves thinking in terms of input, throughput and output. It sounds overly simplistic, and it is, but it provides a way of breaking down some of the details of your business:

➤ Input is the stuff, capital equipment and people that you need in order to make something or provide a service.

➤ Throughput is what your company does with the inputs to create a product or service.

➤ Output is the product or service you provide and the means for delivering it to your customers.

Milestones

Milestones are the things you need to achieve to be successful as a company. They are not the same as activities, nor do they constitute a task list. Activities are ongoing and do not necessarily lead to measurable results. Task lists are at too fine a granularity and a focus on tasks can lose the big-picture view.

For the company, a good number of milestones is one to three per quarter. You will accomplish much more of course, but these milestones are the answer to the question: what do I have to do in that quarter to be successful? Moreover, what milestones must be achieved in this quarter so that you can achieve next quarter's milestones? And so on.

When telling an investor what you will accomplish, keep in mind that those milestones should be critical to success and you might be held to them in an agreement. Don't say that you will rent office space, for example—anyone can spend money. Tell them something like how many sales you will close and of what size, or that you will complete a certain phase of the product and have it ready to ship—these are examples of critical results. Take your milestones seriously, as there may be a penalty for not achieving milestones, depending on the agreement that you strike with investors. Many investors will expect more stock or will withhold future installments of their funding should you not meet agreed-upon milestones. The carrot-oriented investors will offer you additional ownership for meeting them. Either way you might find that something very real depends on passing your projected milestones.

Timelines can make it easier to see where the milestones come in time and also how one follows another. In many cases, you will have to discuss how you will know that you have achieved a particular milestone. Sales numbers make great milestones because they are so easily quantified and measured—although, like any other metric, they can be gamed.

A caution on milestones and metrics: they can cause unintended side-effects. This is especially so if compensation is tied to the meeting of specific milestones.

Employees and vendors get paid cash, not potential for success.

Take the example of sales figures: if bonuses depend on exceeding a number, then the temptation is to set that number low; if they are tied to time, then there is the temptation to push sales into one quarter at the expense of another and there is the temptation to "book" the sales "creatively" in ways that do not tie directly to cash-flow. Employees and vendors get paid cash, not potential for success.

Financial Needs

If you will need to raise money, state when you will need it and what you will use it for. And, most importantly, what value-enhancing milestones you will achieve with it. Sophisticated investors will want to see the valuation increase from the time they invest until the next event that puts a valuation on the company. These events are: subsequent private-financing, IPO, merger or acquisition. These events carry more weight than third-party valuation opinions because these events require someone to *pay* what they think the value is. A valuation from an accounting firm or other hired evaluator doesn't have the same authority as the market. And in startups with little or no operating history, these valuations require a lot of educated guesswork.

Valuation

My opinion on whether to include valuation in your plan is probably the opposite of what you might think. My advice is to not include it for investors but consider including it if the plan is for internal use.

The inclusion of valuation in plans for internal use gives your team and staff a sense of the value they are creating. Regardless of whether this number is increasing or decreasing, it can open some eyes and be very motivating. This is especially so if your team owns part of the company.

> **Myth:** *You should/must tell the investor what your valuation is in the plan.*

> **Reality:** *For a private placement memorandum (PPM) you should, and in most cases must, do so. For a business plan, as opposed to a PPM, you should not. This myth has been propagated by investors because a) they want you to move first in any negotiation and b) they want to use valuation as a qualifier to decide whether to give your opportunity further consideration. You really have nothing to gain from providing the valuation to the investor. Fewer than 1% of venture capitalists will screen you out for not explicitly stating valuation so long as the rest of the summary or plan is compelling. If you come in too high you may get screened without the opportunity to negotiate. If you come in too low you will never be able to increase it.*

Complicating the simple statement of valuation for investors is the fact that it will be used to determine how much equity they can get for a certain amount of money. But this equation also depends on the "valuation" that can be assigned to the investor. In other words, on the one hand, you may be willing to give away more equity for a certain amount of money to a venture-capital firm that has connections in your industry—and so your apparent valuation would be lower in this case. On the other hand, some terms from investors may be more onerous than others and this will also determine your willingness to take their money, which would be reflected in a higher apparent valuation.

Growth Strategy

In most cases, growth is what this is all about. At this stage of your planning, you should be focused on those first one to three products or services and not try to be too clever about your 50-year plan. There are many startups that became so focused on their long-term goals that they neglected completing and selling the first product. They built and hired for growth that never came.

Right now you have one or several customer-offerings that you are working on. How are you going to leverage the near term into the long term? You will have created some core competencies that you want to build on as you create future offerings. You will have captured a toehold with some customers and market segments and you will want to sell them new or expanded offerings in the future and you will want to grow with your customers. You will have established vendor relationships that you can use for subsequent products.

There are myriad ways in which you can proceed following your initial products or services. You need to look at what you are creating in the near term and at the vision you have for your company to determine what your growth strategy will be.

If you foresee changes in the market that will draw you in directions in which you do not have core capability, you will need to allow time to develop it or acquire it. You will also need to have a mechanism for doing so—hiring the right people or financing an acquisition for example.

Let the plan reader know what the future will bring, given what you currently know, and relate the long-term growth strategy to the more near-term focused strategy. If possible, show how this will impact on sales, competitive advantage, customer acquisition costs, valuation and/or profitability.

Risks

Many business plans do not include sections on risks—perhaps because of the entrepreneurial taboo against negative thoughts. Or, if the plans are for investors, maybe because the writers think mentioning risks will hurt their sales prospects—the sale in this case of equity for cash. Nonetheless, this brief section is an excellent exercise, and an excellent communication-tool, for you. It is great for communicating to your team honestly about how it isn't all happy-talk and IPOs. It is great for communicating to your investors that you have not inhaled too much of your own exhaust; i.e. you know that there are risks and you will face them head-on.

While there may be others that apply to your business, the basics are:

➢ technology

➢ marketing

➢ financial

➢ manufacturing

➢ competitive

➢ schedule

➢ execution.

The risks in each category can be stated very succinctly and the mitigation also stated. One way to format this is to have a three-column table in which each risk is named in the first column and explained in the second, and mitigation is outlined in the third. For example:

Risk	Description	Mitigation
Technology	There is significant risk that gravity on earth can not be significantly reduced through positive thinking.	A secondary prototype will be built that will operate in normal earth gravity.

Technology

Technology risk is the risk that you can't make the widget or software work. It includes the case in which physics just won't allow what you are trying to do, as well as the risk that you and your team weren't clever enough to solve the problem with the available resources.

Mitigation strategies might include having backup development for a product that may not be quite as great but for which the risk is far lower. They also might include parallel development-paths using independent technologies, so that you increase your odds of making one of them work. This introduces some financial and execution risk, of course—it makes it more likely that you will run out of money or not be sufficiently focused to execute well.

Marketing

Market risk could include the risk that the market is smaller than you thought or that the market might not accept your product in the numbers anticipated. There is also risk that your marketing strategy may not perform as planned.

The market may be smaller than you thought because you could not segment as you would have liked, because you are timing your product or service for the emergence of a market or you are anticipating market growth to coincide with the release of your product. Acceptance might not occur because you do not meet the market requirements or because users do not behave as you expected. Your marketing tactics might fail to produce the results you expect, either because behavior was different or because your message missed the audience.

Talking to your users so that you know what they want can mitigate acceptance risk.

Talking to your users so that you know what they want can mitigate acceptance risk. It can also be mitigated by talking to the people who currently sell to the same people or by obtaining a commitment to buy from customers. Having multiple paths that you can test with low time- and resource-requirements can mitigate the risk that you miss the mark with your marketing strategy. You can also test your message, brand and other aspects of your strategy in focus groups and marketing interviews.

Financial

Financial risk is the risk that you run out of money. It can be mitigated from both the input and output ends. In other words, by ensuring that money comes in before you need it and ensuring that you manage spending so that your burn rate is controlled.

Mitigation on the input side can include constantly developing relationships with investors, reaching value-creation and risk-reduction milestones that trigger subsequent financing, or solidifying customer and vendor commitments to make it easier to close on investment. If funding is obtained through profits, then this means managing price and margins.

Mitigation on the output side can include controls and implementation of software systems. It may also include hiring freezes or layoffs, depending on the environment. Often startups can control a lot of the output by focusing their development, marketing and sales efforts. In development, the focus comes from the market requirements—by making the one to three products that customers really need and will pay for. In marketing, the focus comes by doing a few things that work really well, rather than having many simultaneous experiments with no proof of which are working. In sales, the focus comes by prospecting efficiently and qualifying potential customers so that time is spent where it gets the greatest return.

Manufacturing

This broad category can include everything from having signed agreements with manufacturing partners to the risks of having sole-sources for aspects of manufacturing or supply. It can also include the risk that processes cannot be developed to keep yields high and manufacturing costs low.

Mitigation includes getting signed agreements or multiple sources. It can also include developing, verifying or acquiring processes to ensure that desirable yields and manufacturing costs are achieved.

Competitive

You have identified your competitors and their strengths and weaknesses elsewhere. Decide which competitors or types of competitor are most threatening and why. They may have existing brand, distribution channels or market penetration.

Mitigation is what you will do to counter what your competitors do well.

Schedule

Schedule risk is the risk that your estimated times for meeting milestones, especially getting to market, have been too optimistic. Mention the bad things that might happen if this is the case. For example, you might run out of money or you might miss a market window.

A common mitigation is to have backup plans or parallel development-plans.

Execution

This is the broadest of the risks, but in some way always comes back to the people—primarily those in the management team—and their abilities to set and achieve realistic and meaningful goals.

To support your team's ability to execute you can mention its past history of delivering on expectations. If you are an early-stage startup— the target of this book—then briefly reflect on the key hires that are in the works or need to be completed.

Spreadsheets

The financials make up an odd section of the business plan in that, to do them properly, you will put a lot of work into them and the result in the business plan will be a few terse pages of financial summaries. Still, the exercise of doing the financial spreadsheets will be some of the most worthwhile time spent in planning.

... the exercise of doing the financial spreadsheets will be some of the most worthwhile time spent in

A word on templates

Most templates are too complicated and spit out data that is largely irrelevant for evaluating or running a company. The problem with complicated systems is that they rarely get used, they are more prone to error and they don't allow the intuition in your company that a simpler system developed by yourself would allow.

Your financials need to be done from the ground up with top-down verification. You may wonder what the hell that means. It means that your numbers should be built on things that you make happen or that already exist.

For example, you might key your dollar sales to the number of sales people, the average time to close a sale, the number of qualified prospects salespersons can meet with per month, the percent of prospects that lead to closed sales and the average dollar sale. While these numbers involve some guesswork, they are easier to get a handle on than more dependent numbers such as market share.

Once you have worked your numbers from the ground up, you can sanity check them with top-down numbers. If the average sales per employee for companies like yours is $300,000 and your spreadsheets show $3,000,000 per employee, then you need to know why. Either you have missed something or you have some very good secret-sauce and you need to know why that secret sauce will give you that kind of operating efficiency or those vastly increased gross-margins.

In many plans and discussions, I have heard entrepreneurs explain away numbers like these by saying that their competitors are idiots. Usually they are bit more diplomatic and point to "industry inertia," or claim that their competitors "don't understand the new-economy reality." If you only have one competitor, then that might be the case, albeit unlikely. If you have more than one competitor, then this is highly unlikely. Although smart people, by definition, are in the minority, there are still plenty of them around and you can expect that your competitor has hired a few—even if by accident.

Tools

Your primary tools are most likely to be either a spreadsheet program or pencil and paper. In most cases the flexibility and capabilities of spreadsheet software will make it the better tool. However, for simple businesses or for doing subsets of your calculations, pencil and paper can be the quickest approach.

There are some sophisticated software tools and spreadsheets for doing projections. Some are free and some are for sale. The value of these tools is in formatting, summaries and metrics. Many of these tools are beautifully formatted with shadings and separations of data. Their summaries are canned and will extract the right data, based on your entries, to create income statements, cash-flow statements and other summary sheets. These tools will often have numerous formulas coded to do financial ratios and other financial calculations such as net present value.

The problems with off-the-shelf or downloadable tools are as follows:

➤ They make assumptions about what your inputs should be. You are then faced with a dilemma: do you try to put your round data into their square holes or do you try to "trick" the tool into doing what you really want.

➤ You will not reach the insights that you will get by doing your own spreadsheets. The tools start looking like a black box and you may lose sight of the interrelationships of the inputs. And the inputs are what you *do*—you risk losing sight of how what you *do* impacts your *results*. Recall that you are not doing the spreadsheets for the sheer joy of spending hours with a spreadsheet program, but rather, you are trying to figure out how best to set up and run your company.

➤ You may not save any time. If the tool is powerful enough to adapt to your business, then it may take time to learn. If it is very simple to use, then it will generally be prompting you to oversimplify or guess at data.

My advice is to do the core work yourself in Excel or an equivalent and keep it simple and focused on the business and what you need to know to make decisions. This may or may not correspond to generally accepted metrics. Then, after doing your own budget and projections and being satisfied with the results, you can decide whether to use one of the available tools if you want some of the metrics, summaries or formatting that they will produce for you.

... do the core work yourself in Excel or an equivalent and keep it simple and focused on the business and what you need to know to make decisions.

Elements

You will probably find it easiest to work on several sheets. In Excel, sheets are represented by the tabs at the bottom left. The sheets could be: budget, revenue, profit and loss, cash plot, salaries and summaries, which can be on multiple sheets. You might want to add other charts or plots to help you see the data. A few examples are: unit sales over time, gross margin over time, valuation over time and dollar sales over time. It is convenient to put salaries on a separate sheet so that you can show budget sheets to anyone without them seeing sensitive salary-information. On the budget sheet you can then simply put a number of people in the row corresponding to a position and use a formula to compute an aggregate dollar number for labor costs by department.

Getting Started

If you still have one foot in the due-diligence phase, it is probably best to start with sales projections and then work iteratively between the budget and sales projections. They are interdependent.

Let's look at a simple example: the way in which you develop a product will determine when and how you sell it. How quickly you sell it will determine your growth rate and ability to spend on marketing and development.

If you are at the earliest stages of startup and you need to do some development or marketing before you can sell, then you might want to start with the budget—at least up to the point at which you have something to sell.

In any case, you will want to start with the aspects of the business on which you have the greatest clarity. Then you have a foundation to build on and starting with what you know or see clearly will also expose the areas about which you are not clear and need to do some work.

If you really can't seem to get going on the spreadsheet, then get some help—see the next section.

Subcontracting

While I think that entrepreneurs should do much of the work on their spreadsheets so that they understand their businesses better, getting some of the right help could really speed you through this task.

Accountants with solid business-experience can ask you a lot of the right questions or work with you iteratively to prepare the spreadsheets. Insist on doing the spreadsheets from the ground up. You may find that your accountant knows to ask you what your sales will be but that you will still be on your own in trying to develop a model for how those sales will evolve. This is where the right consultant or advisor can help.

You will probably find that consultants or advisors with startup experience will be the most helpful. These are people who have been in the trenches and know what to watch for and where some of the planning pitfalls lie. They will know from experience how long it takes to print the collateral, develop the Web site or raise money.

Budget

In a budget I like to set up sections for the various reporting areas—these will depend on your business but an example list is: administrative, development, marketing, sales, manufacturing and operations. Doing this allows you to chunk the exercise so you don't have to think of everything at once. Also, if you have some members of your management team in place, then they can be a great help in planning for their department or group. In addition, this separation can help you in managing your team to budget in the future—giving team members ownership of their parts of the budget.

Elsewhere you have laid out your key results and timing. This is where you need to think through how you are going to allocate resources to get those things done. You have no choice but to estimate here. You can get a good start if you have a lot of experience, otherwise it is best if you can talk to other people who have run these areas within companies. Experience will give you key insights into what it takes to get things done—everything is easy when all you have to do is talk about it and put it on a whiteboard.

The following lists show areas that need to be covered in the budget—either by hiring the person-hours to get things done or by purchasing something. These lists are not comprehensive but are intended to get you thinking at the right level of detail.

Marketing

- ❑ Public relations
- ❑ Trade shows
- ❑ Brochures and printed collateral
- ❑ Web site
- ❑ Advertising
- ❑ Market research
- ❑ Analysis
- ❑ Strategic planning
- ❑ Writing copy
- ❑ Pricing
- ❑ Promotion planning
- ❑ Product management
- ❑ Customer interviews
- ❑ Market-acceptance studies
- ❑ Travel and entertainment
- ❑ Conference attendance
- ❑ Focus groups

Sales

- ❑ Trade shows
- ❑ Collateral
- ❑ Travel and entertainment
- ❑ Sales meetings
- ❑ Inside sales
- ❑ Sales engineers
- ❑ Sales operations
- ❑ Distributors
- ❑ Distributor management
- ❑ Sales training

Development

- ❑ Software
- ❑ Mechanical
- ❑ Human factors
- ❑ Industrial design
- ❑ Electrical
- ❑ Optical
- ❑ Training
- ❑ Software licenses
- ❑ Lab equipment
- ❑ Technician
- ❑ Purchasing
- ❑ Production engineer
- ❑ Quality assurance
- ❑ Information technology
- ❑ Web development
- ❑ Prototyping
- ❑ Parts

Manufacturing

- ❑ Quality
- ❑ Test equipment
- ❑ Operations
- ❑ Logistics
- ❑ Facilities
- ❑ Documentation
- ❑ Process development
- ❑ Industrial engineering
- ❑ Purchasing

Finance

- ❑ Controller
- ❑ Audit
- ❑ Payables
- ❑ Receivables
- ❑ Planning
- ❑ Fund raising
- ❑ Money management
- ❑ Reporting
- ❑ Leasing

Office Expense

- ❏ Rent
- ❏ Improvements
- ❏ Office supplies
- ❏ Hosting
- ❏ Computers
- ❏ Office equipment
- ❏ Phones
- ❏ Utilities
- ❏ Cleaning
- ❏ Insurance
- ❏ Furniture
- ❏ Food and beverages
- ❏ Company events

All

- ❏ Travel
- ❏ Entertainment
- ❏ Conferences
- ❏ Training
- ❏ Consultants
- ❏ Legal
- ❏ Salaries
- ❏ Payroll taxes
- ❏ Insurance: health, dental, vision, life, disability

Your budget should include travel and allowance for payroll taxes and insurance for your employees. Typically, marketing and sales people will travel a lot more and have higher entertainment-expenses than everyone else.

On office expenses, be realistic but not extravagant. If you are working alone or have just a few people, one option is to work out of one of your houses most of the time and to rent office suites when you need a conference room for a meeting. These office-suite companies typically rent offices and conference rooms by the half-hour or the full day—and although the hourly charges can add up, it is a lot less expensive than having your own space before you need it.

On office space, you need to think about the message you are sending to your customers and your employees. Many entrepreneurs overspend on office space and furniture because they think they have to "look big" to customers and vendors. Too extravagant and it can look like you are not focused on the right things. Remember that many of the people that you meet with have started a company.

Sensible spending on office expenses at startup is a delicate balance. If you are really strapped for cash, you might be making photocopies at Kinkos instead of owning your own copier.

The addition of personnel should be timed to allow them to get up to speed in the company and then contribute to the completion of the key results with enough time for them to execute. You need also to allow time to recruit good people. By not allowing enough time, you might make a bad hire in an effort to meet schedule. For a senior-level person it can take several months to find someone that is a really good fit.

In early-stage companies it is common to use many consultants and subcontractors and this, of course, should be included in the budget. The pros of doing this are that consultants can bring you specialized knowledge on a temporary basis, and in using consulting companies you can access a lot of wisdom that you might never be able to afford to have in-house.

> *An example of this is industrial design for products. Industrial design benefits from collaboration amongst a lot of individuals and a designer at a consulting company can walk down the hall and get input from tens of people with broad experience—this is hard to replicate in a small company.*
>
> *Another area ripe for a consulting relationship is PR, because a PR firm can have vastly more valuable relationships than the one or two people you might be able to hire.*

The cons with consultants are that you are teaching people who might someday help a competitor and you might not be adding to your core capability. One tip here is that, whenever you use consultants, you should ask on a weekly or monthly basis how you are making them teach your people and thereby increasing your internal capability.

Progress as far as you can on the budget by using your key results and timeline as guideposts. Just rough it in at first because it will need some fine-tuning as you start projecting sales. Marketing and development lay the foundation for early sales. Supply must be adequate to meet demand and there must be "capacity" to manufacture and provide a service or a place for people to do business with you. Distribution needs to be in place to get the product or service to the customer. When sales are closed they generate cash for further marketing, development or capacity. Financing is an optional input in the cycle.

Sales Projections

Unless you have historical data from which to start, projecting sales is really tough. You have to anticipate customer behavior that is largely out of your direct control.

In a previous section of this chapter, you developed your sales process and sales funnel, or at least a model thereof. Somehow you will generate suspects, or people that you think might be qualified to purchase your product. You might do this by advertising, cold-calling, networking, using your existing contact-list or doing industry research. You will have a certain amount of money to spend on these activities and it makes no sense to generate them at a higher rate than you have people and time to turn them into sales; i.e. in excess of capacity.

Once you have enough suspects, you can start to qualify them to determine whether they are prospects. At first this can seem an odd notion to an entrepreneur without a sales background. Why would you not get every customer you can? Because some customers will generate less income than the cost of selling to them and servicing them. There also is an opportunity cost. With limited money and people, you want to invest these resources where they have the highest return. If your salespeople are spending too much time on low-return customers, then they can't spend that time on high-return customers.

Why would you not get every customer you can? Because some customers will generate less income than the cost of selling to them and servicing them.

From your sales process and funnel, and knowing your available resources and capacity, you can begin to project sales. You will also need to introduce time as a variable. It takes time to close a sale and there may be multiple revenue-generating steps in the progress to a high-dollar sale. To estimate the time it takes to move people through the various phases of the sales funnel you can talk to people.

Identify some similar businesses and call their salespeople in the slow part of their day, tell them (briefly) what you are doing so that they know it is not competitive, and ask them about their sales cycle. Many will oblige you, especially if you can reciprocate by sharing some valuable information or insights with them. If you have salespeople or are recruiting a salesperson to your team, ask them what sales cycles and close rates they would stake their commissions on.

You can also sometimes garner information from SEC (Securities and Exchange Commission) filings, which you can find at www.sec.gov in the "Edgar" section of the site. You will find information only on public companies or companies that are filing to go public but if they are selling similar or competitive products, or selling different products to similar customers, then you might be able to get some valid information. Some of the information might take some sleuthing to put together. You might find the average dollar sale one place in the text and then use the total dollar sales figures from the spreadsheets to deduce the approximate number of customers (total dollar sales divided by average dollar sale). Obviously the right advisors, board members or consultants can offer you insights as well.

> *Let's look at an example of how time can affect sales projections: a customer who could usefully use 1000 of your widgets might take an average of two months to close after first contact. Even then he might only buy three of your widgets and test them for three to six months to see if they work and do not result in unintended consequences or maintenance problems. He then might purchase 50 of them for a year-long test to verify the cost savings that you claimed when you sold to him. After that year, he might only buy 100 per quarter because he is limited by his ability to finance and install the widgets he buys from you.*

This leads to an obvious but important suggestion: think about ways that you can shorten the sales cycle.

> ### Example 1:
> *If you are making a product that the customer will want to test for months before making a volume order then you might be able to sell them pre-production prototypes that they can test. Then they will be able to purchase in volume some months hence when you have the capacity to deliver in volume. Otherwise you run the risk of having capacity and burn rate but very low sales while your customers try before they buy. (A pre-production prototype in this discussion would be one that was hand-built from machined parts rather than one that was assembled on a line from molded parts. In other words, pre-production prototypes can be made before tooling and volume-production systems are in place.)*

> ### Example 2:
> *Suppose that you have a component that goes into products. If you create reference designs that your customers can use to integrate your component, then that reduces their risks and their development times, leading to both a shorter time to a commitment as well as a shorter time to volume sales.*

The Supply vs. Demand Dilemma

When you are in an unpredictable market it is very difficult to reconcile anticipated supply and demand. It is always far better to have a supply problem than a demand problem. A supply problem is solvable, whereas a demand problem may not be. If you have demand that outstrips your supply, there are usually ways to manage it. You can offer coupons to keep customers for delayed delivery or you can offer added services or products as part of your "apology". You will, however, lose some customers by not being able to meet demand. As for the supply shortfall itself: assuming that you have no fundamental difficulty beyond lack of inventory or capacity, the solution is obvious. Purchase more inventory or arrange for greater capacity. Use outside financing if necessary, which should be much easier now that you have shown demand outstripping supply. That is an investor's dream opportunity.

If you can't get financing you now know how demand responds to your marketing and you can scale back marketing to generate demand consistent with the capacity that can be internally financed.

From my experience, most entrepreneurs end up with a demand problem, which becomes an over-supply and over-capacity problem, which then becomes an under-financing problem. The demand problem may be fatal in that you might or might not ever figure out how to get people to buy in sufficient quantity for you to make a business. That is why there is so much emphasis throughout this book on proving that you can sell your product or service.

It is always far better to have a supply problem than a demand problem.

The difficulty with over-supply and over-capacity problems is that they cost money that you could have used to generate demand. Moreover, the reason for the demand problem may be that you had the wrong product or service, in which case you might have to abandon some of your supply or capacity. With your money already spent on supply, you might not have the money left over to wait for or generate demand.

> *This was a common mistake made by Internet-bubble companies. Too many startups thought that they were the next eBay and they planned and paid for the capacity to meet that type of demand. People selling to these eBay wannabes would point to some of the well-publicized outages at eBay in its early days and strike fear into the hearts of entrepreneurs: "You wouldn't want that to happen to you, would you?" Consequently, there were many $1,000,000 sites developed for businesses that needed only $100,000 sites.*

> *It would be interesting to know whether the early outages at eBay were actually signs of good management. That is, the managers were frugal in their capacity build-out while they tested demand.*

Cash

Your spreadsheet should have some rows devoted to your cash position on a monthly basis. Moreover, it is a good idea to plot your monthly cash so that you have a very good sense of where you are and where you are headed. This, in turn, allows you to respond to any dangerous turns in cash flow. The surest way to go out of business is to run out of money.

The surest way to go out of business is to run out of money.

If you are selling stuff, then you need to think about who will carry and pay for inventory. Try to find out what is standard with the vendors you use and, if you have special relationships, see if you can get vendors to fund your inventory

You need to think also about the receivables and payables cycles. Accrual accounting can tell you a lot about your business, but every week or two you have to meet payroll with real money. Once you have closed the sale and booked it, there will typically be a delay in when you really get paid. Likewise, you can often stretch your payables in the same way, but again you need to know what is acceptable to your vendors. You can refine this by including in your projections uncollectable invoices, credit-card fraud and finance charges. But for most startups, these refinements fall into the noise and your time is better spent refining your budget or your sales projections since they will have a vastly greater impact on your business.

The receivables/payables timing provides an opportunity for some cleverness.

> *One company I worked with sold products through a Web site and had a fulfillment partner. Customers purchased with credit cards and the company was credited immediately with the cash. A few days to a week later the fulfillment partner would ship the product. The company would then be invoiced twice a month with payment due in 30 days. They were selling stuff and getting paid long before they had to pay for the stuff. In a rapidly growing company this can be a significant source of funding.*

Assumptions

As you plan and do your spreadsheets, you should keep track of your assumptions so that you can easily go back and check them on a monthly or quarterly basis. An easy way to do this, that also makes for good presentation in a business plan, is to put the assumptions in a table. The left-hand column shows the assumption, the second column the value or range of values assumed and the third column shows rationale and comments. The third column is the best justification that you have for that assumption, or, if it is weak, then what you can do to test it. Some of your entries will be "guess". This has value also in that it is good to know what you don't know.

Some of your entries will be "guess". This has value also in that it is good to know what you don't know.

The following is an example assumptions table for a new-category product for which relatively little was known about market adoption.

Assumption	Value	Rationale
First revenue in vertical	Month 19	Allows time to close and customize after prototypes.
First revenue in test market	Month 23	Allows time to make major account sales within consumer e- companies.
First revenue in consumer market	Month 31	Allows one quarter of results from test market to justify volume commitment. May be aggressive.
Typical vertical volume	500 units per month per customer	Becomes qualification criterion.
Typical module price	$250	Supports a $700 to $1500 consumer product.
Typical test market volume	1,000 units per month per customer	Estimate that is considered conservative. Needs support.
Typical test market module price	$150	High but justified by time to market benefit.
Typical volume shipment	10,000 units per month ramping to 35,000 units per month over four years per customer.	May be low if market explodes. On low end for consumer product— conservative.
Typical volume module price	$50 decreasing to $25 over 18 months	Enables end-user product price of $200 to $300. Realistic ramp-down with expected competition.

Your Plans and Projections Are Wrong

So, after all that work these bozos are saying that your projections are wrong? If they're right, then why did you go through this? The primary reason why you went through all this is so that you understand

... the bad stuff is harder to anticipate but that doesn't make it any less likely to happen.

your business inside and out, and have some intuition about the dependencies that drive your business. There are three primary reasons that the projections could be wrong:

➢ The real world is different than you may have assumed and customer behavior and external events will probably be different than you have assumed.

➢ Your projections are probably optimistic because you know in advance about 80% of what can go right but you only know about 20% of what can go wrong—the bad stuff is harder to anticipate but that doesn't make it any less likely to happen.

➢ There is a bias towards success in your projections. There has to be, otherwise you would never start this company or any other.

So what do you do? Pad your numbers so that you don't run out of money, or have a backup plan if things are not going as you projected. As for padding—this is insurance and it may require that you give away more of your company upfront so that your ownership does not go to 0 in dollar value. It is obviously a fudge and should be larger the riskier your venture is, the less confident you are in your projections and the less successful experience you have with planning. The better strategy is to have a backup plan, or even a series of backup plans, together with decision points that tell you when to put them into effect. You need to choose a metric that tells you if you are getting in trouble and change course before you head into the abyss. It's better to think about this in advance, rather than under the stress of impending failure.

In an interview with Entrepreneur.com, Jim Collins, author of *Built to Last* and *Good to Great*, related the following:

> "There's a great, maybe apocryphal, story about Gen. Dwight D. Eisenhower. Once the troops landed on D-Day, he threw the plans in the wastebasket, saying, 'Planning is priceless, but now that we're moving, plans are worthless.' You want to do a lot of thinking, but that's very different from adhering to a plan. It's like mountain climbing: You can get killed if you don't plan or killed by not learning to adjust."

Presentation

In many ways, the presentation is more instructive and valuable than the plan. This is so because the presentation will force you to make choices—choices about what is truly important. When you are limited to 12 to 15 sheets of paper, a

When you are limited to 12 to 15 sheets of paper, a few bullet-points per chart and a few graphs, you have to really drill down to find what matters.

few bullet-points per chart and a few graphs, you have to really drill down to find what matters. If you are getting stuck in writing the plan and find that it is getting more muddy than clear, then you may want to try to draft the presentation to get refocused.

The charts in a presentation should not be cluttered with text—it is not a copy-and-paste exercise to go from business plan to presentation. They should be concise, with the expectation that you will talk—not read—about the underlying detail. Focus on why you and your company will succeed. The charts should include:

➢ what it is that you are selling

➢ why it is superior

➢ what is good about it

➢ who will buy it

➢ how will you reach buyers

➢ whether there are enough buyers

➢ critical milestones to success

➢ vision

➢ financial and/or sales projections

➢ management team

➢ competition.

While the charts are written at a very high level, you should be prepared to go three to five layers deeper than the charts. Answering questions, whether for investors, vendors, employees or customers, is where you get to build their confidence in you and your company.

In presenting, you should know your business so well that you smell like self-assurance—not arrogance. If you have worked through the last chapter and this one, this self-assurance will be justified. Try not to ramble or impress people with your knowledge or facility with details. Speak naturally, and while you should prepare and even rehearse, don't memorize or read what you want to say. If you memorize what you will say then it will usually result in a very stiff delivery. Moreover, people speaking from memory are noticeably irritated when events deviate from script. Events *will* deviate from script and the best way to deal with this is to be fully present rather than reciting from the bowels of your brain.

When a person in your audience asks a question, you should address it in real-time rather than telling them that you will get to it later or that you will be open to questions at the end. This is not *your* presentation, it is your audience's presentation. The information that audience members want is more important than the information that you want to deliver. In almost all cases, your audience consists of a customer—someone to whom you are trying to sell something for their money, their support or their time.

After you have given the same presentation a few times, you will find people diving into detail in similar areas. This begs you to prepare back-up slides that help you address those details. You just need to keep those slides handy, in case the detailed discussion should develop. The reason you don't just include such detail in the main presentation is that it hasn't been requested yet. Whether at a presentation or on a Web site, "customers" do not like to be hit with unexpected and unrequested material; they need to invite you to present it. This is why you get so irritated when you are looking at stock quotes online and a pop-up window covers your monitor trying to sell you sea monkeys.

Your presentation should be tailored to last 15 to 30 minutes. This is especially true if you have a one-hour meeting with investors. If they have any interest at all, you will want 40 minutes to talk to them, answer their questions and ask them some of your own. Usually, you will be interrupted so many times with questions that you might only interject the occasional chart between lengthy discussions.

Always have some paper back-up packages that you can either leave with your audience or use in case you have difficulties with presentation equipment. Usually, it is best not to hand out the paper copies in advance of your presentation unless they are your only presentation means—people will be reading ahead instead of paying attention to what you are saying. If you are using other people's equipment, arrive early and learn how to operate it and make sure that your charts have been loaded properly and have not suffered formatting changes in the conversion from your computer.

Summary

This chapter took you into some of the details of planning for your business and built upon the information you gathered as part of the quick screening process of the last chapter.

Remember that the map is not the territory and that the planning is more important than the plan.

People often get stuck when they start to plan their company—the equivalent of writer's block, where weeks go by and they stare at blank paper or only get three paragraphs into the outline. If this happens, then you can often get around this block by working on spreadsheets or the presentation.

The spreadsheets can be invaluable in forcing you to clarify your thinking. They should be done from the ground up; i.e., by constructing a model, rather than from the top down. The top-down numbers can be used to check your results to verify either that they are in line with comparable companies or that you know why you will outperform the comparable companies.

As you start and run your company, the spreadsheets and plans become the instrument panel for your business.

5. TESTING THE OPPORTUNITY

In previous chapters you have evaluated yourself, evaluated one or several opportunities and started or completed your planning. Through this, hopefully, you have found some areas that you want to explore further or in which you do not have enough information. If you haven't, then you are not trying hard enough.

To some extent, the first step in "proving the model" is to try to disprove it; i.e. to look for its fatal flaws. The reason that this makes sense is that if there really is a fatal flaw, then it is better to find out early and at minimal expense rather than later. Fortunately, looking for flaws can usually be done in a way that moves your business closer to success.

... if there really is a fatal flaw, then it is better to find out early and at minimal expense...

For example, to determine whether people will buy, get a commitment from a customer. This tests the value proposition and buying behavior, but it also moves you closer to your goal of a successful business.

The longer you wait to find flaws, the easier it will be to fall into a sunk-cost trap. The sunk cost trap is the trap wherein you are tempted to continue on a path simply because you have already invested so much time and money. However, that time and money is already gone and there is nothing you can do about it. What you *can* control is where you spend the next months and the next dollars; you need to evaluate your current opportunity on those terms.

The sunk cost trap is the trap wherein you are tempted to continue on a path simply because you have already invested so much time and money.

In proving or disproving a model, a lot of the work will involve refining your information and, as a result, often, refining your plan. Most entrepreneurs are tempted to just jump in to *do* it, which in most ways is a great impulse for an entrepreneur. However, since you are taking a risk, you might as well evaluate every opportunity carefully so that you enhance your likelihood of success and so that you pick an opportunity that is worthy of your investment, your energy and your talents.

Over-confidence

I have seen the greatest humility and confidence in serial entrepreneurs and the greatest arrogance and insecurity in first time entrepreneurs and young venture-capitalists. Some of the greatest arrogance was observable during the Internet bubble. There were some pretty silly business models and anyone who pointed this out "just didn't get it".

Once you know what you need to do and what your back-up plans are you can move forward with well-earned confidence.

Entrepreneurs, by their nature, are optimistic and have a can-do attitude. That is mostly great but it is best not to forget that you might not be able to *make* people buy your product, you might not be able to *make* your product inexpensively enough and you might not be able to *make* the laws of physics change for your benefit. This is why it is important to know how you are going to make things happen. Find out if others have tried and failed. If they failed, why did they fail, what are you doing differently and why are you going to succeed? More specifically, what do you need to do to succeed? Answering questions such as these is empowering. Once you know what you need to do and what your back-up plans are you can move forward with well-earned confidence.

This chapter is about testing the waters a little, rather than jumping in with the assumption that the world and people's behaviors will be exactly as you have assumed in your business planning. Then you can either move forward with justified confidence or explore and test another opportunity. This may be a time-consuming process the first time around but if you have to do it more than once you will get pretty quick about it.

Weaknesses

In your financial and risk sections of your plan you will have identified three categories that can lead to failure:

➢ weak assumptions or guesses

➢ assumptions to which your business is very sensitive

➢ business risks, as outlined in the risks section.

The weak assumptions should be firmed up if they are likely to have a significant impact on your business. Assumptions to which your business is sensitive should be tested as soon as possible, because being wrong could lead to failure. If you are assuming that sales will ramp at a certain rate and they don't, then you might run out of money before you ever get off the ground. If you are assuming that you can license technology from XYZ Corp and it turns out that you can't reach agreement with them, you could be out of business if there is no reasonable alternative. For each of the business risks outlined in the planning section you should be thinking about how to make them go away, how to go through them or how to go around them.

There are three primary ways to deal with assumptions:

➤ Verify whether they are correct through a source. In many cases this can be as simple as talking to the right person. In other cases you may be able to pay for the answer or hire someone to get it for you. In most cases you can find a way to find it at little or no cost.

➤ Test assumptions directly.

> *For example, if you have assumed a 3% response-rate from an email campaign, then just try it. Prepare the sales letter, buy some names and send out the emails to see what the response is. Using a thousand names or so might not be enough to satisfy a statistician but it will tell you if you are in the ballpark.*

➤ Make the assumption irrelevant. You can do this by reformulating your baseline plan so that it doesn't depend on a particular assumption. Or, simply develop some alternatives that you can move to if your assumption proves incorrect.

Backup Plans

When looking at risks and assumptions, the first and best way to deal with them is to find good backup plans that may not be quite as desirable but which you are more sure you can execute. Without a backup plan, you can either get stalled because you were not prepared when the world did not behave the way in which you wanted it to, or you can continue in a failing direction because it is the only way that you think you can make things work.

To use backup plans effectively, part of your planning needs to include metrics for success.

> *For example: You want to test an email campaign. You know that the list you want is $0.25 per address and so you decide that you can get valid results with 1,000 emails. In other words, you have decided in advance to risk $250. You are in the early stages of your company so you don't know exactly what your unit operating profit will be but you do know that your gross margin is $20 on your product. So, for the email campaign to even*

be in the ballpark, it has to return 13 buyers per thousand emails or 1.3%. Based on your projections, you think that your unit operating profit will be $15, which would imply breakeven at around 17 buyers per thousand emails or 1.7%. From this, you decide to test the email campaign with ten separate mailings to see if you can get the buy rate higher than 1% for the aggregate. If one of the ten mailings is 1.5% or better, then you might be able to play with your message to improve the response to better than the hurdle of 1.7%. Or your margins might allow this type of marketing or there might be some ancillary benefits to building sales at low margins. If all mailings result in a response less than 1.5%, it's not working and you move to one of your backup plans.

Note: An admission for the algebra whizzes out there—this is a little bit of a fudge since the costs of sending the email are counted twice, once in the reduced operating margin and again in the figure showing the breakeven for the email cost. This is the same as assuming that the emailing itself is a small part of your operating expenses. Since your numbers are estimates right now anyway there is not much harm in being inexact here.

Commit?

… count on surprises, embrace them, and turn them into opportunities. You can't stop them anyway. You need to practice startup-judo.

Unfortunately there is no formula for when you know enough or the risk is low enough for you to commit. Part of the answer depends on how much risk you are willing to take on at this point in your life. At the end of the day, you will have to make a judgement call for yourself. Throughout this book, I have tried to set some realistic expectations so you have a pretty good idea about what you are getting into. Nonetheless, count on surprises, embrace them, and turn them into opportunities. You can't stop them anyway. You need to practice startup-judo.

Part of your decision will depend on the availability of backup options, should something not work as you plan. But in the end you will not *prove* your business in any absolute sense—if you could reduce the risk that far, then it would hardly have enough reward to be worth doing.

Testing

Decide in advance what you are setting out to test and what results of each test you must get before you know that it is a go. Alternatively, or in combination with this, find a way to start your business incrementally so that you continuously test your assumptions and improve your strategy while either making money or not putting too much money at risk at any one time.

This doesn't have to be terribly complicated. You have gone through some fairly detailed planning in the previous chapter and you now know what your key assumptions are and what key milestones you need to hit to succeed.

The following is a sequence like the one you might construct to decide when and how you are ready to commit:

> 1   *If assumptions A, B and C are correct, I am confident to start doing this in the evenings and invest $100,000.*
>
> 2   *If I can achieve sales of $120,000 and get a letter of intent from BigCo within 6 months of doing this part time, I will hire Joe and Sally, quit my day job and invest an additional $75,000.*
>
> 3   *If we are on track to have sales of $300,000 by the end of the first full-year, then I will try to raise $1,000,000 through individual investors.*
>
> 4a   *If I can raise that money, then I will target $2,000,000 in sales for the second year.*
>
> 4b   *If I cannot raise the money, then I will grow organically with a target of $800,000 in sales by the end of year two, while I spend 15% of my time trying to raise additional capital so that I can jump to step 4a if and when I raise money from outside investors.*

Assessing Information and Advice

You need information to make decisions. While you will never have as much of the *right* information as you would like you will usually have too much information from which to choose from. As a Dean of Harvard Business School said: "The art of management is the art of making meaningful generalizations out of inadequate facts."

… there is so much information so easily accessible that you might never get to action, let alone results, if you were to try to sift through even a small fraction of it.

One problem with information is that it comes through filters. An example is this book. I have a point of view based on experience and I filter the information and present it with a certain bias. Sometimes this is intentional—the intention is to get you the right information and illustrate it in the right way so you can quickly move to action and results. But there will surely be many times that I have filtered the information unintentionally and unknowingly.

The same is true for any information you get, and there is so much information so easily accessible that you might never get to action, let alone results, if you were to try to sift through even a small fraction of it.

So how do you sort through it?

Be Skeptical

Be skeptical about what you hear, especially when you first encounter a source. Ask yourself if it makes sense and if it is consistent with truths that you already know. If it isn't, then at a minimum you should discount that source in that area. However, some sources that spew nonsense in some areas are quite credible in others. You just need to know the limitations of the source. Another thing to remember is that we all misspeak or get our facts wrong at times, so be a little forgiving but let those slip-ups be a warning never to let your guard down totally. If a source consistently provides information that violates common sense or is contrary to what you know to be true, then move on—you aren't getting any value for your time invested.

Discount Credentials

I have seen some horrible information come from people who you would think, based on their credentials, would be great sources. It is easy to get misled here. There are academics with no practical experience that claim to be market seers or who claim to have a "process" for entrepreneurship. There are venture capitalists who may have zero operating-experience and little venture-capital experience but yet purport to know how "things are done".

One class of credentials that always has weight however is the successes of current and former CEOs. These people are often great founts of information and wisdom in specific areas. However, they may have run a very different company than yours and therefore will be fighting their last battle, rather than your new one.

I have been on boards with former fortune-1,000 executives and CEOs. I found that in some areas their instincts were phenomenal but in other areas unique to startups they were at a loss. They had just never had to grapple with those areas before.

Recognize When Popularity is a Contrary Indicator

Some sources of information are very popular partly because they provide quality information. CNN is a great example of this. Other sources are popular because they provide lousy information in a popular package—look at the tabloid rack next time you are at the supermarket checkout.

The same holds true in business. Look for information that shows some thought and, while it may be positive, is not designed exclusively for your approval.

For example: I have visited some entrepreneur newsgroups where people are a bit too supportive, along the lines of:

Wow John! A banana slug plantation! What a great business idea! I bet you could use some of my fantastic recipes! ☺ That's just the kind of new delicacy that sells itself!!! BTW: are banana slugs members of the yellow food group?!

Beware of Truth by Repetition

Most conventional wisdom is true and it perpetuates because it rings true to so many people. However, a lot of conventional wisdom perpetuates because some group *wants* it to be true. There are many examples of this throughout this book, so enough said here.

… a lot of conventional wisdom perpetuates because some group wants it to be true.

Note the Better Sources that Do Filter

Sometimes you just need accurate information so that you can filter and draw conclusions on your own. However, more often, you have limited time and a more valuable source is one that does some filtering and draws some conclusions for you. Of course you need to know already, through your experience from some other means, that these sources are credible. But having a few credible sources that filter information and give you what you need is invaluable. This is part of the function of a strong executive-team. A second choice is a board or consultants that can serve that filtering function.

Look for Recommendations, Conclusions and a Point of View

These are important in working out whether the information and advice you are getting is useful.

> *For example: A company I worked with was preparing for an acquisition deal and had hired a consulting firm to do competitive research. The CEO threw up her hands and tossed me the market-research report. It was an alphabetical list of summaries obtained by going to competitors' Web sites. It wasn't totally worthless because the consultants had done some filtering and organization. However, because there were no pros and cons, no metrics on which to compare the offerings and no recommendations, the report was nearly worthless to this time-pressed CEO.*
>
> *A good source would have stepped back and asked what was important in comparing the competitors; i.e. what metrics could be used for a valuable comparison. In this case, as consultants, they should have asked their customer what she was looking for. They could have rated all competitors along those metrics and have provided several options for action and the pros and cons of each. And they could have made a recommendation with the reasoning for that recommendation. Now that would have been truly useful.*

Know that Better Sources Answer the Questions You Didn't Ask

I don't mean that they tell you why the sky is blue while you are discussing the value of a strategic relationship. I mean that they look ahead to issues that you may not even know exist. Good attorneys with business sense excel at this, as do advisors with relevant experience—especially the ones that have made some mistakes.

> *For example: We had a meeting with a company and an attorney to set up their LLC operating agreement and "stock" incentive programs for employees. The attorney agreed that the best option at present was to set up an LLC. However, he also pointed out the tax disadvantages that would result in a merger if it were to occur some years down the road. In thirty seconds he*

had transmitted some very useful and relevant information that none of the rest of us were even thinking about.

Realize that Common Sense is Too Uncommon

We now come full circle. Your sources should, primarily, make sense to you, their reasoning should be sound and their views of objective reality be accurate. Secondarily, they should have some experience in the areas about which they speak or enough experience in related areas that they can filter and synthesize information.

This last point also is important. If they can't filter, then you might as well do a search on the Web and take your chances. If they can't synthesize, then they won't give you any insights but only regurgitate information at face value.

Finally, their information has to be useful rather than only correct. This lighthearted story circulating on the Web seems relevant here:

> *A helicopter was flying around above Seattle when an electrical malfunction disabled all of the aircraft's electronic navigation and communications equipment. Due to the clouds and haze, the pilot could not determine the helicopter's position. The pilot saw a tall building, flew toward it, circled, and held up a handwritten sign that said "WHERE AM I?" in large letters.*
>
> *People in the tall building quickly responded to the aircraft, drew a large sign, and held it in a window of the building. Their sign said "YOU ARE IN A HELICOPTER".*
>
> *The pilot smiled, waved, looked at his map, determined the course to steer to SEATAC airport, and landed safely. After they were on the ground, the co-pilot asked the pilot how he had done it.*
>
> *"I knew it had to be the Microsoft Building, because they gave me a technically correct but completely useless answer."*

Market Acceptance

You may be able to find a way to test the market. If it is simply the sale of a product, then can you sell someone what you plan on making. You can do this by test-marketing or selling to a customer in advance of availability. The reason that this latter approach can be so compelling is because it is usually far more difficult than selling product that you already have.

You can do focus groups and other interactive marketing-studies but it is best to recognize their limitations. There is much you can learn from such market studies.

> *Examples are: what people expect the price to be, where they would expect to find it, what experience they expect based on their own assumptions and the marketing copy, what features they would like to see, how they think they might use it, whether they might gift it to others—the full list could fill its own book.*

What focus groups and marketing interviews are often not good at is judging demand and real purchase behavior… These methods also divorce the pain of spending real money from the desire to have something.

What focus groups and marketing interviews are often not good at is judging demand and real purchase behavior. Participants typically want to please the interviewer or facilitator and far more people will say they will buy than actually will do so. These methods also divorce the pain of spending real money from the desire to *have* something.

If you are trying to determine buying behavior the best way to test it (duh) is to get people to buy. With business customers, you might be able to get a contingent purchase or at least a letter of intent. With consumers, you can pitch them non-existent product and measure the response to your sales letter, brochure, email or advertisement.

Sales Agreement

The best proof you can get is actually to receive money for what you plan to sell in the future. This is very difficult to do, but if you can, you:

➢ are one hell of a salesperson

➢ know you can communicate the product's benefits

➢ know there is customer demand

➢ can predict sales for a given amount of effort.

Assuming that you can't yet deliver the product or service, you should have an agreement with your customer. That agreement should spell out what you are delivering in terms that are of importance to the customer. Customers don't care what titanium alloy you are using but they do care about the benefits of using it—that your product is corrosion resistant and weighs less than x grams.

You should commit to a delivery date and if your customer is a business, then you will likely be subject to some penalty for not fulfilling your commitment. The agreement is your opportunity to set expectations with the customer and you need to learn to do this in a way that does not disappoint.

The agreement is your opportunity to set expectations with the customer and you need to learn to do this in a way that does not disappoint.

If you are dealing directly with the consumer, then your pre-sales will be a little different and probably less formal. Nonetheless, the principles of expectation-setting and commitment are similar.

Letters of Intent and Memoranda of Understanding

Letters of Intent (LOI) or Memoranda of Understanding (MOU) are usually the next-best things to an actual sale or binding agreement. Of course these only apply if your sales are to businesses. The equivalent in the direct-marketing world would be for customers to register to purchase, register to be notified of availability or agree to be billed when your product is shipped to them.

The MOU typically lays out an understanding between at least two parties, saying what either party will do or provide as part of an exchange of value. The MOU is signed by all parties concerned to formalize and add some weight to the understanding. Generally, the MOU may or may not call for specific action. However, for the purposes of supporting your business, MOUs should call for specific performance and action.

The LOI is typically a letter from one party to another telling the second party of the intent of the first party. LOIs are typically signed by only the first party.

Both MOUs and LOIs are usually explicitly non-binding, which raises the question of whether or not they are Barney deals (see below). It is true that they are mostly unenforceable and do not represent contracts. If you can get a contract or written agreement at this stage, then by all means do so—MOUs and LOIs are by far secondary alternatives.

So what are these things good for? For one, they serve the purposes implied by their names. Let's focus on the LOI. A well-crafted and signed LOI explicitly states the intent of the person signing it. It is a communication tool that should be specific and written with an implied "if-then". I am assuming that this LOI represents a precondition to a sale.

A good LOI says that if YourCo's product weighs less than sixty pounds, can be delivered within twelve months, costs less than $1,400 and goes faster than one hundred miles per hour, then the customer intends to buy fifty of them.

Even though LOIs are non-binding, you would be amazed at how seriously most CEOs take them. If the company is small, LOIs should be signed by the CEO; if large, by the CEO or by someone running the division you will sell to. At that level, executives typically take LOIs very seriously and will do them only if they expect them to lead to results. In my experience, people are careful to make sure that LOIs truly do represent their intent. They view them as precursors to agreements, which can be pursued when you have reduced the risk enough for an agreement to be worth their time.

Another purpose of the LOI is that it gets you a "yes" from the customer and therefore increases the probability that, when you can deliver, you will be able to close the sale. Thus the LOI should be good validation for you or others that you probably have a viable business and can get sales. Because they are non-binding, you should try to obtain at least a few LOIs from people who mean what they say—just to hedge your bets.

In crafting LOIs you should have developed a relationship with the customers and know their needs very well. If they want your product then they should want you to succeed. If they want you to succeed then, in many cases, they will be willing to sign a letter of intent.

>*An approach that I have used successfully many times is to identify the needs of the customer and to talk to them about what I have in mind. That is, find out how many widgets they have projected to buy if the widget meets their requirements, and make absolutely sure that I understand their requirements. I then ask them if I can send them a soft-copy of an LOI that reflects our conversation. I ask them if it reflects what we discussed, and if so, to please sign it or change it and sign it as they see fit. In most cases they make a few minor changes and send the draft back to me; I say, "Great, that is exactly what I needed," and they then send me a printed and signed hardcopy*

>*Quite a few times customers have taken my draft and strengthened their intent or added complimentary details that are to my benefit. You need to balance making this type of thing easy for them with not being too pushy— they don't have to do this and there might not be much you can do for them right now. I should mention that I have never had anyone decline to sign a letter of intent that I drafted using this simple approach.*

LOIs can be used in many contexts as aids in understanding and in decreasing the risk as you venture forth. You might want them from vendors that you need, customers, marketing partners and others.

It should go without saying but I'll say it anyway: don't confuse intent with commitment. Get the commitment as soon as you think you have lowered your customers' risk to the point where they will sign. Even *binding* written agreements can be evaded—but that's another issue.

> *It should go without saying but I'll say it anyway: don't confuse intent with commitment.*

Barney Deals

Beware the Barney deal. Barney deals are content-free, everybody-feels-good "deals". Typically, they are non-specific, leave crucial details for some future and unspecified date, and are used to get interest from investors, vendors or customers—saying that you have an "agreement" with a well-branded company does get attention. However, at some point that "agreement" will be subject to due-diligence before any real commitment is made. It is at that point that you might lose significant credibility: when the people doing due-diligence see that the "agreement" is a Barney deal.

> *Beware the Barney deal. Barney deals are content-free, everybody-feels-good "deals".*

> *I remember an "agreement"—between a startup and a record company—that did not specify price, quantity, dates, performance or the specifications of the service to be delivered. Technically, an agreement had been signed but it left all the important details to some future mutual agreement. The CEO looked foolish in due-diligence for having claimed that he had an "agreement". This agreement was weaker than a specific, even though non-binding, letter of intent because it did not clearly accomplish anything except prove that in some fashion the startup had been in contact with the record company.*
>
> *The startup was referring to this Barney deal in presentations to investors as though it represented a likely sale. This supposed deal got investors' attentions but it couldn't pass the scrutiny of due-diligence. It also destroyed the credibility of the management-team members because they either did not know that it was a Barney deal or they knowingly misrepresented it— neither is the sign of a winner.*

Validation and Information Gathering— Guerilla Tactics

This section on validation and information gathering is subtitled guerrilla tactics because many of the examples in this section are more dependent on resourcefulness than resources. In other words, there are often ways to get what you need without much time or money.

Give to Get

… you will learn a lot by talking to people. By doing this, you learn about the things that you didn't know you were looking for.

A consistent theme in this book is that you will learn a lot by talking to people. By doing this, you learn about the things that you didn't know you were looking for. Or you may find that someone puts something in a perspective you had never considered.

So, how do you get time-pressed people to open up to you and give you those gems? In a way, it is fairly simple. You just need to be someone that your source wants to talk to. That means several things:

➢ It means being pleasant but businesslike. No one wants to talk to a jerk and few people want their time wasted. Make the experience pleasant for the other party.

➢ It means you need to provide some value to the other person. You are calling to ask for something of value to you and *taking* the time of the person to whom you are talking. Before you initiate the call or contact, think about what you have to offer. Since you have been doing planning and research in an area of interest to your contact— otherwise their knowledge would not be of interest to you—you probably have learned some things that the other person will find useful or interesting.

➢ It means not making it hard for people to talk to you by asking them to sign a non-disclosure agreement before you will say "good morning". Also, find ways to talk to people openly without giving away anything that is truly confidential. Usually there is much you can say without giving away anything about your secret sauce. If you will not open up, then you will find yourself isolated from the information you need most—the kind that comes from the folks in the trenches.

➢ Don't be a know-it-all or argumentative. I have had people I didn't know call me for information or advice and then try to start an argument with me about it. That was zero added-value for me; those conversations ended quickly.

Marketing Data

The easiest way to find market information is the old fashioned way—by accident. This happens more often than you might expect. When you are reading a lot on a particular subject, it is not unusual to find market numbers that you need quoted in magazine or newspaper articles.

The easiest way to find market information is the old fashioned way—by accident.

If you are not so lucky, then there are alternatives. One of them is to find people and companies in areas of interest. Look through their Web sites under the "investors" and "about us" sections for starters. But especially ripe are press releases. When people issue press releases with the frivolous quotes that journalists won't use, they often let their guard down in favor of self-importance and will drop some good information.

If all you need is one or two numbers, then you might be able to get them from a high-priced market-research firm for free. You can often find out which market-research firms might have the data you want by reading the abstracts or tables of contents of the reports that they sell for thousands of dollars. The next step is to call salespeople or analysts and tell them what you are doing and what data you are looking for. You might as well be up-front with them about the fact that you can't afford their reports. In many cases they will try to help you out. There are three reasons for this:

➤ You may have some insights that are valuable to them through your research or experience (give to get).

➤ They should want you as a future customer and realize that you can become one only if you get your company going.

➤ They realize that they aren't losing a sale in giving you the information for free because you couldn't buy it anyway.

Customer Data (Business to Business)

One of the obstacles in talking to potential customers is the difficulty of figuring out who they are. Finding the companies is usually pretty easy but finding the right individual within a company is not. The "system" is usually set up to guard individuals' precious time.

The best way to reach someone is through a personal relationship; i.e. through an introduction from someone you know. Second best is being able to call and say that so-and-so gave you the contact information and suggested you call.

If you can not get an introduction of some sort, then you can often—but not always—get through to someone by calling—but you still have to find out who to call before you can do this.

Press releases are excellent sources of contact names and titles. The names that you would not be able to get if you called the company's main number might be right in front of you in a press release. Interviews, company reports and SEC filings are also great sources of contact names.

Competitors

If you are professional about it and give to get, you can often obtain great information from competitors. Some topics will be off limits—their customers, their sales figures and other proprietary information.

However, there are some topics that might be of mutual benefit: information on a third competitor, general industry-information or information about a generally known supplier. Especially in the case of a competitor, you need to have something to give. And in this case it has to be something that does not damage you or is of too much benefit to your competitor. No doubt this is a delicate dance.

> *Note: It doesn't hurt to keep civil relationships with your competitors even as you try to destroy them in your field of competition. They may be your acquisition, acquirer or strategic partner at some point in the future.*

Vendors

The best tactic to use to get in bed with vendors is to refer them to other prospects.

Vendors can be excellent sources of industry and market information. Often they will have a broader view than any of your customers or competitors. In many cases they will talk to you simply because they want your business in the future. However, in many other cases, they will be reluctant to spend much time with you because you are not a "qualified" customer. They would rather wait until you are closer to the point at which you can become a paying customer.

The best tactic to use to get in bed with vendors is to refer them to other prospects. Not prospects that can compete with you, but other companies or people that you know that could become their customers. This is about the best give-to-get exchange that you can create for vendors.

As always, make it easy for them to help you. Know what you want to ask and do it in a way that does not sound like the inquisition. Don't ask them for proprietary information about themselves or be too nosy about your competitors. In early contacts this will just make them uncomfortable. Earn their trust and build a relationship before you pry too much. Know beforehand who you may be able to connect them with to their benefit.

Customer Data (Business to Consumer)

Again, talk to people. If you are interested in what people are buying, go to a store where people are buying competitive products and strike up conversations with people who are shopping. Go to stores during their slow times and talk to salespeople about what is selling and what pitches work. Tell the salespeople what you are doing and get their feedback. You can get amazing insights from the people who are selling directly to the end-user.

> *If your customers are early adopters, then visit a Sharper Image. If your product will depend on its styling to jump the adoption hurdle, then visit the Porsche store and look through fashion mags to see what thought leaders are telling people is "leading edge".*

Summary

Given that this is business, not science, you can't prove in an absolute sense that your opportunity will be a success. The best you can do is to inform yourself and reduce the risks before you put much at stake.

There are some opportunities that absolutely do not make sense.

> *For example, if you could create a great search-engine that would have to charge people twenty dollars per search to be successful and would cost fifty million dollars to develop, then you could be pretty sure that it wouldn't succeed. The price of the search would limit the market opportunity, which might be a good business if it needed little investment. However, the high investment-needs would not be justified by the limited opportunity.*

Having backup plans and alternatives can greatly increase your comfort level.

More typically, you will end up in a gray zone and have to make a gut call on whether to move forward with your opportunity. Having backup plans and alternatives can greatly increase your comfort level. Also, knowing yourself, and what you are willing to put at risk, will help you in making this tough decision.

Much of this chapter has been about how to get the information you need without going to great expense. It doesn't make much sense to move ahead as the only possible route when there is so much you can do to check your assumptions and reduce your risk.

Whatever you decide to pursue as your great opportunity will have risk. Once you have made that difficult decision, you may need help, financing and advice—the topics of the next three chapters.

6. HELP

No matter how good you are. No matter how smart you are. No matter how rich or well connected you are. You are going to need help.

You are going to need help, both because you don't know everything and because you don't have enough time to do everything. Most entrepreneurs are very quick learners and already have very broad capabilities. But they will still need help.

You are going to need help, both because you don't know everything and because you don't have enough time to do everything.

> *One entrepreneur in particular was good, not just piddling, at the following: Web site development, graphic arts, writing ad copy, database development, book authoring, developing strategy, finance, negotiation and planning. He, unlike many entrepreneurs, realized that his days were only 24 hours long and he had to get help in some of these areas so that he could focus his efforts on where he added the greatest value. This entrepreneur was also unique in that he sought out help in areas that were new to him or where he wanted another view.*

Unfortunately, this entrepreneur was the exception. More common are entrepreneurs who try to do everything themselves and run out of time or run out of ability. The bottom line is that, regardless of how much you *can* do—you will need help.

The bottom line is that, regardless of how much you can do—you will need help.

You will need help internally from your team. You will need help from external sources so that you can take advantage of their specific skills or so that you can benefit from their wisdom—without having to make the mistakes that made them wise. As a wise old saying goes:

> *Wisdom results in good judgement. Most wisdom is the result of poor judgement.*

External vs. Internal

There are four primary issues to consider when deciding whether or not to get help by hiring a permanent team-member or by using an outside source:

- cost
- duration
- bandwidth
- value creation.

Cost

If you can't afford to pay someone to do something that needs to be done, then you have a pretty easy decision. You just have to do it yourself or have someone else in your company do it. If it is wisdom that you need, then you might have to use some guerrilla tactics to get it from an outside source at little or no cost.

Duration

If your need is just temporary, then it will usually make sense to get help from the outside. Such help may cost more per hour, but may cost less overall. This is because it might take less time for an outside consultant to do the work and you will not have to pay for benefits, supplies, space, payroll taxes, tools and hiring and termination costs.

Bandwidth

There will be times when you are growing so rapidly that you just don't have enough work-hours in your company to get something done by a certain date. In this case, outsiders can be good sources of back-up bandwidth either while you recruit someone into your company or until the urgency passes.

Value Creation

If something needs to be done that is part of your core capability, then it should be done internally if at all possible.

This is the more difficult and more strategic issue. In most cases, you will not only be selling widgets but also building intrinsic value in your company. Remember that this is how your company becomes worth more than receivables plus hard assets.

If something needs to be done that is part of your core capability, then it should be done internally if at all possible. If you don't have the expertise to do it in-house, then hire it done but assign one or more of your people to work closely with the service provider so that they conscientiously acquire the expertise and bring it into your company.

Using outsiders to teach your company while they accomplish something can be very valuable. You will almost always learn more from good people than you will from even the best books or Web sites. If there is a capability that you want to develop within your company, then using consultants can be a fast and inexpensive way to jump-start that capability within your company.

In a later section I will discuss how to hire and use consultants so that you actually get something of value rather than a lengthy, leather-bound report whose primary use is to collect dust.

You will almost always learn more from good people than you will from even the best books or Web sites.

People Screening

This chapter is about getting help from good people. Hiring or using bad people is usually counterproductive in the sense that negative work gets done. Negative work results when the service provided is not only worthless but also sets back your company by eating up work-hours, sending the company in a bad direction or irreversibly screwing something up; e.g. a key business-relationship.

Obtaining and managing people is going to be your biggest and most important challenge. It is important because it gives you tremendous leverage. If you haven't seen it already, you will be amazed at what a difference a single person can make in a startup—both negative and positive. The trick is in defining what is "good", and this will depend on your needs as well as on the type of company you are creating.

Resumes are notoriously bad devices for screening people who are not being hired for specific technical skills. References are not much better for helping find good people, although they can help you root out some bad ones. In the end, again, you will have to make a judgement call based on your intuition and experience. So here are some thoughts on how not to get fooled.

Salt-shaker Syndrome

The story of the salt shaker is one of those persistent urban legends that I've probably heard ten or twenty times in some variation. It goes something like this:

> *Bob, who was president of the Tornado Attractor mobile-home park, was recruiting a grounds supervisor. He took the recruit, Leon, to dinner so that he could get to know him a little better and see if he passed the "salt-shaker test". At the T-bone Diner they both placed their orders and talked over sodas until the food arrived. After*

> *the food arrived, but before Leon had even picked up his fork, he salted his steak. Right then Bob knew that he wouldn't hire Leon. He knew from the fact that Leon salted his food before eating it that Leon was impulsive and likely to show up late for work—and* naked *no less. You see, the way a man salts his food tells you a lot about how he'll perform on the job.*

I've always thought that stories like these say a lot more about the Bobs than Leons. For one thing, Leon's job was not salting food, so why did the salt-shaker test have anything to do with it? Moreover, there could have been many reasons for Leon's salting his food before tasting. He could have eaten at the T-bone Diner many times before and known that their food was always bland. He could have found that throughout his life he'd always had to salt restaurant food and saw no point in wasting a bland bite on the unsalted version of his steak.

What does this have to do with this book? This: there are many instances in which absolutes don't apply in judging a situation or a person. Moreover, you need to determine what qualities and skills a person really needs to possess in order to add value for you and be careful not to infer that from irrelevant data—such as salting behavior.

In most cases one has to go beyond the superficial to get at what counts. Consider the case of Dennis and his homerun…

> *Dennis was a prospect who contacted me when I was a business-development executive. He called me the first time and talked for a half an hour about how great this company that he was starting was and how I had to work with him because he had a "homerun". I dismissed it as a lot of hot air and left it to him to follow up with me.*
>
> *Dennis called me about a week later telling me about his "fucking homerun" and how he had a number of business deals sewn up already. He went on for about twenty minutes and I knew I should qualify him before he ate up too much of my time. I said, "Dennis, this sounds pretty aggressive, are you well funded?" To which he answered that he was self-funding the deal and his funds were "fucking unnnn-limited!"*
>
> *I let him go on for another twenty minutes or so and he asked* me *how much funding he had. I said, "Your funds are fucking unlimited." To which he yelled into the phone, "Right, you're a fucking genius!" (There was uniformity in Dennis's use of adjectives.)*

> *On a business trip about a month later I stopped in to see Dennis. When I arrived in the meeting room there were six men in white shirts and ties, some of them smoking cigars. There was one guy with a black, turtleneck shirt, multiple gold-chains, wearing sunglasses in a dark room, smoking Kools and drinking a beer. Yes, that was Dennis.*
>
> *At the end of the meeting I got Dennis to agree to do some things that cost money to show his commitment. I figured I would never hear from this nutcase again. Instead he followed up within a few days and did everything he committed to. I also developed a good, and always entertaining, relationship with the guy. He wasn't crazy, he was just having fun and had a great sense of humor about himself.*

The moral of the story is that there was no way for me to know early on whether Dennis was for real other than by giving him a chance—albeit on a shorter leash than usual.

So, with people as with most things in business, you are well served by staying focused on what matters, on knowing what to measure and on when something meets your criteria; this will lead us soon to the Bozo filter.

Seeking A-People

The main reasons why you want particular people—whether permanent or temporary—on your team are:

➢ their skills

➢ their abilities

➢ their wisdom

➢ their insights

➢ their cultural fit

➢ the fact that they are not bozos.

Skills

Especially if you are hiring someone as an individual contributor, you may be more interested in the person's specific skills than anything else.

If you are hiring a programmer, then does the person know how to program in the languages you are using?

If you need an operating agreement, does the attorney you hire have the basic skills to write one?

If you already have some people with the skills you are seeking in your staff addition they can usually give you a pretty accurate assessment of someone's skills.

Ability

Ability is different from skills. If someone is a permanent hire, you may be more interested in the person's ability than the person's specific skills.

In one instance we hired a woman who was self-taught in several computer-languages and had good examples of her work. We hired her more for her ability to learn than for the specific coding-skills she already possessed.

This is why some companies go to such lengths to hire smart people with broad interests. They have the basic backgrounds and temperaments to pick up new skills.

Wisdom

Experience is worthless unless it gets processed to become wisdom... Insight is even more valuable than wisdom. It is the ability to draw from wisdom and underlying experiences to come up with truly unique conclusions and theories.

You may have noticed that experience is not on the list. This is because experience by itself is not worth much. I have experienced a hockey game but I would suck as a professional hockey player. Experience is worthless unless it gets processed to become wisdom; i.e. unless the person gaining the experience learns and draws some perspective from the experiences.

So, rather than looking at people's resumes to see where they have been, you need to probe to see the wisdom they have derived from their experiences. You want added value—not just people that can recount stories about past experiences, or try to do everything the way they did it at Prehistoric Technologies.

Insights

Insight is even more valuable than wisdom. It is the ability to draw from wisdom and underlying experiences to come up with truly unique conclusions and theories. Insight produces ideas and concepts that can be applied to new situations because the person has moved beyond the surface and been able to synthesize new thoughts based on past experience.

Cultural Fit

Presumably you have chosen the culture for your company so that it supports your company's success. Why would you hire anyone who is not a good cultural fit?

You will be tempted to deviate from this criterion and when you do you will usually end up regretting it. Poor cultural fit results in ineffective teamwork, destructive conflict and poor communications. Ineffective teamwork happens because people work from different perspectives and with differing personal goals and sources of satisfaction. Destructive conflict happens because the disagreements arise from fundamentally different objectives, rather than from different ideas about how to accomplish the same objectives. Poor communications happen because people's basic assumptions differ and so words take on different meanings and suffer from interpretations that are not in line with the team's intentions.

Not Bozos

This refers to the next section, which discusses the Bozo Filter. Very briefly, the Bozo Filter is a way for you systematically to score people on the ten or so personal qualities that are most important to you and your company's success.

Bozo Filters

As you seek out help and especially as you gain some level of success, people will crawl out of the woodwork to "help" you. Anyone can type "management consultant" on a business card and even credential programs will often be more marketing gimmicks than screens for you. Even when there is a credential body there can be huge variations within the credentialed group. The American Bar Association and American Medical Association are probably the two most well-known credentialing groups and they have done a great job of setting a minimum level of standards, but even a little experience with either profession will prove once again that you are on your own.

Over time, you will develop some intuition about who can really help you in an efficient way. To help you, someone has to have skills, insights or a mode of thinking that you do not have. But their basic principles need to be aligned with yours and they have to mesh with your work style. Otherwise every communication will result in moderate to severe brain-damage. This often manifests itself when you have the urge to say, "Just flipping do it," after arguing with people and realizing that they will never understand what you are talking about because their basic premises are out of phase with yours.

If people's principles are similar to yours, you will find that communication is far more efficient. There are so many things that need not be said because they are taken for granted by both you and your help.

There are some qualities that I think anyone helping you at a peer level should have. These are:

➢ self-assurance

➢ intelligence

➢ flexibility

➢ clarity.

Self-assurance

Self-assurance is important because insecure people will waste your time by telling you things to impress you rather than get to a useful result. Insecure help will also be defensive when challenged, rather than engaging in constructive conflict. And, finally, it will be easier to communicate with self-assured people since they can focus on what you are saying rather than the brilliant gem they should speak next or the name they should drop.

Intelligence

People who help you should be intelligent so that they can understand what is going on in your company and what your needs are without taking a lot of your and your team's time. They should not need a lengthy education at your expense.

Flexibility

You want them fighting your war rather than their last war.

Your help should be flexible so that people do not try to blindly apply a previously successful formula to your situation. You want them fighting your war rather than *their* last war. You want them to adapt to your company and its ebbs and flows so that both they and your team can work together efficiently.

Clarity

Clarity is so essential in communication that it would be easy not to mention it. But clarity here means, firstly, that people know what they are saying and, secondly, that they can explain it to you in terms that you can quickly understand. They can relate what they are saying in a way that is relevant to you and your business. This is where chart thinking comes in handy—can they draw the single diagrams and write the few bullet-points that make their points so obvious as to appear inevitable?

Other Qualities

You should probably think about other qualities that your help should have so that they don't drive you nuts. Or worse, cause some permanent damage. It might even be a good idea to make a list of ten or twenty principles someone must hold to be in sync with your company. I know this sounds a bit anal-retentive, but being specific about such things can save you the grief that you might incur by hiring people based on the firm they come from, their education or some other superficial qualification. And, after all, they might be absolutely fantastic at what they do but not be a good fit for you because your principles are not aligned.

... they might be absolutely fantastic at what they do but not be a good fit for you because your principles are not aligned.

Creating a Bozo Filter

I developed what I call my Bozo Filter after I found myself in a couple of business relationships that left me shaking my head and wondering how I let them develop. I knew intuitively, early-on, that something didn't smell right, but, because I couldn't reason why, I ignored the signals. My Bozo Filter helped me clarify what was important and provided some discipline in screening people.

I developed my Bozo Filter in a spreadsheet and listed in the left-hand column the qualities that were really important to me. I then made a series of columns for several people that I had worked with. With some of these people I had fantastic experiences and the experiences with others were pained or outright bad. I then scored each of these people from -1 to +1 on each quality, to see how they ranked. I added the scores so I could then check them against the way things had actually turned out. I used this system for about a year until it became almost second nature to reflect on the Bozo Filter before I engaged and invested any time or money in a business relationship. This greatly improved the quality of my business relationships.

While your Bozo Filter should reflect your priorities, mine is shown below as an example:

Bozo Filter						
	People					
Quality	A	B	C	D	E	F
Clarity	1	0	-1	1	1	-1
Self-assurance	1	1	0	1	0	-1
Results-orientation	1	-1	-1	1	1	-1
Urgency	1	-1	-1	1	1	-1
Honesty	0	0	-1	1	1	-1
Sense of humor	0	1	0	1	1	0
Trustful	0	1	-1	1	1	-1
Smart	1	1	0	1	1	-1
Quick	1	1	-1	1	1	-1
Flexibility	1	1	-1	1	1	-1
Integrity	-1	0	-1	1	1	-1
Bozotility	6	4	-8	11	10	-10

My relationships with A and B were awkward at times but generally positive and my business life was better for them. Relationships with D and E were absolutely fantastic. Column C refers to an evasive CEO who turned a great opportunity into a multiyear directionless slog, and F was the closest thing to pure evil that I have ever experienced.

Attorneys

We'll cover this early because you will need an attorney soon—even before you have fully formed your company or your team. And, for the small amount (hopefully) spent on attorneys, they can have an enormous impact on a company.

Some of the main reasons you will need an attorney are:

➢ An attorney will have far more technical legal knowledge than you can ever reasonably acquire on your own.

➢ Within their firms, attorneys will have access to partners that can answer specialized questions even when the attorney you consult cannot.

➢ An attorney will have experience doing things many times that you may only need to do once in your lifetime; for example, you might set up your company only once, whereas your attorney might have set up a hundred companies.

Acceptable Attorneys

We'll start with some minimum requirements, then move on to desirable qualities and then discuss how to manage your attorney(s) effectively.

The minimum requirements are:

➢ experience

➢ integrity

➢ problem-solving ability

➢ efficiency.

Experience

Your attorney should have some experience with businesses. While a divorce attorney may have taken the same law-school courses as a business attorney, the experiences of the two will be vastly different. Experience ensures that you will minimize your contributions to your attorney's post-graduate legal-education fund.

Experience also means that your attorney doesn't need to start everything from scratch on every project. If you need a non-disclosure agreement (NDA), the attorney should have several previously completed that you can either use immediately or with minimal editing—this will save you time and money. The attorney's job then is to provide you with the pros and cons of various terms and make a recommendation based on your particular business and your way of doing business. Depending on your preferences, you might want a one-page NDA out of principle or because it represents a low barrier to doing business with you, or you might want a longer NDA that covers some special cases or provides greater protection.

Experience also means that your attorney will have made some real-world observations. For example, the attorney will have seen many operating agreements and know the pros and cons of the many ways that a buy-sell section can be written. Attorneys can tell you what they have observed as a result of companies having, or not having, specific provisions in their agreements. With their business experience they can tell you how these events impacted the *business*—not just the legal ramifications.

Integrity

As I introduce this, I can hear you snickering and I am resisting the urge to insert several lawyer jokes. Even though attorneys' perspectives are shaded by the adversarial and somewhat mercenary environment in which they operate—they can, and many do, have integrity.

In particular here I mean that they have the integrity not to milk you for fees. They don't create or arbitrarily expand scope. They move you closer to completion rather than further away from it. They do not do things without your permission and then bill you for them. They do not nickel-and-dime you at every turn to see just how much they can get away with. It's an unfortunate fact that these behaviors are common at both large, well-known firms and small ones.

> *I once had an associate develop an agreement for me. Not only did she take an eternity to do it, but she started doing things I hadn't asked her to. She decided to take some initiative and review a Web site and tell me what I needed to change. Firstly, I hadn't asked her to do that. Secondly, I had written things for clarity and was comfortable, as a business decision, with the slight increase in risk associated with writing in a way that a real person might like to read. She thought my business should be governed by her priority to minimize risk. Ten thousand dollars later I had learned that I would have been far better off having a partner do most of the work, even though his rate would have been three times the associate's rate.*

Some firms will charge you a considerable amount for making photocopies or for organizing your files. Some of this is justified—it does cost money and take staff time. However, make sure that these charges are reasonable and related to work that you requested—and are not just a billing exercise.

Milkers will make up work, ask a lot of irrelevant questions, use the phone when an email would suffice, and manufacture dragons that they then need heroically to slay for you. These behaviors are insidious because you can't prove the milkers' intents. But you don't need to prove their intents: you are the boss and it's your time and your money. Your judgement is all you need—so use it.

Problem-solving ability

The risk in doing a deal can be minimized by not doing the deal. Unfortunately, this is also a great way to minimize your reward.

Another minimal requirement is that your attorney does not become a roadblock. Part of the reason that you hire attorneys is to raise issues. This is especially valuable for entrepreneurs because they think in terms of future possibilities and creating value and are incurably optimistic. Attorneys are typically great at raising issues and that is part of their value—but, to be truly valuable, they should be able to solve problems.

Businesses, and business relationships, are inherently risky and your goal is not simply to minimize risk. Your goal is to minimize risk while increasing your reward. The risk in doing a deal can be minimized by not doing the deal. Unfortunately, this is also a great way to minimize your reward.

Attorneys you use should at least try to understand your business issues and solve your problems. They should know that the world does not revolve around a thick codebook full of fine print and scary things.

Efficiency

The three preceding requirements all increase efficiency. However, there is one other aspect of efficiency to consider here.

Attorneys' jobs are not to tell you what you can and cannot do. They should tell you that if you do a particular thing, you can go to jail. Or, if you do something else, you could have a multimillion-dollar obligation if the other parties exercise their options. It's *your* decision whether it is worth the risk.

> *If you find yourself arguing or negotiating with your attorney once he has presented you with the pros and cons and you have made your decision, take your business elsewhere.*

If you find yourself arguing or negotiating with your attorney once he has presented you with the pros and cons and you have made your decision, take your business elsewhere. If people working for you behaved that way you would fire them. Why should it be any different for a service provider?

If attorneys have the minimum requirements, you can probably work with them and get a reasonable job done. This will cause you some brain damage at times but will keep you from making egregious mistakes.

Good Attorneys

Now we move on to what to hunt for in that rarest of business beasts—a good attorney. Good attorneys are efficient, prepared and able to think clearly. When you meet with them, they stay on task and get quickly to the point. Before you meet with them, they have done their preparation. They do what you ask them to do and they respect your way of doing business.

> *For example, in one negotiation in which I was involved I knew it was going to be a lengthy process with a lot of trivial back-and-forth before we got close to a*

final agreement. I decided, since the source of the dickering was the other side's attorney, I would let them finish fiddling at their expense before I got my attorney involved. I asked my attorney to look through the first agreement and tell me what issues he had. He spent about half an hour and sent me a pointed email with some insights I had not considered. This was true added value!

Then, after about three weeks of wrangling, I had an agreement that I thought I could sign and I asked my attorney to review it. In about half an hour he read through it, and, rather than raising numerous issues so he could create a billing opportunity he said that he might clarify a few things but, since it was in other respects a great agreement, I should sign it rather than open the door to further negotiation. This was great: he was thinking like a businessperson. Rather than trying to milk me or create a risk-free agreement, he understood that there was an upside that might be lost if we opened the door with secondary, technical issues.

This highlights the main criterion that separates the good attorneys from the mediocre. Good attorneys have some business sense. Mediocre attorneys see the world in terms of zero-sum transactions.

For example, I dealt with one company's mediocre attorney to create an operating agreement that distributed ownership to founders and employees. The attorney saw this as two transactions: employee start and termination. The business objective of the shared ownership was to provide incentives and retain employees and founders.

Evidently this notion was incomprehensible to the attorney. Whenever left to his own devices, he inserted clauses that created a liability or loss for the employees and founders. This would have been obvious to people reading the agreement, or at least to their attorneys. If this hadn't been corrected, it would have bred cynicism and had the opposite effect to what was intended. Eventually, we replaced him and he'll never really know why.

Good attorneys understand that you must take risks to be successful in business. They also understand that business is often more about relationships than transactions. There is a fundamental distinction here.

> *For example, in a transaction, say selling my car, I don't care how slimy the buyer is. But I don't want a business relationship with slime.*
>
> *Likewise, I will sell my car for the absolute highest price I can get. In a business relationship I want to maximize the long-term value created, so I may not play quite so rough on price in order to get a greater return in another area.*

The following diagram illustrates this distinction.

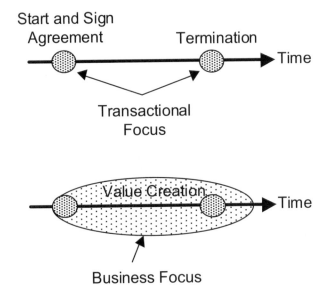

Good attorneys will not insert friction into your business. The type of friction I am talking about is the type that creates a barrier or resistance to doing business with you. Onerous and long non-disclosure agreements are one example of this. Firstly, the longer the agreement, the more likely it is to go unread and unsigned, which may mean that you never even get the opportunity to start a beneficial business relationship. Secondly, onerous terms will not go unnoticed and may be seen as a red flag that you may be hard to do business with.

Other sources of friction:

➤ Using legal terms or awkward concepts where common language will suffice.

➤ Referring too often to codes or laws by number, so that a reader is then obligated to look up or, more likely, pay someone to look up and interpret.

➤ Nesting references to multiple documents where agreement A refers to agreements B and C and B refers to A and C and C refers to A and B.

> *I have seen this done with as many as five agreements. Not only did it give me a terrible headache but I chose not to work with the person because he and his attorney refused to consolidate the agreements. My call was that if they did not value clarity enough to consolidate the agreements and make their meaning clear, then they didn't deserve to get past the bozo filter. I'll never know whether they were trying to hide something, intentionally creating ambiguity to weaken their obligations in case something went to court, or if they were simply unclear on their objectives.*

Finding an Attorney

How do you find a good attorney? How did you find your spouse or partner? Some luck, some skill, some trial-and-error and some courting. Ask other business people with whom you connect which attorney they use and whether they are satisfied. Go out of your way to meet attorneys at networking events and develop relationships with them.

Think back to agreements you have read that seemed especially businesslike or clear—then call the attorney that drafted the agreement.

You should talk to attorneys before hiring them and if you aren't totally sure about them then test drive them with a small task such as preparing a non-disclosure agreement. If you are concerned about their billing, then get an estimate in advance. Interviewing attorneys and getting an estimate before they start work is not unusual, so don't be intimidated if they balk. But do try to respect their time—only talk to them if you have a genuine intention to hire, and keep it brief and to the point. Your time and their time are both valuable.

By interviewing and getting an estimate you also set the tone for the relationship and are less likely to find mystery charges on your invoice. By respecting their time and getting to the point, you are more likely to find they return the favor and keep the billing time low.

If an attorney isn't working out then find another one. The work attorneys do for you is too important for it not to be done properly and if they make mistakes, these could be huge ones whose full costs do not emerge for years. And, as I said before, they work for you and you should not allow them to abuse the relationship.

Finally, if you are pleased with your attorneys' work, then refer them to others at every chance you get. This works for everyone. You get to help someone find good attorneys and the good attorneys build their businesses. This has the side benefit of culling the herd because you will have made it more difficult for bad attorneys to get work.

> **Myth:** *Attorneys will introduce you to investors.*
> **Reality:** *A few will, such as the large, coastal technology firms. However, most cannot or will not, so don't make that your primary criterion for selecting an attorney. An attorney's job is providing good legal-services, so make that the primary criterion. There are more than a few attorneys who use the implied promise of funding as a way to get new entrepreneurial clients. If this is the promise, then get at least one funding success story or several introductions before you hire that attorney.*

Large vs. Small Firms

Consider the following table which shows how to score large vs. small firms (large firms have hundreds of attorneys and small firms have from a few up to ten attorneys):

	Small Firm	Large Firm
Contacts	+	+++
Breadth	+	+++
Service	+++	++
Availability	+++	+
Rates	+++	+
Financing	++	+++
Clout	+	+++

A large firm, simply by virtue of the number of attorneys it has, will have a better network. If you are seeking someone or something, chances are that someone in a large firm can give you the contact for which you are looking. A large firm can have considerable breadth, with specialists in everything imaginable.

The service at a small firm will usually be better. You will be dealing with the same one to three people all the time, whereas at a large firm, as a small client you may get shuffled around. This can be costly, because every time you get new attorneys you pay them to learn.

The availability at a small firm will be far better than at a larger firm. At a larger firm, if an IPO comes in, you may have to wait awhile to get your phone calls returned.

Rates at a small firm will almost always be lower than at a larger firm. However, a large firm can still be great value. For example, it may have done so much work in your area that it takes the attorneys in the large firm far less time than those in a small firm to obtain the same results.

On the one hand, large firms' abilities to connect you with financing may be great; large firms may even have institutional mechanisms for this. For example, one coastal firm has regular breakfasts for clients who are seeking funding to present to clients who are looking for investments. In small firms, on the other hand, the attorneys may have fewer but very close relationships with their investor clients.

While clout is fairly superficial, the brand name that comes with some large law-firms can look good to some investors, vendors or customers. In litigation it can intimidate your opponent or show that you are playing to win. The main thing is that you have a respected law-firm, even if it is small and/or regional.

While I have used a comparison of small and large firms to make the differences clear, midsize firms can be great options. These are firms with 30 to 60 attorneys. They are large enough to have most of the benefits of large firms and small enough to have many of the benefits of small ones. This of course depends mostly on the individual firm and then the individuals with whom you work within that firm. Using a midsize firm has worked out well for me, but to some extent I got lucky by getting introduced to some excellent attorneys there.

Partners vs. Associates

The use of partners as opposed to associates is something that you need to manage. Associates can be a real bargain on some straightforward work but they often don't have the experience and wisdom to offer you sound advice or to find a clear path to solving a tricky problem.

Even though partners are usually far more expensive on an hourly basis, they can turn out to be the least expensive route to a quality result.

Managing Your Attorney

This company is yours and your team's. You have responsibility for its success and failure. If you have chosen your attorneys well they will be highly competent professionals who sincerely want you to be successful. However, they will usually not be shareholders or have anything at risk in your company.

Many firms do now invest in or encourage their partners to pool funds to invest in client companies. I think this is a very healthy development since it moves the emphasis from activity to results. The attorneys get paid for activity, but they get ROI for results they help create. However, the amount of money invested is usually relatively small.

I have seen some startups turn over responsibility for some business matters to attorneys. This can be disastrous. If the attorney is transaction oriented and negotiating a deal for you, the work done can irreversibly damage a business relationship or botch the deal altogether.

Because they don't eat, sleep and breathe your business as you do, attorneys won't have the same information that you have about your business. This results in less agile deal-making because they do not have the appropriate backgrounds to come up with a creative and winning deal. They will not have the knowledge to see where value can be created simply as a result of a business relationship.

Another reason not to pass all responsibility for deals or agreements to attorneys is that it is not their relationship to manage for the long term. This is simple "account management". The person within the company who owns the long-term relationship should be involved every step of the way. In the startup stages that person will almost invariably be you.

The person within the company who owns the long-term relationship should be involved every step of the way. In the startup stages that person will almost invariably be you.

When an attorney prepares an agreement for you, you should understand the terms in that agreement. This is often not the most exciting reading, but it is your responsibility to understand the agreement, to understand the implications for your business and to make sure that the terms of the agreement are honored by all parties—including your own company. You don't have to deal with the what-if scenarios relating to the various terms entirely on your own—your attorney can usually help you.

You need to allow a reasonable period of time for your attorneys to complete their work, as you would with your team. To provide some perspective, the following times are typical when you account for the mismatch in schedules and the need for some iterative problem-solving between you and your attorney:

➢ NDA: 1-3 days

➢ operating agreement: 1-3 weeks

➢ stock-purchase agreement (private): 1-2 weeks.

These times are calendar periods. It should not take the attorney this many person-hours to do the work. The times given also assume that you have done your homework, have a good idea of what you want and have communicated well with your attorney. Even the best attorneys are not telepathic.

Before you start on some legal work, do some expectation setting. Let the attorney know when you would like the work completed and find out whether that is realistic and what you need to do to make it possible. This assumes that you have developed enough trust with your attorney that you don't feel the need to pin the attorney down to a certain number of hours. This is a point you should reach after one, or at most two, projects.

Recruiting the Team

The simple version: recruit great people who are culturally aligned and work well as a team.

The simple version: recruit great people who are culturally aligned and work well as a team.

Ideally, you are working through this book and planning your company with some like-minded people that are going to be part of the team. You have all been through Chapter 3 and, although some of you are stronger in some areas than others, each person's strength complements someone else's weaknesses.

In the real world, it is more likely that you have been doing a lot of vetting on your own and have a handful of people you would like on your team but most of them will not commit until you have proved the model, can pay them or have received financing.

Make sure that you are hiring some people with the wisdom to get you to the next major, value-creation milestone or further. Again, wisdom is not experience—just having been there is not enough. There are plenty of older people with vast experience and little wisdom and plenty of young people who have little experience but have learned a great deal from it. This wisdom-vs.-experience distinction is why resumes are notoriously bad screening tools. Unfortunately, I'm not clever enough to come up with a better introductory tool than the resume or bio.

Someone with startup experience should be one of your requirements. If you don't have that experience, then do your best to find someone who does. There are so many things about doing a startup that cannot be learned except by having lived it. It's analogous to looking at pictures of Yosemite Valley rather than going there.

There are so many things about doing a startup that cannot be learned except by having lived it.

The pictures are beautiful and they are accurate representations of what you would see if you were there. But there is a huge difference between looking at the pictures and being immersed in a deep valley almost entirely surrounded by massive, granite formations.

Preferably, the startup experience of someone in the company will include failure as well as success. People learn more from failure: if all they have known is a single success they may be confusing skill with luck. Multiple successes are a different story—they are rarely luck.

People learn more from failure: if all they have known is a single success they may be confusing skill with luck.

Paradoxically, the right person from a large company can be a great team member. For the person who wants to learn, a large company allows exposure to many people, skill-sets, temperaments and management styles. The key is whether the person did, in fact, take advantage of this and acquire some wisdom, or just acquired a big-company mindset. Big-company experience can also be helpful in understanding the way your business customers or vendors do business. Also, a person from a big company might be able to see ahead clearly to the day when you do need more process or operational focus.

As you form your team, try to find ways to work with the people you are recruiting before you commit. Have them help you solve a problem or ask their opinions on a real strategic problem you are chewing on. This allows you to see how quickly they learn, how well you can communicate with them and how smoothly the give-and-take goes. You might even want to include other members of your team to see if there is any friction among them. Choosing a real problem here is far better than a hypothetical one. This is because it *matters* and isn't just a test of the wits. It is also better in that you will have incomplete information and it will be as consistent as the real world allows. This is difficult, if not impossible, to simulate fully in a hypothetical situation.

Think ahead about how the management team will evolve over time. It will change as you need additional capability and as your company changes. Talk openly about how roles might shift over time. This is not a question of people "growing into" roles. Some people are better at different phases of a company than others—neither of them needs to "grow".

> *One company that I helped start was set up from the start to have CEO and VP roles that would change when sales started. The initial CEO had extensive startup-experience, had built teams and knew how to get a product quickly developed and to market. The initial VP had a lot of experience running a company with moderate growth and little development and which needed solid, operational management to maximize sales and profitability. The CEO and VP decided in advance to switch roles a few months before sales began so that the company would always have the best leader in place for the phase that it was in.*

You should try to find out what the long-term goals of your team members are. You have no obligation to help them achieve those goals and their first responsibility is to make the company successful. However, when you can help your team members in achieving their long-term goals and benefit the company at the same time, you will have a more motivated and loyal team.

On recruiting friends—don't do this on the basis of friendship alone. The one example I have seen of a CEO recruiting a team of friends, without regard to their abilities, was an absolute disaster. Before you recruit a friend ask yourself: can I hire this friend? And, more importantly, can I fire this friend?

The real question is how much value they add, not how much they cost.

Some entrepreneurs have unrealistic expectations of what they can pay people. Don't assume that, because you are giving them some stock options, your team will be willing to work for $20,000 per year. Good people cost money and you may be short-changing yourself by being too cheap in hiring. The real question is how much value they add, not how much they cost.

> *I remember helping a CEO set up a sales-compensation system. At one point in designing the incentives he said: "I can't do that. If she exceeds the second sales milestone she will make more than me." I pointed out that if the sales VP exceeded the second sales milestone, she would have doubled the company's sales, more than doubled its profit and more than doubled the company's valuation. Moreover, with the money that VP of sales could bring in, the CEO could either use some of the profit to give himself a raise or leave it in the company to fund growth. In a nanosecond*

this CEO decided that his desire to grow his company was greater than his desire to keep compensation low.

Finally, don't hesitate in recognizing your recruiting mistakes and terminating people's employment when you need to. But try to learn from those mistakes so that they are infrequent. High executive team turnover is always an indication

... don't hesitate in recognizing your recruiting mistakes and terminating people's employment when you need to.

that something is wrong. Terminations take a lot of energy from the team before they are completed but can be very energizing once they are in the past. I have never heard CEOs say that they fired anyone too soon.

Consultants

Management Consultants

It seems as though everyone is a management or marketing consultant—it's pretty easy to print the words on a business card.

Good consultants—those with both wisdom and insight—are worth their weight in gold. With respect to risks, they will save you from making mistakes, save you time, save you money and help with alternatives and backup plans. With respect to rewards, they can help you find points of leverage and ways to exploit them profitably. They can help you identify opportunities as well as areas of focus.

One of the things that good startup-consultants bring, and which is hard for you to replicate, is breadth of experience. Because they will have worked with many companies they will have good instincts. They will have seen what succeeds and fails—from a phenomenological viewpoint instead of a theoretical one.

When you are in the startup phase and looking for startup-specific, strategic-level assistance, I believe that you will usually get greater value from the right individual than from a large firm. The emphasis is on "right". On the one hand, there are many more bozos than there are good consultants, which means that it may take some effort to find that right individual consultant. On the other hand, you are usually assured of a certain minimum-level of quality with anyone in a large and well-respected firm. You may end up with someone who is mediocre from a large firm but probably not bad.

The large firms often have their "startup experts" or "startup practices" within their firms. People who can survive in large consulting-firms are almost by definition not entrepreneurs. They also often lack real-world experience because they don't get too involved with their clients. Their mode involves studying, drawing on some research, and providing you with a report from which you can either draw your own conclusions or take some action. They also often lack any real startup-experience and are too process-oriented. Simply following a series of steps will not make you successful. There are many processes that can lead to success but it isn't the process that makes you successful—in fact most processes are pretty obvious. It's the way in which you work through it that makes you successful.

Simply following a series of steps will not make you successful... it isn't the process that makes you successful—in fact most processes are pretty obvious. It's the way in which you work through it that makes you successful.

You are usually better served by small management-consulting firms or individuals when in the startup stages. Later, the collective organizational experience and contact base of a large firm can be of benefit as you move to operations-oriented stages of your company's development. In fact, at those later stages, a midsize or larger firm has clear advantages over an individual consultant.

It is rarely necessary to apply the proprietary, 8-Point, ABC Company Startup Process to your business. It is even more rarely necessary to have a fifty page report with helpful advice such as, "Motivate your staff for better results," "Raise more money as a safety cushion for economic downturns," or, my personal favorite, "To set a valuation, get five or six investors competing for your deal and then compare term sheets." It's hard to disagree with any of that advice, but how many companies have five or six term sheets to compare at their leisure? It's obvious and correct but the real art is in doing such things rather than saying they should be done.

Good consultants will have startup experience at an operational level. That is, they won't just have learnt about starting companies from this book and Red Herring—they will have lived it once or several times. They know, for example, how hard it is to qualify opportunities in a startup, and that some of the greatest changes in your company will come about by hiring or terminating the employment of a single individual. They know how high the risk really is. They know where the bodies are buried and know enough not to believe without question what is in print or comes from the lips of self-appointed experts.

You should have chemistry with business consultants, as with any service provider. If you have very different values, then it is hard for them to act or recommend in your best interest. As has been repeated over and over in this book, their ideas and observations have to make sense to you. And some of these should provide insights and wisdom that are not obvious or that you don't already know—else, what's the added value? Business consultants should have many of the same qualities as good entrepreneurs—and be good entrepreneurs. Especially important are:

> ➢ results orientation

> ➢ a sense of urgency

> ➢ clarity

> ➢ intuition

> ➢ resourcefulness.

Especially valuable is insight.

> *I was working with a company that was starting a wireless integrator. We met over lunch with a consulting firm that we thought might be of some help. It billed itself as having technology and marketing experts who were well connected with investors and the technology community. During the lunch, I kept asking the consultants simple questions. After the lunch, when we were alone, the CEO asked me what I thought. I answered with a question: "Did you hear a single insight in that hour and a half, from two of their senior partners, while they were trying to impress us, that you didn't already know?" The answer was, "No". And the obvious course of (in)action was to not use that firm. There was no reason to believe that they would add significant value in ten or one hundred hours if they could not add any value in an hour and a half.*

Skills-based Consultants

Skills-based consultants are people you bring in because of their specific skills. They need to be mostly self-managing and able to get to speed quickly so that you don't have to pay them to learn too much. Then, of course, they need the specific skills. They might be Java developers or bookkeepers. They should know their stuff and preferably be able to teach some things to the people in your company. They should be efficient and hard working.

Skills-based consultants don't necessarily need to be great cultural fits—the level of need here will depend on how long you will use them. Their interaction with the company is temporary, and because they have little or no impact on the management team they are not likely to confuse or dilute your culture. Because their job is to work as highly competent, individual contributors, they tend to avoid any type of conflict—but especially destructive conflict.

You can hire skills-based consultants reasonably well from resumes and even brief interviews. After all, the risk is relatively low. If they don't work out or don't have the specific skills they claim, then terminate their contract sooner rather than later.

Project Consultants

Project consultants are individuals or firms that take on full projects. Two examples are product development and Web development.

The most common use of project consultants is to get a non-core part of your business up and running without having to build or manage that capability in-house. This allows you and your team to stay focused on your core business.

> *In the earliest stage of company creation it is not unusual to use project consultants to do even core parts of the business. This may be because you want to get part of your business running to test the market before fully committing yourself and your money. Or, you may need financing before you can really get started and you realize that the shortest route to financing is a strategic relationship, which requires completion of a prototype. So you hire a product-development firm to get you through the early product-development phases*

The theory of how project firms like to work is that they work with you to develop a specification at your expense. Then, if you agree with the specification, they will build to that specification. If you want changes, then you will be charged for those changes.

In reality, what happens is that you are doing everything in parallel in an uncertain environment. You are refining your view of the customer and the market requirements on a weekly or daily basis. Consequently, your idea of a specification is changing at least as quickly. You are also developing new ideas that you want to incorporate in the project. So what was supposed to be a carefully thought out and nearly static specification is nearly obsolete by the time it leaves the laser printer.

Much of the art of successfully starting a company is knowing the balance between getting ready to do something on the one hand and pulling the trigger and doing it on the other.

This "process" of moving ahead with incomplete information, which is every bit as messy as it looks, is usually the most efficient way to get the result you need. If you planned enough and did enough research then the specification would be fairly static and the *development* would be efficient. But, as a whole, you would have spent more time and money due to the up-front work and end up with a result that took longer and cost more than the iterative fire-drill that is more common in startups.

This is not to say that you shouldn't do some planning and research. Much of the art of successfully starting a company is knowing the balance between getting ready to do something on the one hand and pulling the trigger and doing it on the other. Pull the trigger too soon and you could end up with a patchwork that won't work as a whole. Too much preparation and you never really get started and run out of time or money, or miss your market or funding window.

The project-consulting firm also knows that things will deviate from specifications and that it won't be able to charge you for every little change, so it will pad its quote if it is a fixed fee. If the quote is for time and materials, the firm will often leave the estimate low and then blame you, rightly, for the increased costs due to your changes and scope creep.

Project-consulting firms can help you prove your model and get you jump-started with their skills, breadth, infrastructure and tools. However, they might take your time and money and leave you with a product that you need to throw away so that you can start afresh. To avoid the latter takes some high-level thinking about objectives and specific deliverables, a lot of interaction and communication with the consulting firm and frequent checking of the work to make sure that it is on track.

My advice is that you make your decision based on the following flowchart:

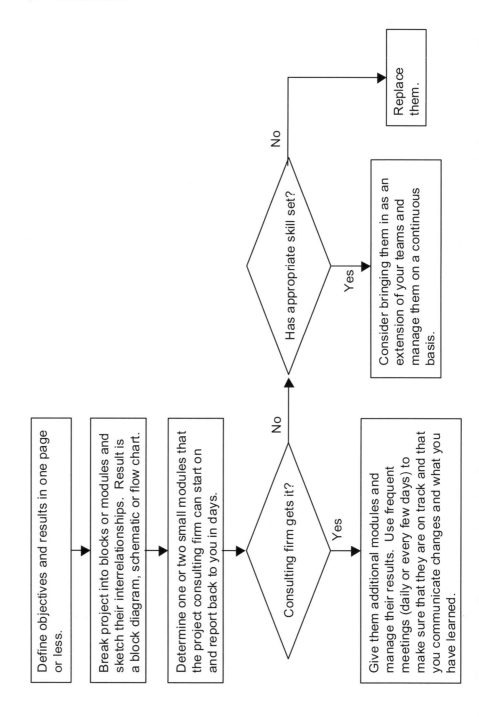

Finders and Investment Bankers

Finders

Finders find money for you for a fee (often a percentage of the deal—4% to 10% of both the dollars and the equity in the transaction). It is tempting to think that these people can find you money. But consider these questions:

➢ Why would they present your deal better than you can?

➢ Do they have a verifiable record of success?

➢ Or, do they have the contacts to get you the money?

➢ Who is taking the risk in their fee structures? If they are charging a large up-front fee and a retainer, then you are taking the risk—it's all upside for them because they are making good money off of you whether they succeed or not.

I would much rather see finders get large percentages than take up-front fees that are unconnected to how they might perform.

Investment Bankers

Investment Bankers are usually associated with firms that have broker dealer licenses. You can check with the SEC to find whether they have had any disciplinary actions or whether there are any complaints pending against the principles. The term "investment banker" covers a lot of ground. It includes people who are just finders with broker dealer licenses and people who can solicit and manage acquisitions or initial public offerings; one-man shops and large firms with research and legal departments. Investment bankers range from relatively slimy rent-seekers to highly skilled professionals who kill what they shoot at and skin what they kill.

Investment bankers range from relatively slimy rent-seekers to highly skilled professionals who kill what they shoot at and skin what they kill.

For the purposes of this book, it makes sense to focus on private fundraising since that is likely to be where you would use an investment banker. Good investment-bankers should be very well connected and have vast networks of people that they can draw from in trying to match funding with businesses. They will have business sense and not just be money salespeople—they will be able to help you position your business plan and refine your pitch. They will often want to prepare a private placement memorandum. This provides some additional liability protection for them and their firms. Make sure that the PPM does not suck the life out of the description of your business.

Investment bankers typically get paid at least a percentage of the cash they raise. This is usually in the range of 4% to 10%, with 6% probably the most common percentage. Many investors will not allow more than 6% of their money to go to a finder or investment banker and this will be in the term sheet and definitive agreement—don't let an investment banker screw up your deal by creating a contractual obligation that puts off investors. Some investment bankers will also take a percentage of the equity transacted that is about the same number of points as their take of the cash transacted. Some investment bankers require an upfront fee and a retainer. Ostensibly, the upfront fee is for preparing documentation, financials, business plans and private placement memoranda. Some investment bankers will ask for $20,000 to $30,000 for this work, which I think is far too high for preparing material that you can do largely on your own.

Some investment bankers will ask for retainers. It is argued that a retainer makes you more committed to the process and pays some of the investment bankers' expenses. This is a valid point, since there are so many people who want to come up with an idea, have mountains of money given to them and then cash out in a few years. They tend not to fare well under investor scrutiny, which makes it hard for the investment banker to close a deal. Retainers with top firms should be in the range of $5,000 to $10,000 per month or less. But do careful due-diligence before parting with any money. Also, if the investment banker really can deliver, you should expect her to do careful due diligence on you and your company since she really does make her money on the transaction rather than the retainer.

Chambers of Commerce

This is a short and equivocal section that can be summed up in this way: some great value but beware.

Chambers of commerce are extremely variable. They are often not in a position to judge the quality of their service providers and volunteers. Also, they try to serve such a broad range of interests that you may struggle to find relevant programs and services. They are often serving Fortune 500 companies, one-person hair-salons, hundred-person technology-companies and raw startups.

Chambers of commerce can offer some excellent, low-cost programs and advice; the trick is figuring out what is good and what is not.

Incubators

At their best, incubators can give you access to talented people, investment, advisors, and other incubator companies. They might be run by serial entrepreneurs who have vast experience that they can share with you and a talent for finding clarity. They might be parts of venture funds or corporate ventures. They can be great sources of advisors because of their contacts and their visibility within communities. Unfortunately, not all incubators live up to this potential.

At their worst, they are overpriced office-space with self-appointed experts that, though well-intentioned, will lead you in the wrong direction. Then, not only do you have the task of building a company, but also of recovering from the time and money lost in going in the wrong direction for a while.

Incubators fall broadly into two classes—non-profit and for-profit. In either case, the quality is highly variable and you need to do some due diligence before you make a commitment. Part of that due diligence is asking yourself whether you really need to be incubated—regardless of how good the incubator is.

Rather than believe the success statistics of the incubator itself or assuming that if it is associated with a well known individual or institution it must be good, you will need to talk to present and former clients of the incubator to be able to set your expectations realistically.

Non-profit Incubators

There are some good non-profit incubators that clearly add value to their client companies. This added value usually takes the form of advice or connections. The better incubators have vast extended networks of advisors and have talented entrepreneurs on staff. The trick of course is to not confuse quantity with quality and you will need to screen advisors and others that you find through the incubator much as you would if you were independent of the incubator.

The better incubators have vast extended networks of advisors and have talented entrepreneurs on staff. The trick of course is to not confuse quantity with quality...

To some extent, non-profit incubators are a la carte office-suites of the type you find now in even moderate-sized cities. The tenants pay a monthly rent, and pay for photocopies and so on. But this is often not enough to pay staff salaries and expenses and so they use fundraisers and/or public funds to keep the doors open.

This brings to the fore a reason that many non-profit incubators are limited in their ability to add value. They aren't businesses in the usual sense. The people that would help you often have a limited stake in your success and therefore may not have the commitment to your success that someone you pay or someone who has invested in you.

This is not to say that a good non-profit incubator is not the right place for you to start. Just realize that no one and no incubator can *make* you successful. Before entering an incubator it is important to understand clearly what you will gain from the relationship by talking to other entrepreneurs that are in the incubator as well as some who have left and now have a more distant perspective. If all that you are going to get from an incubator is space and photocopy privileges, then you can probably find a better bargain elsewhere.

For-profit Incubators

Many for-profit incubators have been founded by successful, serial entrepreneurs. Many of them also invest in their companies and then offer the services of an experienced team to these companies. Historically, many of these efforts failed because too many of the staff were less experienced than they thought they were and because they were built on the assumption that the wild IPO market would persist indefinitely. Their business model was predicated on a quick return from incubated companies of one to three years—those days are over.

Because the individuals at for-profit incubators have economic interests in your success, they are pretty hard-nosed about who they admit to their incubators. However, once you are in the incubator they have an incentive to work hard to help you succeed. They also have incentives to help you find additional funding. The flip side of this direct connection to your success is that for-profit incubators will also tend to be ruthless in cutting you off if they don't think you will succeed, whereas most non-profit incubators will let you stay as long as you pay your bills.

In the current funding-environment, venture-capital and corporate-sponsored incubators can give you a significant advantage in getting funding from them. Some are only funding opportunities that have passed through their incubator. In the time you are in the incubator, they get to know you and your business and this allows them to lower their risks compared to a first-, or seed-round deal that comes in from outside their walls. And the hurdle for entry into the incubator is usually much lower than that for first-round funding without going into an incubator.

Summary

Whether or not they are on your payroll, you will need help from people—advisors, consultants, customers or vendors—if you are going to be successful. In this chapter we have discussed the pros and cons of internal vs. external sources of help. The reality of a startup is that in practice you might have to do some things that, in a perfect world, would not be in your long-term strategic interest.

Picking, managing and leading people is very difficult and is what separates the great successes from the zombies (the living dead) and failures.

The people who will have the greatest impact on your company are those on your team. However, especially in the early stages, attorneys and management consultants can have huge and lasting impacts. They can help you set up the company properly to reduce long-term risk and maximize your opportunity. This affects not only the company structure but also the planning, strategy and organizational development that will help your company to maintain an upward slope. Too often, companies do not set stable foundations and so they make great progress for six months to a year and then stall while they keep trying to make the old mode of operation work for a new phase. They then decline or figure things out and resume the upward slope.

In this chapter you will have read some approaches that will help you pick people without wasting your time or money. You will also have realized that there are no seven-step processes or magic formulas for doing this. Picking, managing and leading *people* is very difficult and is what separates the great successes from the zombies (the living dead) and failures.

7. FINANCING

In some cases, companies simply cannot be done without financing of some sort. In other cases, companies are at substantial competitive risk unless they can fight hard in the marketplace. In still other cases, it is a question of leaving money on the table; i.e. even after the dilution that results from selling equity to investors the company can provide a greater ROI to the entrepreneur with funding than without it. And finally, some ideas are so grand that they really cannot be done on a small scale. An example of this is companies that require infrastructure (think cell-phones) or standard setting (think video chipsets).

Some companies want financing to cushion some of the risk. There is nothing wrong with this and it provides a win for both entrepreneur and investor. However, know when this is your reason so you can objectively weigh the pros and cons of taking investment.

Bringing financing into your company can allow you to ramp more quickly and recruit better people from the start. It will give you clout with the companies with which you need to work. If you are not well established, a common qualification-criterion that vendors will have before they spend much time with you is that you have raised significant capital. On many occasions the source of the capital will also be a source of wisdom and have an extensive network.

... as soon as you take someone else's money you have an obligation to provide them with a good return on investment.

On the minus side, as soon as you take someone else's money you have an obligation to provide them with a good return on investment. In most cases, you will eventually give up control through fundraising and it is not uncommon for founders to find themselves unemployed after a couple of years (this is not generally a bad thing, however). If you have unsophisticated investors, and too many of them, they can take a lot of your time or be difficult to work with.

To put things into perspective, here are some sources of funding for startups in order from the most common to the least common:

➢ yourself

➢ friends and family

➢ debt

➢ vendors

➢ customers

➢ sophisticated individuals

> ➢ venture capital

> ➢ strategic investors.

We'll discuss these and other sources in the course of this chapter.

Planning

If you have decided to look for outside financing and want to keep your sanity, then you will want a plan.

If you have decided to look for outside financing and want to keep your sanity, then you will want a plan. This plan is basically a sales funnel. Instead of selling a product or service, you are selling part of your company. Your customer is the investor.

You start with how much money you need, your exit strategy, your business type and your business objectives. From these you can develop qualification criteria. Among your qualification criteria are:

> ➢ the type of investor

> ➢ the typical investment size

> ➢ the availability of money

> ➢ whether the investors do investments in your "space"

> ➢ the place of investment

> ➢ the fact that the investors do not have competitive portfolio companies.

From these qualification criteria you can start identifying prospects. This is especially easy with venture capitalists because you can find them in listings and then do research online on their portfolios and activities. If you are looking for individual investors, it is harder to fill the top of your funnel.

Decide in advance on the intermediate results you need to obtain to achieve your final objective. You might have to set limits on what you are willing to do or how long you are willing to pursue this.

> *For example, contact 30 well-qualified venture-capitalists through introductions within six weeks, get five or more meetings and close one or more investors. Obtain meetings within ten weeks of start and close financing within sixteen weeks. If this does not work then scale back VC search to 20% of time and move to plan B.*

A plan will tell you whether or not you are making progress and will also let you know what you need to do to achieve the major milestones. And, if you start with a plan in mind, you are more likely to develop multiple financing-options at about the same time. Having multiple investors interested at the same time is the best way to move a close along and maximize your valuation. This is especially true if you need to syndicate the investment.

Having multiple investors interested at the same time is the best way to move a close along and maximize your valuation.

As with all planning, it's important to develop alternatives in advance:

➤ If you can't get venture capital in a reasonable time frame, then do you pursue individuals for a scaled-back business plan or do you get a line of credit on your house?

➤ What are the backup plans and at what point do you jump to an alternative opportunity?

> **Myth:** *Real entrepreneurs do whatever it takes to get venture capital.*
>
> **Reality:** *There are many VCs who, if asked, "At what point should an entrepreneur give up on trying to find funding?" would reply, "If you give up on raising funding then you aren't an entrepreneur."*
>
> *This is a facile answer and ignores the fact that continuing on a path that is demonstrably not working is not a smart business-decision. The smart thing to do is be resourceful in moving to a successful alternative. The corollary to this myth, by the way, is that entrepreneurs who keep looking for financing will eventually find it— yeah, right!*

These comments hold only for first-round funding. If you have already taken money and need more to succeed, then you have to do whatever it takes to raise additional money. You owe this to the existing shareholders if they agree that with that money you would likely succeed.

If you have already taken money and need more to succeed, then you have to do whatever it takes to raise additional money.

Types of Financing

Venture Capital

Venture capital is probably the most well-known source of financing for early-stage companies and somehow this has bred the false notion that it is the most common. The many books devoted to finding venture capital and the emphasis of "startup" seminars on venture capital leave many entrepreneurs with this false impression.

...there is much more to starting a company than raising money and the focus on financing sometimes leads entrepreneurs to think that all they need is money.

Firstly, there is much more to starting a company than raising money and the focus on financing sometimes leads entrepreneurs to think that all they need is money. Secondly, your odds of securing venture capital are quite low if you are a first-time entrepreneur with a seed-stage opportunity. That doesn't mean you shouldn't try, but you will age more gracefully if you recognize this and develop alternatives from the start.

Even during the Internet bubble, the raising of venture capital was much more rare than people were led to believe by the popular press. This misconception was partly fueled by the numerous examples of 22-year-old CEOs with what seemed like goofy ideas. These made great stories that were over-reported by the media. For every one of those goofy ideas that was funded, there were 10,000 other ideas that were no goofier but never received a dime in funding. Those weren't very good odds.

If you follow the words of venture capitalists in the press or at speaking venues, you will hear them say things such as: "An A-team with a great idea will get funded in any environment." This is a feat of circular reasoning and defies the statistics. The circular reasoning looks something like this:

> *I am a good venture-capitalist*
> *Good venture-capitalists recognize A-teams*
> *Good venture-capitalists recognize great ideas*
> *I fund A-teams with great ideas*
> *Therefore all A-teams with great ideas get funded*
> *and if I don't recognize a team as an A-team with a*
> *great idea then it must not be one.*

The statistics on the likelihood of raising venture capital are that even in the best of times, the number of first fundings from venture-capital firms in a year can be counted in the hundreds. The number of good business-ideas and teams is orders of magnitude larger. Needless to say, there is some luck involved in raising venture-capital—and you should keep as much of your business as possible under your direct influence if not control. So, you may want a "plan-B" that does not involve venture capital.

The most common alternative to obtaining venture capital at idea or seed stages is to use other, smaller sources of capital to move your company through some of the early milestones. Of course, there are also many things that you can do for little or no money that will move your company forward. Most of the work that you do in testing your model (Chapter 5) will also make you more fundable.

About Venture Capitalists

It is worth spending a little time to provide background on what venture capitalists are like and what their perspectives and motivations are. This should help you in interacting with them as people rather than as caricatures.

Depending on whom you listen to, you could easily come to believe that venture capitalists (VCs) are entrepreneurial geniuses that can commonly pick winning companies and that, through their entrepreneurial genius, they can make the difference between a company's success and failure. In general, neither is true. Some VCs are very good entrepreneurs; more of them are not. And even those that are great entrepreneurs will not be spending much time with you or your company. As for their abilities to pick winners, there are some VCs that can consistently do so, but there are many more who cannot. As a startup attorney put it when describing the pre-bubble, venture-capital environment: "Did anyone really believe that you could succeed by having 28-year-old venture capitalists investing in 26-year-old CEOs?"

There has been a tendency over the past five years to elevate the venture capitalist to rock-star status. Venture capitalists are quite fallible and most will gladly admit this. At a very good firm, they may be able to screen well enough to narrow their universe to the top few percent of the plans and teams they see. But within that group they really don't have effective crystal-balls. It doesn't usually matter too much because they can still obtain excellent returns by picking randomly within that top few percent. There is a lot of skill in what they do but also some luck.

You will find that venture capitalists are as varied as entrepreneurs. You will also find that most of them have higher-than-average intelligence and think very quickly. Many of them, however, overestimate their abilities to evaluate opportunities and add value to their portfolio companies. A fairly common career-trajectory for venture capitalists is to get MBAs from name schools, spend several years in consulting and then somehow hatch themselves in venture-capital firms.

This type of VC often does not have much to offer you besides money and will focus on parts of the business that are secondary or tertiary in their relevance to success.

> *I remember a meeting with two such VCs in which they kept returning to how much the executive team would be paid. They were quite adamant that a "good" CEO could recruit a team to work for equity only. They brought this up no less than five times in a two-hour meeting. It turns out that this firm's world-view was based on software firms that were started in someone's house while the founders all had full-time jobs. This is an entirely valid way of starting a company and a fine model for a VC firm. However, it does not prove that "good" CEOs get their team to work for equity alone.*
> *This VC firm was recently dissolved.*

On the one hand, you will get a lot of "This is the way it works" advice from venture capitalists—give it the same scrutiny that you give to advice from any other source. Their own, sometimes-narrow, experiences or motivations can shade the advice they provide.

On the other hand, you will find that some VCs have considerable operational experience and this, coupled with the breadth of experience that they get in working with many companies, makes these VCs significant value-adds. Between their minds and their wisdom they can provide a high level of clarity in a short period of time. In my experience these VCs are also the ones that are most likely actually to spend some time with companies—probably because they know they are having impacts and find that satisfying—not to mention that it is in their self-interest.

Realize that VCs do not really share all of your pain.

Realize that VCs do not really share all of your pain. In most cases, they are receiving a good salary derived from management fees—so have no risk of personal loss—and they receive part of their returns on the winnings of the portfolio (the "carry"). Moreover, while you are betting on one company, they are betting on tens of companies, so they are more likely to have positive returns—on average. They talk a good game about you hanging it out there and taking risk, and they certainly put other people's money at risk, but their advice is shaded by the way they are compensated.

> *Note: Many VCs have more entrepreneurial arrangements whereby they are paying their own expenses and/or going without salaries until there is a return on their investments. VC-compensation schemes*

are more varied than many of the books and magazine articles would lead you to believe.

One way in which VCs do share your pain, and which is often overlooked by entrepreneurs, is that VCs have to raise money too. They usually start small or join other firms and then raise money from institutional and accredited investors. Based on their successes, they can raise larger funds or start over elsewhere. They may not always be in the same boat as you but that doesn't mean that their life is easy.

Other ways in which entrepreneurs and VCs are similar are that both categories work incredibly hard and for long hours, both have obligations to provide returns to their investors and both have the stress of knowing that they are only a few bad decisions from failure.

So, while it's fun to bash VCs because of their legendary arrogance, they are often just people working their butts off to create great companies. Sound familiar?

So, while it's fun to bash VCs because of their legendary arrogance, they are often just people working their butts off to create great companies. Sound familiar?

Even though VCs will structure their deals so that it is unlikely that anyone can screw them through legal maneuvering in the agreements, they will still be putting a lot of faith in you: faith that you will not steal and will not spend the money like a drunken sailor, and faith that you will answer their questions truthfully so they know the real state of the company. This information might help you avert a crisis and without this honesty you might drive the bus over the cliff.

The following table indicates the ways in which VCs may be compared to entrepreneurs:

Comparison of Entrepreneurs to VCs		
	Entrepreneurs	**Venture Capitalists**
Added value	Ideas Network People	Money Network Credibility Advice
Role	Execution	Advice
Knowledge	Deep knowledge	Broad knowledge
Diversification	Singly invested in one company	Diversified over tens of companies
Pre-money representation	Represents self, founders and employees	Represents limited partners
Motivation	ROI, satisfaction of creating	ROI through single exit event

Education	Technical degree or MBA	Technical degree or MBA
Experience	Entrepreneur, company exec.	Consulting, entrepreneur, exec.
Arrogance	High	Higher
Sense of humor	Normal	Twisted
Intelligence	High	High

Working with VCs

Don't oversell them on your opportunity as they have heard every pitch imaginable—their eyes don't even see the words "revolutionary", "first-mover-advantage" or "no competition", so don't bother saying them …

VCs are very busy and need to find ways to get through all of the business plans and meetings that come their way each day, while still serving on boards and working on portfolio companies that are in trouble. If you are going to talk to them, show them clarity and focus in your communication—this reflects well on you as an entrepreneur. Let the small talk wait until they initiate it. Don't oversell them on your opportunity as they have heard every pitch imaginable—their eyes don't even see the words "revolutionary", "first-mover-advantage" or "no competition", so don't bother saying them or writing them. Tell them in real terms why this is a good opportunity.

When presenting to VCs, show them clarity but be prepared for detailed questions. Many VCs can dive into excruciating detail—technical, financial, sales, marketing and so on, but first give them the view from 30,000 feet. Keep your presentation short so that if you were uninterrupted you could get through it in 15-20 minutes without strain. Most likely you will never get to the end of it if there is any interest. Good VCs will be jumping ahead in their thinking and will engage you with questions pretty quickly.

A big part of your sale is both that you are able to succeed but also that you can be trusted.

I have never seen a presentation go all the way through without major interruptions. Don't let this bother you: this is where you get to show what you are made of—that you can think on your feet, that you know your business inside out, and most importantly that you say, "I don't know" rather than bullshitting when you don't know an answer (yet). On this latter point, a better approach is, "I don't know the final answer but we know we have that hole and so we have called five customers and have ten more to call. So far the average of their answers is five." Or, "I don't know and it's something that I really need to find out. Given that you have invested in XYZ Corp it seems like you might have some insight you could share with me." A big part of your sale is both that you are able to succeed but also that you can be trusted.

One good technique to raise funding is to build your credibility with venture capitalists over a period of time. A typical scenario for idea- or seed-stage entrepreneurs is that they talk to venture capitalists about their opportunities and they get answers such as: "It's a bit early for us but keep in touch with us about your progress."

Take this as an invitation to communicate your milestones and build your credibility by meeting them. Over a period of months, as you move through your milestones or prove important aspects of your model, let the venture capitalist know. In this way you build a relationship and you build your credibility by showing that you can obtain results. This is not an invitation to be a pest, to write lengthy emails or alert VCs to trivial progress—show that you know what is important.

> *For example:*
> **Good:** *This market is currently $400 million annually distributed over unit sales of 250,000 and with an annual growth-rate of 30% projected over the next three years. [Source: High Falutin' Marketing Research Company]*
> **Bad:** *The size and growth of this market is absolutely unfathomable.*

Also, keep in mind that your relationship with investors is firstly a business relationship and you shouldn't forget that. That doesn't mean you shouldn't have a beer or dinner with investors and enjoy yourself—but it does mean that you still have to perform if you want continued support.

... your relationship with investors is firstly a business relationship and you shouldn't forget that. That doesn't mean you shouldn't have a beer or dinner with investors and enjoy yourself—but it does mean that you still have to perform if you want continued support.

Venture capitalists are not investing their money. They have what are called limited partners who have invested in their venture funds. These limited partners are typically large, institutional investors such as retirement funds, mutual funds and wealthy individuals. The general partners who are referred to as the venture capitalists—a bit of a misnomer, since it is usually not their capital—represent their limited partners first and especially before they invest. They have both legal and moral obligations to invest the funds wisely. They also have obligations to get the best deals that they can. Most VCs are smart enough businesspeople to know that it is not in their or their limited partners' best interests to milk you for the very lowest valuation. Doing so can sour good relationships and enough equity has to remain to recruit great talent. Still, expect that negotiation may be a little rough at times—be professional about it and there should be no hard feelings on the part of either party.

Many venture-capitalists are quite nice folks and they, as much as you, would like to do business with people that are enjoyable to be around. So don't try to impress VCs with how tough you are.

The bottom line in dealing with venture capitalists is:

➢ be clear

➢ be honest

➢ be respectful and expect the same

➢ treat the relationship appropriately for what it is—a business relationship

➢ show that you are a worthy risk.

"Sophisticated" Individuals

These are people who are generally capable of evaluating business opportunities. They may or may not have extensive investment experience but they have solid business savvy. They usually know what they don't know and will seek advice where they need it from professionals or other investors before they commit money to a deal.

They are often synonymous with "accredited" investors (this term actually has a legal definition beyond any plain-English definition). Very briefly, an accredited investor is one that has either $1,000,000 in "nearly-liquid" assets (stocks count towards the total but real estate does not) or $300,000 in annual gross income including spousal income. There is no book or list of accredited investors and no accrediting body—it isn't the same as getting a driver's license. Accredited investors typically "accredit" themselves by signing documents that explain what "accredited means" and ask them to check off the boxes that apply to them.

You must be wondering what this technical explanation has to do with anything. It is very important because it determines the nature of your investors, how you raise money, how you solicit investors and the documents you need to prepare. If you have investors that are not accredited, then your "deal" may fall under another set of SEC regulations that would restrict your subsequent ability to raise funds— and might put you on the wrong side of the law even in your current fundraising. (See the SEC Website and consult a *good* attorney.) This is the sort of early mistake that could hamstring you later in your company's development. Suffice it to say here that your life will be much smoother if you can restrict your fundraising to accredited investors.

Individual investors come in so many flavors that they almost defy description.

> *I was talking to an investment banker about the range of individual investors and he told me about his father-in-law. He said, "My father-in-law gets up every morning around 5:00 am and operates a backhoe most of the day. He is worth millions through the large and successful excavation company that he has built, but he doesn't know squat about investing in technology startups."*
>
> *Yet he was an excellent businessperson and had no illusions about his knowledge or abilities. He was an ideal candidate to mix his money and experience with other investors who were complimentary to him.*

Individual investors include people who have inherited money, have earned it as executives of huge corporations, have cashed out of technology startups, have built less-than-famous companies that they sold for a tidy sum, have invented and licensed technologies and on and on.

You need to find out if they are really ripe to invest so that you aren't just entertainment for someone who is tired of golfing. In most cases, these people, because of their backgrounds, are respectful of your time. They also are comfortable enough in their skins that they will usually be respectful and direct with you. Next, you need to know in what ways, other than with their money, they might contribute to your company and how they want to be involved. As in any sale, you need to qualify and evaluate your customer.

Some of the non-financial ways in which they can contribute are as varied as they are, and include:

➤ interim CFO (chief financial officer)

➤ introductions to customers, vendors and investors

➤ technology advice

➤ strategic-marketing advice

➤ clarity

➤ mentoring

➤ legal

➤ manufacturing

➤ international issues.

If they have earned their money, then chances are they have some special knowledge or talents that could be of value to you and your company if they choose to be so involved.

Individual investors, even more than venture capitalists, do not want to invest in jerks. They want to have fun as part of making their money. They want you to respect their privacy and lifestyles.

Finding individual investors can be very difficult. Depending on where you live, there may be organizations of sophisticated, and usually accredited, investors in your area. They often have formal procedures for introducing new plans to the group. And, even though the identities of the individuals are closely guarded, the organizations are relatively easy to find and contact.

In most areas of the country there are few, if any, formal groups of individual investors. In this case you just need to network like crazy. Talk to CEOs and other entrepreneurs. If you know some venture capitalists, ask them to introduce your deal to individual investors. Also, use the consultants and professionals that you work with, e.g. your attorney. When there are no formal groups, you will often find that one individual investor does not know very many others—meeting other investors is usually not a primary activity. Most entrepreneurs are surprised to learn this.

Another consideration is that individual investors are not professional investors. That is, they may do one to three deals and then may not do another deal until they exit one of those investments. In other words, the fact that people were investors yesterday does not mean they are investors today.

Individual investors are accountable only to themselves, whereas venture capitalists are accountable both to their general partners (other VCs at the firms) and to their limited partners (investors in the VC funds). This means the following:

➢ Individual investors have much more latitude in the deals that they do and why.

➢ They can sit on the sidelines for as long as they like.

➢ They can put more time into helping companies because they have fewer investments and commitments.

➢ They can spend *less* time with their investments because the risk is entirely theirs and they have no obligations to anyone else to *make* their investments successful.

> They have more options in how they receive returns on investment; e.g. shares of profits may be acceptable instead of single liquidity events such as acquisitions or IPOs.

> They may not be comfortable with setting company valuation, both because they lack industry information and experience.

On this last point, a common way of circumventing the valuation issue is through convertible debt. In a convertible-debt deal, the investor loans you money at a certain interest rate with payments on principle and interest due at some point in the future. This is unlike a loan in that the investor can also exercise warrants rather than, or in addition to, getting paid back. The warrants typically convert at a price that is some fraction of the valuation set by VCs in a subsequent round. This allows individual investors to receive premiums for investing when the risk was higher, reduces their risks of loss, allows them to participate in upside at their option, and relieves them of the job of valuing the company.

Friends and Family

Friends and family are the most common source of funding other than founders. While funding from friends and family can be very convenient, it can also create some problems.

It can cloud your business judgement because you now have an emotional connection rather than a purely business connection with your investors. You might feel obligated to act on bad advice to make Thanksgiving dinners more enjoyable.

When taking money from friends and family, I strongly suggest that you use convertible debt. This is because friends and family often overvalue a company. This is fairly innocent in that it usually occurs because they aren't too concerned about multiples and, so long as they do not lose their original investment, they are happy to help you out. But this is equivalent to overvaluing the company. The risk to you then is that later investors do not want to enter the deal because they can give you only a lower valuation, which is often problematic. Convertible debt makes "business" investors set the valuation. It also makes it more likely that your friends and family receive a return in line with the risks they are taking.

With all investors you need to set expectations on what you will do and how they will get a return. However, with friends and family you might have to provide more information and education. While sophisticated investors might understand business, your uncle might not. While a venture capitalist takes for granted the risk associated with a technology, your

My advice is to over-communicate and make sure that your friends and family investors really understand what they are getting into.

brother-in-law might not even know that it is risky. My advice is to over-communicate and make sure that your friends and family investors really understand what they are getting into.

Venture capitalists or sophisticated investors may not want your deal if they know that they need to contend with Aunt Harriet in board meetings.

If you have friends and family on your board you should consider whether that will always be appropriate. Venture capitalists or sophisticated investors may not want your deal if they know that they need to contend with Aunt Harriet in board meetings. I suggest that you let any friends and family on your board know that their positions may be terminated when new investment comes in. And let any sophisticated investors or VCs know that your board formation is subject to their approval and you expect that the friends and family members of the board will leave the board.

Your Fellow Citizens

Many companies have been started to take advantage of government subsidies or contracts. The most common of these for technology companies is the Small Business Innovative Research program.

Government money always looks as though it is free and a great way to fund your company. In reality it often comes with so many strings that it was hardly worth the effort and it diverts you from your core business.

My feeling on government funding is that it is usually not worth the brain damage. The people who would take money from your fellow citizens and give it to you have no stake in creating a successful business. Their motivations often have little to do with results and they and the rest of that system can be infuriating to deal with. My advice is that government money be your absolute last resort.

The curse of government funding of your development is that you may end up in the business of writing proposals and winning contracts. Meanwhile you could be creating a company that provides so much value that people will *voluntarily* purchase its products.

I have seen numerous examples of companies that built significant revenues off of SBIR contracts and were able to provide a decent wage to their founders and employees. They even developed some interesting or leading edge technologies. However, they hit a wall when they tried to branch out into the commercial sector and sell products rather than technologies to free-market customers rather than contract monitors. The wall was created by a culture and management team that were not tuned to the rigors of the marketplace.

Fools

The good news is that most entrepreneurs and investors are honest and have good business-sense. On the other hand I have seen several examples illustrating the adage, "You can't buy

I have seen several examples illustrating the adage, "You can't buy brains."

brains." To which I would add the corollary that you can't buy character. From entrepreneurs I have seen some slimy behavior that, although it was not fraudulent, was misleading. The moral principle I am talking about here is that if you take people's money as an investment you have an obligation to do everything in your power to make them a return on their investment.

I have seen proof that you can get people to invest in just about anything or anyone—especially if that anyone is willing to stretch the truth a little bit. These deals always end up in the toilet or the entrepreneur ends up in a locale without an extradition treaty with the US.

So, assuming that you are honest and have your moral compass rigidly set to provide a return to your investors and treat their money with more care than your own—you should avoid fool investors at all costs. The pitfalls are many:

Negative work

Fool investors do negative work for your company and they make suggestions that you have to pretend to take seriously and then reject. Or, worse, they make bad suggestions that you follow because they are investors.

> *I recall one company with several attorney-investors who were inexperienced in business. They focused on ... legal issues. The company got mired in legal technicalities rather than running its business. Fully half of their expenses were on legal costs and all that is left of the "company" is ongoing legal actions.*

Higher-than-deserved valuation

Fools will often give you a much higher valuation than you deserve. This sounds great until you go to raise subsequent financing from more sophisticated investors. Then your deal gets shot down from the start because the sophisticated investors know how difficult it will be to do a down round. Or you do the down round and the fool investors are upset at their "loss", at best, or sue you, at worst.

One company that I was familiar with had a number of fool investors who hadn't done their due-diligence. I was talking to one of the investors who was concerned about someone buying the company, which had not even completed a technology prototype and had a single issued patent. He asked what I thought a good return would be and I said that 100% annual return would be awesome and 50% annual return would be great. He nearly choked at what he thought would be a paltry return on his investment and said that there was no way that he wanted the company to sell at such a return. This showed both his lack of sophistication as an investor and that his expectations had been set inappropriately by the CEO, his own unrealistic hopes and his very real gullibility.

Thwarted success

Fools will scare away other investors because the new investors just plain don't want to have anything to do with the fool investors.

They will make it hard for you to recruit solid management. Good management-team candidates will do their own due-diligence and run when they see fool investors.

The main pitfall, of course, is that they will make it nearly impossible for you to succeed in the long term even if they make it possible for you to write your own paycheck in the near term.

Yourself

If you don't believe enough in what you're doing to invest then why should anyone else?

This is the most common funding-source and it should be. If you don't believe enough in what you're doing to invest then why should anyone else?

I am not of the school that you need to risk personal bankruptcy to show your commitment. This just isn't worth it and it will often force you to make desperate decisions even while it can be a great motivator. While we have all read countless tales of entrepreneurs who max out all of their credit and put their homes at risk to build their businesses, most of these stories—those that go untold—end in personal bankruptcy. Most near-death experiences result in death.

Entrepreneurs that have ideas but either cannot or will not put any money at risk have failed 100% of the time in my experience. This is for several reasons:

➤ Their resistance to investing is evidence of uncertainty and lack of commitment.

➤ They are unprepared for their venture in many ways and a lack of money is just the most measurable.

➤ They have not been successful in their careers and have therefore not made or saved much money.

Customers

Customer financing can come in several forms. The most obvious is that you have some customers that want your product so much that they will literally invest in the company.

This has the advantage of having your customer fully committed to your success. You will get honest, well-considered requirements as well as market insight from the customer. There is some trickiness too, however:

➤ You will probably want to sell to a broader market than a single customer. Will other customers be hesitant to buy from you because you are funded by their competitor?

➤ As part of a complex or strategic sale, you will often have privileged information about a customer. How will you safeguard that information?

➤ As an investor your customer might ask for a board seat. This could lead to a conflict of interest since the interests of that customer might not always be entirely aligned with the company.

➤ There is also the risk that proprietary information about your or your customers' companies is discussed in a board meeting which will allow your customer-investor to obtain information they should not have. To deal with this potential board-conflict, you could appoint a board member to speak in the best interest of the investor without disclosing inappropriate information. This can actually work reasonably well and is worth considering if this becomes a sticking point in negotiations.

Another way that your customers can finance your company is by paying you for your goods before you have to pay your vendors.

An excellent example of this was an e-commerce company that sold direct to consumers. The consumers provide their credit-card numbers and the company received payment, with little or no receivables risk. The order then went to a fulfillment partner that billed the

> *company once a month with payment due in thirty days.*
> *This meant that the company was able to receive money*
> *for goods shipped and for which* they *would not need to*
> *pay for 30 to 60 days.*

For a high-growth company this can be absolutely magical because if it has to pay before it receives it can end up limiting its growth by its inability to finance purchases ahead of increasing sales.

Another approach is to form a consortium with some competitive safeguards so that the customers' industry as a whole has access to your product or service. This works when they see that your product or service will increase the overall market for their own products or services.

And, finally, you can identify an industry leader and then contract for this leader to invest in exchange for a limited exclusive. That is, where you provide the leader with exclusive rights to your product. This should almost always be limited in a number of ways to reduce your risk:

➤ Limit it to markets in which the leader already sells and has some proven success, and put in safeguards so that the leader cannot create a gray market in other markets and so that other customers you have cannot sneak product into the leader's markets.

➤ Limit it geographically to areas where this customer can provide maximum benefit and maybe give the customer some regions to develop where you may not have the resource for some time anyway.

➤ Limit it by time so that it does not continue indefinitely but only serves to provide the leader with a head start over competitors within the leader's market.

➤ Limit it by performance so that the leader has to meet sales or other milestones on a quarterly or semiannual basis to maintain the exclusive terms of the agreement.

Vendors

As with customer financing, vendor financing can range from direct investment in the company to financing inventory for a period of time. Also, as with customer financing, there are pros and cons. Without going into detail on the same or equivalent points in the previous section, the main points are:

➤ You probably don't want to get married to a single vendor to the exclusion of all others.

➤ Within your company or in board meetings you might know things that are proprietary to other vendors of yours and to your vendor-investor's competitors, and you need to safeguard that information.

➤ Vendors commonly "finance" by giving you terms on your purchases and this can be magical to a high-growth company that must have inventory to operate.

Vendors, more than customers, lend themselves to strategic relationships. A vendor might provide a key added-value that is not core to your business. Likewise, your company might add a key piece of value that both enables a new market and which is not core to your vendor. Thus, the key ingredients for a good, strategic relationship may obtain.

A caution in this is that even though vendors might have an investment in your company, they usually will not be as committed to your success as you and your team are.

Strategic Investors

Strategic investors are those who gain by virtue of the existence of your company and its working with their companies. In some cases, you may enable a market for your strategic investor's company simply by providing a key component that has never before existed.

> *For example, laptop manufacturers are enabled by liquid-crystal display manufacturers. Without the liquid-crystal display, there would be no viable laptop products.*

Likewise, your strategic investor might provide a key enabler to you, might be able to market your product, or might be able to integrate it into a complete solution to meet the needs of a market segment.

As mentioned at the end of the last section, your strategic investors might be far more committed to your success than would be the case if you had a simple, buy-sell relationship. However, it is a mistake to think that they will be as committed to your success as you and your team will be.

> *At one company that manufactured a complex component we found a manufacturer that had a key manufacturing-process and infrastructure in place to move the company to volume manufacture quickly and at minimal cost—in theory. In reality, because the company with the complex component did not have sales, its needs were always at the bottom of the partner company's list of priorities. Moreover, the larger partner would not listen to the complex-component company on refining its quality assurance and manufacturing process. And finally, because it had invested, it had a sense of*

entitlement that meant that it would not respond to the complex-component company as it would have done to a regular customer. In the end, the relationship was dissolved due to non-performance by the larger partner.

With strategic investors especially, you might need some creative, performance-based terms—for either side of the agreement. And your valuation will be more complex than the percent of the company for a certain number of dollars. There is value brought by both companies to a greater whole, and this might greatly influence the dollar-per-share figure.

While they take some creativity and more effort than straight dollar-for-ownership exchanges, strategic investments can be the best of any type. Still, they are not risk-free and require that you or someone working with you (an attorney or consultant) has some corporate-development wisdom.

Valuation

Valuation of early-stage companies, and especially startups, is more art than science.

Valuation of early-stage companies, and especially startups, is more art than science. The fact that you end up with a specific number makes it no less an art.

There are many excellent books and sections of books on valuation. There are also companies that will do a valuation for you. The books are often most relevant to more mature companies and the companies that do valuations are not likely to give you a number that is not easily negotiated up or down.

The simplest explanation of valuation is that it is the price that a willing buyer will pay a willing seller. This is technically accurate—even obvious—but totally useless to you. We can do a little better by saying that it is the present value of future cash-flows.

Valuation is usually referred to in the context of investment but also has relevance to many strategic relationships, in that you may trade some equity for some non-cash value from a strategic partner. For simplicity, here I will focus on investment.

Valuation comes into play in determining how much of the company you will have to sell to attract a specific amount of money. You will hear the words pre-money and post-money valuation. The post-money valuation is the pre-money valuation plus the amount that was invested. This makes sense.

If your company is worth $500,000 on January 4th and you take investment on the afternoon of January 4th, *then by the morning of January 5th there probably hasn't been much change in the company's circumstances other than the investment you have received. So your post-money valuation should just be the valuation as of January 4th plus the additional money in the bank on January 5th.*

To start to get a handle on the value of your company you can break it down into elements that might be considered valuable as they reduce risk and/or increase the potential upside:

- ❑ proprietary technology

- ❑ patents

- ❑ prototypes

- ❑ completed product

- ❑ customers

- ❑ switching costs

- ❑ recurring income

- ❑ letters of intent

- ❑ memoranda of understanding

- ❑ business plan

- ❑ management team

- ❑ advisors

- ❑ manufacturing capability

- ❑ proprietary relationships

- ❑ proprietary processes.

These are all things that could either be sold for cash or that lower risk for an investor. They are also hard to put a value on, but at least by breaking things down in this way you will have a more realistic estimate. The value of this list and what you could sell it for will typically give you a lower bound on your valuation.

If you do a net present-value (NPV) analysis, this will give you an upper bound on your valuation. You don't need to get too obsessed with this calculation. If you look in the better books on valuation, they will show you what is technically the "right" way of doing it by taking into account risk-free interest-rates, among other things. However, for an early-stage enterprise, the annual ROI should probably be in the neighborhood of 50% to 100%. That, coupled with the fact that this is a rough estimate at best, means that it really doesn't matter whether the real ROI is 97%, 100% or 103%. They are all equivalent for this exercise.

To do a back of the envelope NPV analysis, begin with the exit in mind. Look into the future to the year that you expect to get acquired. Now figure out your valuation at that point in the future. You can base this on price-sales ratios for comparable companies, or on a price-earnings ratio if your growth has leveled off; if you have high growth, a price-to-sales-to-growth ratio might make the most sense. Try to pick companies that are comparable. It would be nice to know acquisition prices but, in the absence of that knowledge, you can do a little research to get the ratios for public companies. Now you have the value in that future year.

> *For example, let's suppose that future valuation is $32,000,000. The next step is to work it back to the present. For the case of 100% annual return, the valuation needs to double every year, so, supposing that your exit is five years hence, your current valuation needs to increase by 2*2*2*2*2=32 times. That means your current valuation is equal to $32,000,000/32=$1,000,000.*

More generally: $PV=FV/[(1+AR)^Y]$, where PV is present value, FV is future value in year Y, and AR is annual return rate (expressed as a fraction, e.g. 100%=1, 37%=0.37, etc.). (The symbol $^\wedge$ means to raise to a power, for example: $3^\wedge 2=3*3=9$.)

... any precision in annual return rate is the equivalent of counting angels on heads of pins.

Now you can see why any precision in annual return rate is the equivalent of counting angels on heads of pins. Because of the huge multiplier in going from future value to present value, the projections on which that future value are based are the most critical numbers in the calculation. Unfortunately they are also the most uncertain.

> *A typical scenario is that you have a prototype that, after talking to some people who have experience, you think you could license for $700,000. You have done an NPV calculation and you came up with $5,000,000 valuation. That's quite a range but at least you have narrowed it down and you are unlikely to get $5,000,000 or higher valuation. The valuation that the capital market will give you will be $700,000 plus the value of your management team, customers and other items from*

*the list above. Just where you end up between $700,000
and $5,000,000 is subject to negotiation.*

Now we'll come up with another number for a minimum acceptable-valuation. To compensate you and your co-founders for your talents and the risk you have taken, you need to preserve enough equity for it to have been worthwhile. You also need equity to attract top talent and provide incentives for employees. Think about how much you will need to raise through the progression of the company and what the valuation will be at each step. What valuation in this first round will preserve enough equity to achieve your operational goals? Some typical equity percentages for an IPO exit are:

➢ 10% to 15% for founder-CEO

➢ 5% to 10% for co-founders

➢ 15% to 20% for employee pool

➢ 3% to 5% for non-founding CEO.

At what valuation can you achieve this? In other words, what valuation do you need to get in the current round so that you retain 30% to 50% for employees at exit? If this valuation is greater than your present value number, then you are maybe raising too much money in the current round. If you give away too much equity now, then you will not be able to recruit a top-notch management-team and future investors will see this and be spooked off the deal.

You may need to scale back your growth or decrease the time period between rounds of financing. Note that *your* needs do not change the valuation, but they might change the way in which you raise money.

Another angle on valuation is to get comparables for companies that have been funded at a similar stage to yours. This information is very hard to come by. However, by talking to enough people, you can start forming a picture. Some of the companies that will do valuations for hire have access to these comparable data. The better investment bankers have both collected and carefully analyzed these data.

Finally, the best way to get the highest valuation is to have multiple funding-offers and play them off against each other. This is pretty hard to do in the current environment, but if you can, you will get the best valuation and the quickest close as you will have created a sense of urgency—if VC-One does not take the deal then VC-Two will take it.

As stated before, you have little to gain by putting your valuation in your business plan or executive summary. However, when you talk to an investor you should have a well-formed idea of what you are looking for in valuation and *why*. Double-check with people to find out if you are being realistic.

I was talking to a venture capitalist about a company with which I was familiar and which I knew he had met the week before. I asked her what she thought. She said the company had a good idea and the management team had deep domain-expertise, which were two of her primary criteria for investment. Then she said, "But I asked what their valuation was and they said $20 million while I was thinking $3 million. I didn't see much point in talking after that."

This investor thought that the entrepreneur was so unrealistic in his valuation figure that it wasn't even worth negotiating. The entrepreneur will never know why that investor was "not interested at this time".

Summary

All investors are going to ask you more or less the same questions. They will differ, however, in how they weigh your answers, based on their own interests, motivations and tolerance for risk.

Venture capital is the most well-known source of financing but also one of the most unlikely. It is especially difficult to obtain when you are in the idea-to-startup stage. However, it is not impossible and has many advantages. This chapter should have given you a good background on venture capitalists so that you understand their needs and can therefore work better with them—both in seeking investment and after receiving investment.

There are other, more common sources of capital such as friends and family, individual investors and yourself. Each has its pros and cons and its limitations. However, unless you are willing to invest in your opportunity, you should not be surprised if others will not. You should also question why you are doing it at all.

If you take investment, you will need to address valuation in some way. You can do this by simply deferring the issue until a later, more professional round of investment, or by coming up with a number.

8. FOUNDATION FOR SUCCESS

This chapter offers tips, experience-based solutions and cautions against common mistakes. The sections are somewhat disconnected in that they don't link smoothly. Rather, they make up a collection of recommendations that will help you lay a foundation for your company and your way of operating it. The unifying theme is that they all address issues that very commonly arise in the first few months of company formation.

One could write an entire book on one or just a few of these sections. However, they are pretty easy to grasp and put into use. It might be worth coming back to skim this chapter every now and then, as it may give you some ideas as you get consumed by the day-to-day challenges you face in starting your company.

Commitment

At some point you just have to go for it. This chapter assumes that you are fully committed. In the previous chapters

At some point you just have to go for it.

you have taken the first step by vetting, planning and testing. The second step is exhilarating and sometimes scary—with it you leave the past behind. You lose something; sure its intentional, but a loss all the same. This may include your job, savings, location and a part of your identity. You may be moving from secure Engineering Manager Grade IV to CEO of an innovative startup, or from VP of Marketing to CEO of a technology startup, and relying on people with whom you have worked only within a secure environment.

Vision

By now you will most likely have a clear vision of where you are headed. Can you now articulate it in two or three sentences? It has to be specific enough to have meaning but be broad enough to encompass an uncertain future.

> *Microsoft has a great vision-statement: "Microsoft's vision is to empower people through great software - any time, any place and on any device."—Microsoft Web site*
>
> *It is succinct, meaningful and independent of year-to-year changes in business and technology.*

But note this final thought: it makes no sense to get obsessed with the "vision-thing". It is important to know where you are going and have something grand that you are trying to achieve as a company. However, no great vision will save a company that has lousy people, execution or strategy.

... no great vision will save a company that has lousy people, execution or strategy.

Mission

At the start of the movie *Animal House*, the camera is panning the ivy-covered campus-buildings and stops briefly on a pretentious statue with the inscription "Knowledge is good" at its base. I am often reminded of this when I read company mission-statements—especially mission-statements of large companies. They are often as profound and meaningful as the *Animal House* one; e.g. "Our mission is to create a safe and diverse environment for our associates."

Your mission statement is an expression of what your company is about—what you do and even how you do it. It should support the company vision. All in a few sentences.

You don't have to have a mission statement from the start, but you should be thinking about what your company is about. Discuss this with your co-founders. It should be something that can last beyond your tenure and the currently envisioned products.

This is something to work on as you have time, but it is important. Not so much because it gives you something to put on a business card or a banner, but because of the clarity it expresses about your business. And if it does not ring true, it can be counterproductive.

A good example of a mission statement is the Terra Lycos mission: "To be the most visited online destination in the world."—Terra Lycos Web site.

Culture

Whether you want one or not, you will have a culture in your company.

Culture is tied in with principles but is distinct. Culture might or might not be the basis for decisions or actions. Whether you want one or not, you will have a culture in your company—this doesn't apply just to big companies that hire expensive management-consulting firms. The advantage of thinking about culture from the beginning, and explicitly, is that you will hire better people and the people you hire will have a better understanding of what is expected of them. When someone is doing something to which you object, then you have basis for telling them explicitly why it needs to change—based on a stated culture.

Getting to the core of your culture takes time and it is not tied to a specific near-term result. Yet it is results oriented in that it makes everything from hiring, negotiating, teamwork and communications go more smoothly. When well thought out it makes it easier to achieve results.

In almost all cases, there are many cultures that can be successful in a business. This doesn't make culture any less important but it does make it clear that this is up to you and your founders, executive team or others who should be making this decision. In fact, the people who are involved in setting your culture are themselves indicative of your culture. Culture is something you have rather than something you make up or copy from successful companies.

Think about what you and the founders like about doing a startup. Why did you choose each other? Why do you think that the founders' attributes will make you successful? These questions can help you get started in thinking about culture.

Communication for Execution

The most common complaints in a startup concern poor communications. It is amazing how, with just a handful of people, you can have communication problems. Nothing will slow you down like bad communication. This is manifested in many ways.

The most common complaints in a startup concern poor communications.

At times companies fall into a cheerleading mode in which every meeting degenerates into a rehash of how wonderful the vision is and how the company is going to revolutionize an industry. Meetings that should have taken ten minutes take an hour and nothing new is really communicated because a meeting that should have resulted in a decision is hijacked by the "vision-thing". While culture and vision need to be over-communicated, this can really be overdone—and you have the "execution-thing" to worry about.

Sometimes hierarchies are formed or develop all on their own. If they are based on ownership and accountability, they can be good things. However, when they turn into communication funnels, it can quickly turn into a muddle.

For example, Joe the CEO tells Sally the CTO that he wants Development to look at redesigning the home-page, then Sally tells Mac the lead

Serial communication in a startup should be minimized.

> *developer, who tells Lisa the designer, and in a few days the word trickles back up the chain that Lisa has deleted the home-page at Joe's request. Serial communication in a startup should be minimized.*

Documentation, which solves the problem of miscommunication in the chain, has its own overhead and doesn't allow for convenient feedback. Usually, the right kind of verbal communication works great. This problem can be dealt with by having five-minute meetings, as I'll describe below.

Another common problem is that *everyone* has input and changes are made on a whim.

> *Joe looks over the designer's shoulder and says he thinks the background should be yellow. A couple of hours later, Sam looks over the designer's shoulder and says that the page might look better with an Arial font. Joe owns the product and also knows that if you use Arial font on this particular page the purchase rate decreases by 4%. Joe finally gets the design and is wondering how in the hell it ended up with Ariel font. This is another instance where the 5-minute meeting would greatly help.*

The Five-minute Meeting

In the startup phase, when people are literally feet away from each other, it is easy to grab all of the people who might have input in a decision. The trick is to really make this a five-minute meeting. To do this you need to state clearly, at the outset, the decision that needs to be made. Then you or someone else can briefly lay out one or several options being considered. You then get feedback, which may include things you didn't know: "Yes, that way is best but it will take two weeks, whereas this way is almost as good and can be done this afternoon."

You need to leave with a decision and a direction for action and the meeting must stay focused on that single issue. You can do these meetings in a hallway, someone's cubicle or a conference room. After you get good at them, they allow you to avoid a lot of the communications miscues that occur on a day-to-day basis. And, for the most part, people don't mind these types of meetings—because they accomplish something. They aren't about building consensus (gag!), soothing egos or dealing with large, strategic issues, or issues that need to be dissected in detail. However, for a lot of the tactical stuff that needs to get done from day to day as part of your execution, they can be invaluable. These meetings also set some important cultural tones:

urgency, results orientation, open communication, accountability and clarity.

You need to set aside time to discuss strategic issues in the detail that they require. Here, whoever is running the meeting can do much to grease the process by having some notes and having done some homework. If you are discussing an agreement, have copies for everyone and a bullet-point summary of the decisions that need to be made. You want to leave the meeting with decisions made or actions to be taken to move in that direction. By the end of the meeting, you should know who will do what, and by when it will be done. After the meeting, an email summarizing the key decisions and accountability can be helpful to people: they can refer to it in the future.

Many times companies, especially technology companies, get so caught up in the day-to-day activities that they never take the time out to deal with strategic issues. These then become last-minute crises when a deadline looms.

Communication

To figure out how good communication can be made to happen you can follow a path based on a few questions:

➢ What results do you want?

➢ What actions do you need to take in order to achieve those results?

➢ What decisions must be made as precursors to those actions?

➢ Who makes those decisions?

➢ What does the person need to know to make those decisions?

Presumably the nature of the results and actions will determine whom you need to communicate with most. Ultimately you might need to communicate throughout the company, but in the initial stages you probably will communicate more efficiently with the handful of people who can add the most value. A good starting-point is to communicate the result you wish to achieve. Your team can usually help you identify actions that might lead to a successful result. Now you need to decide which actions you will actually take; this requires information. Now we get to where this process often breaks down—getting the right information.

You and your team should make a habit of clear communication—even at the expense of completeness. This means thinking in bullet points.

You and your team should make a habit of clear communication—even at the expense of completeness. This means thinking in bullet points. The section on creating a presentation for investors is a good guideline. A good presentation should include, at least, the pros and cons of any action or decision, its cost, its return, and a recommendation and reason for that recommendation. By stating all of this clearly, you now have given the rest of the team specifics to consider. Do they agree or disagree? Do they have additional information? Do they interpret the information differently to come up with a different recommendation? Now you can get somewhere quickly.

It's worth remembering the following

➢ Whining is not good communication because it is not directed at taking positive action.

➢ A little happy-talk goes a long way. Too much self-congratulation within a company signals that tough issues could be sublimated. It can also take a lot of time as people try to out happy-talk each other until they are all repeating each other.

➢ Personal attacks are horrible communication. They can cause substantial damage within a company and can silence people who should be heard. People need to stay focused on the issues—then some emotion can be good.

➢ Talking behind people's back is a tough one. (Some people prefer more politically correct euphemisms.) It is the nature of business that you need to assess others' strengths and weaknesses, decide where they can add the most value and even decide whether to hire them or fire them. This very often means talking about them behind their backs—or whatever you wish to call it. The damage is done when people assume that this is the default and generally acceptable behavior, rather than the exception for legitimate, business reasons.

➢ Trying to impress is a common occurrence in companies and it is even somewhat effective for *individuals* in many. It isn't, however, very effective in achieving *company* results.

Consensus Decision-making—NOT

Consensus is like socialism, an idea people want to like and want to think could work. But of course for either to work, people have to behave differently than they really do.

Consensus is like socialism, an idea people want to like and want to think could work. But of course for either to work, people have to behave differently than they really do. So, in reality, consensus, like socialism, has the same, failed record.

What people really mean by consensus is usually one of the following:

> ➤ *I will smack everyone else around until they say they agree with me and we will have consensus.*

or

> ➤ *We will meet endlessly and compromise to achieve a mediocre solution that everyone can agree that they disagree with equally.*

or

> ➤ *The outcome of the meeting will lack any accountability or clear goals to be achieved and so whatever "consensus" we reach is largely irrelevant to the participants.*

Every now and then everyone will agree and that is wonderful when it happens. If it happens all of the time, then you have either hired too many clones or something bad, that is suppressing valuable alternatives, is happening inside your company.

More often, some people have well-reasoned and differing opinions but someone needs to take responsibility for a decision and that somebody will probably be you a lot of the time. In a well-functioning company, people then agree to do everything in their power to support the decision on which they had input but with which they may not be entirely in agreement.

Consensus in practice is a recipe for compromise in lieu of optimization: it doesn't make any sense to declare 2+2=4½ because I think 2+2=5 and you think 2+2=4. Compromise is a recipe for mediocrity. Or consensus means that any type of conflict is avoided to the detriment of the company. You need constructive conflict and the airing of alternatives to make good decisions.

> *Consensus in practice is a recipe for compromise in lieu of optimization: it doesn't make any sense to declare 2+2=4½ because I think 2+2=5 and you think 2+2=4.*

Principles, People and Process

All companies depend to an extent on the people they have, but startups depend almost entirely on their people to create competitive advantage and execute. This is why some people are attracted to startups—because they can have a significant impact on the success of the companies rather than the big-company experience that can best be described as trying to push cooked spaghetti uphill.

One of the magical things about startups, and the reason that they can go head to head with Microsoft or 3M in certain areas, is that they are nimble and have great people that can execute in unison towards a common goal. The people within these companies have the freedom to do things in new ways. This is how they overcome the disadvantages of lacking resources and industry positions. This is why they can innovate and find resourceful paths to success. They can develop new business-models that work better for the customer, rather than doing business the same way as it has always been done. There are no entrenched interests who might lose power or their jobs as a result of doing things in a new way.

One of the magical things about startups, and the reason that they can go head to head with Microsoft or 3M in certain areas, is that they are nimble and have great people that can execute in unison towards a common goal.

However, this "magic" will not occur just by bringing together a bunch of great people. That leads to intellectual random motion. Nor will it happen if people are constrained by processes.

The theme of this section is that principles, people and process have to be brought together in the right way at the right time for a company to be most effective. The foundation comprises the principles for the company. People, who are the most important of the three elements, need principles on which to act. Finally, the least important element is process, which is needed for the smooth and effective functioning of the company. This hierarchy is illustrated in the following figure:

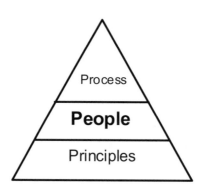

Process has its place in a company of any size. However, occasionally I have seen individuals within startups try to create process *over* people. In other words, they try to concoct some clever, fool-proof *process* for success. The idea is that if people just follow this great process, then success is inevitable. Sometimes people make up names for these processes and even claim them to be proprietary. Consulting firms love to talk about things such as their proprietary "7-Step Sans-Souci Process for Managerial Bliss".

Process should be used to enable people to do their jobs. If you need processes to control people or keep them from cheating in a small company, then you have the wrong people and no amount of process is going to make things right. Rather, process should free people to do higher value-added work for the company.

> *For example, you should have some sort of simple process for making sure that invoices get paid. Otherwise it has to get reinvented all the time, invoices go unpaid and a lot of work is expended in trying to straighten out the mess.*

Process should also be used to keep things from falling through the cracks. Firstly, a process needs to be simple enough that people will actually use it. If a list on a white board will suffice, then don't bother with a document that needs

Think about what you are really trying to accomplish through the process and use the minimum number of requirements to get that done.

to get updated. Think about what you are really trying to accomplish through the process and use the minimum number of requirements to get that done. A danger of process is that people can come to believe that their job is to follow a process, inherently an activity, rather than achieve results.

Now we move on to principles. Clearly stated principles are consistent with the culture and allow people to act within their spheres of influence in the best interest of the company. For some people, that will mean that they negotiate with vendors based on those principles. For other people, it will mean that they don't use pop-up windows on the Web site, or that they run meetings that are consistent with the company principles.

> *As an example, consider a company that has a new-category component that needs to go into a product in order to generate sales for the company. One of the company principles is that, whenever it makes good business sense, it enables the market. Then, when your VP of business development is working on a strategic relationship, he might include a term that allows him to give other companies access to some of the technology on a non-exclusive and royalty-free basis. He might be able to close a sale just for having the presence of mind to offer it and knowing that it is all right to do so*

because it is consistent with the principles on which the company operates.

Principles form the foundation for action by people.

Principles form the foundation for action by people. The principles establish how your people interact within the company and with the outside world. There are many paths from a starting point to a result but principles allow your people to follow the right path for your company.

This also allows people to have more autonomy, and an explicit understanding of your principles provides a basis for your feedback to individuals. This also gets rolled back into lessons learned. In many cases, when something has gone wrong, you will find that somewhere in the chain of events you strayed from your basic principles about how to make your company successful. If you find that a mistake was made by following your principles, then perhaps those principles need to be reexamined.

A good place to start in discovering principles is to think about why you started this company and why you think it will be successful. You can also think about how your approach is unique when compared to others. Two of the best areas to find principles are in what you have taken for granted or where you have made assumptions.

The following are some examples of principles:

➤ In any communication with customers we make sure that they are receiving value before they are asked for anything.

➤ Our strategy is to enable our customers so that, through their success, we become successful. This includes our business processes, acquiring and sharing enabling technologies and doing cooperative marketing.

➤ We encourage constructive conflict whereby all employees are encouraged to voice their opinions and their reasons for them without personally attacking other individuals.

Ownership vs. Process

In any company, but especially in a startup, you will find that ownership works better than process. What I am talking about here is that you make individuals responsible for achieving results and completing tasks. There is just too much that comes your way on a day-to-day basis that could not have been foreseen or planned for and for which you could not have devised a process to give the "right" answer. However, if you assign ownership to an individual to get something done, then they have some latitude in doing what it takes to get it done and you know exactly where to go to monitor progress and who to hold accountable.

This is also motivational. Startups attract people who like to get things done without the constraints of history, institutional process or politics. Giving someone ownership of a result and the

Giving someone ownership of a result and the time and resources to achieve it is empowering.

time and resources to achieve it is empowering. In my opinion, there is no greater reward than being able to push one's limits and achieve something without irrational hindrances to one's efforts.

Action-Feedback-Learning-Intuition

You go into any situation with a certain level of knowledge, intuition and confidence. A large part of decision-making is having a sense for when you need more information and when you just need to pull the trigger and make the decision or take the action. In startups, it is often the case that action will need to be taken sooner rather than later. This means you will make mistakes—so what!

In startups, it is often the case that action will need to be taken sooner rather than later. This means you will make mistakes—so what!

In large companies, there is an emphasis on error avoidance instead of on opportunity maximization. Mistakes are identifiable and even measurable, while missed opportunities or mediocrity go unnoticed and unmeasured. People in large companies get fired for making mistakes. They typically don't get fired for risk avoidance, for moving too slowly or for failing to recognize opportunity. That startups do not have these constraints is the reason why they tend to be the engines of innovation. But, to succeed, you must make mistakes smartly.

So long as you learn and correct any mistakes as soon as possible, it is usually better for the company to take action than to collect information or invoke a process. An empowering loop, which you can enter at any point, is shown below. For sake of explanation lets start at "action".

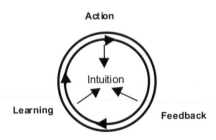

➢ **Action:** A situation demands that you take action. You know what you are trying to accomplish. You try to determine how you will know as quickly as possible whether that action was the right one or whether you need to take corrective action.

➢ **Feedback:** After you take the action you start getting feedback on whether it is having the desired effect or whether there are some unintended consequences—good or bad. From this you can determine how good your decision was and whether it needs some work or whether you need to back up and reset course.

➢ **Learning:** Now you can go into the learning phase. What assumptions did you make in your decision or action that turned out to be true? Which turned out to be false? There may be areas, previously unidentified, in which you need to do further learning or research. Maybe this means doing some reading, talking to an advisor or having someone mine some data already in the company.

Now you know how well you did. You have that feedback and you've gone back to do your learning. You should now have a higher level of confidence when you make the next decision and take the next action.

Through this cycle you will also have refined your intuition. You acted first, at the outset, based on your knowledge, intuition and confidence. Now you have increased all three of those and are ready to act again with a higher probability of getting it right.

To develop intuition you need to ground it with reality—there's nothing mystical about intuition.

The intuition developed through this loop is crucial, because without it you cannot make decisions quickly enough to compete against executives who do have well-developed intuition. Too often, people do not invoke the feedback loop and so do not have opportunities to refine their intuition. The situation then is like intuitively knowing that your intuition is great, in which case there is no feedback from reality. To develop intuition you need to ground it with reality—there's nothing mystical about intuition.

I have seen some intuitive decision-makers who do not fill in the loop by observing feedback and learning—this is called shooting from the hip. They make quick decisions repeatedly based on bad intuition or bad assumptions. These companies *move* quickly, *do* a lot, *spend* a lot of money but *accomplish little.*

In addition, the action component is essential to developing intuition. Without action, you never test that intuition. This is also how you expand your comfort zone without having to panic that you don't know everything for every situation. You develop the confidence that you can take an action and even make a mistake without damaging the company, so long as you observe the feedback and quickly take corrective action.

Lessons Learned

You will make mistakes as an individual and as a company. You could implement processes to make sure that mistakes are never made, but this inevitably leads to processes whereby risks are never taken, and if risks are never taken, then rewards are small. Instead, for any reasonable effort that is not pure routine, take a few moments to reflect on what was learned:

➤ If you did what you set out to, what did you do right that you want to keep on doing?

➤ Who did you rely on that excelled?

➤ Are there some things that you want to fine tune?

➤ If things went poorly, then, as a team, what did you learn?

Obviously you can't do this for everything that the company does, but it is worth doing it on even moderate-scale efforts. By doing the lessons-learned exercise, you signal that you are interested in improving and growing. You are signaling that it is all right to make mistakes (once), admit them and then dissect them to see what you can learn from them. Also, by making lessons-learned standard operating-procedure, and so long as they don't become public stonings, you create an environment in which people are not defensive about mistakes. This makes it less likely that mistakes will get glossed over, hidden or ignored and less likely that the feedback part of the loop will get filtered.

By doing the lessons-learned exercise, you signal that you are interested in improving and growing.

Course Corrections

Part of the cycle of quick action followed by feedback and lessons-learned is that quick course-corrections are also required. If you make a habit of learning lessons and responding to feedback, then you have the reasons for making a course correction. Communicating these reasons, along with the change of course, is essential in a startup.

While planning is essential so that you understand what you want to achieve and how, you will be working in an uncertain world with partial information. This means that no matter how much you plan, you will need to make course corrections. Mastering the art of quick course-correction within a company can increase your velocity and lower your risk.

It is not uncommon for startups to make quick course-corrections but to fail to communicate the rationale behind the changes. This then appears to some within the company as capriciousness and they may even lose some faith in the management team. If you communicate the reasons for changes, people can understand that the changes are not being made on whims and are not purely emotional responses.

Some people who are either new to startups or who are not on the management team will not be comfortable with rapid changes. When talking with them, you might find that they think that management is shooting from the hip and, with proper planning, the company would never need to change from its intended course. In general, these people will either learn to embrace change or they will become so uncomfortable that they will leave the company—whether voluntarily or not.

Comfort Zones

Some people are more able to push outside their comfort zones than others and entrepreneurs must do this on nearly a daily basis.

We all have comfort zones and there are some situations that make us uncomfortable. Some people are more able to push outside their comfort zones than others and entrepreneurs must do this on nearly a daily basis. This means that you need to do things you've never done before with the confidence that you'll figure it out and get the right people to help you. You will end up in social situations that are uncomfortable because you have never been in them. If you take the time for some introspection, you will usually find that there are areas in which your company will benefit if you take on some personal growth.

So, this is not the same as merely being confident that you can do anything; rather, it is taking action in a direction in which you feel awkward. This will need to become a common occurrence for you and your company. You need to reflect occasionally to determine whether you and your company are pushing the envelope or settling into a comfort zone.

There will be many challenges with which you will have to deal for the first time and you just need to embrace them.

For example, your first meeting with a venture capitalist can be intimidating until you realize venture capitalists are just other people with genuine concerns that they need to have addressed. If they are rude to you, that's their problem, not yours. Your measure is whether you got results:

> *Did you get a next meeting?*
> *A follow-up on more information?*
> *Some kind of next step that signifies that you are moving forward?*

As discussed at greater length earlier, you will get more mileage out of these encounters of the out-of-comfort kind if you create feedback loops to increase your confidence and refine your intuition. It becomes liberating when you realize that you can do this.

Backup Plans

Backup plans are one of your keys to success. As I have discussed previously, if you are pushing yourself and your company, you will hit some roadblocks or unforeseen circumstances. Giving up is usually not a good option.

One way to approach such problems is to wait until they occur and then devise a new strategy. But most problems are not immediately apparent in a grand flash of blinding light accompanied by sirens. The line between good intention and failure is usually wide and gray. The onset of failure is insidious. This is greatly exaggerated if you do not have backup plans before you need them. When there is no clear alternative to the current path, the tendency is to say, "It still might work, let's stay the course. It's not that bad."

The line between good intention and failure is usually wide and gray. The onset of failure is insidious.

When the backup plans are devised in advance it is much easier to say, "This isn't meeting our criteria for success. Let's move quickly to our backup plan and apply what we've learned about this." Of course, you did establish criteria for success in advance, didn't you?

As an example of backup plans, consider risky technology development. You have path A for an optics design, which results in the fewest parts and the best field of view but no one will know whether they can make it until they try. So you develop plans B and C. Plan B is still pretty good; it has one more part in it, but two manufacturers have told you that they think they can make it. Plan C uses still one more part and is heavy and bigger than you would like but it uses design elements that you know have been made before.

Taking this route has numerous advantages. It allows you even to try plan A, which might have been too risky to consider were it the only option. It means that if plan A does not work, you can immediately switch horses. And if you also work plan C, you will have something to show or even take to market with no technical risk and that can almost surely be done on schedule.

Time Management

As your company picks up, you will find that you are trying to cram more and more into every day and still trying to keep your head clear enough to make good decisions. Every business is different in terms of its demands for individual contribution. However, in all cases there will be a significant interactive part of the job. As soon as you try to do something a bit grander than stuffing envelopes, you need people. People to help you, people to buy from you, people to sell you stuff and people to help you market and sell. These people will be looking to you for guidance and decisions and, in some cases, motivation.

Usually, your style of interaction is the area where you can gain or lose the most time.

Usually, your style of interaction is the area where you can gain or lose the most time. This is truly art, since the way in which you interact with people will depend on your style and what you are trying to accomplish. On the one hand, the same direct and abrupt style that seems natural and is even expected of one executive could come off as artificial and smack of "One-Minute Manager" syndrome to *your* team. On the other hand, if *your* natural style is to be direct and to the point, a lot of "How are the wife and kids" talk could come off as smarmy and manipulative. In other words, there is nothing wrong with either of these styles but there is something wrong with being inauthentic. Even if no one can put their finger on it, they will "smell" that something is not right and might mistrust you or question your ability to lead as a result. So, with that caution, let's move on to some ways to save time.

Saving time in interactions of course starts with you. You have to know *what* you want and *how* you want things done. This is one of the areas that is very positively impacted by the planning you have done and your efforts in defining principles, mission and vision. You and your team have thought these things through carefully and now you don't need to reinvent them every time something comes up.

A good goal to have in interactions is, as far as possible, to reach a decision and a call to action by the end of the interaction. This objective then determines the level of the interaction. You are in a startup and you will at times need to dive into details that the CEO of Exxon would never even consider. Note however that this is not the same as micromanaging.

Simple time-sinks are doing things that don't need to be done.

Simple time-sinks are doing things that don't need to be done.

> *I have seen CEOs waste hours formatting documents that will be used only for internal communication, or designing graphics when they could easily have sketched them on whiteboards, or selecting packing-box design for demonstration hardware.*

Other wasteful areas are low-intensity networking. If you are golfing every week with the same two people, that's great. Just realize that you are doing that because you enjoy it and that in that same time you could be doing things that would have a greater impact on your company. (It is different if you are actually talking a deal with those people, or if you are meeting new people every week.)

Demand vs. Supply

Because entrepreneurs are naturally optimistic, they sometimes worry too much about potential supply-problems. And many times they build up capacity in anticipation of demand that is never realized.

This was a recurring problem in the Internet-bubble days but persists even now. This is one of the reasons that companies such as Viant, Scient and MarchFirst are suffering so badly. Back when everyone thought that they would be the next eBay or Amazon, and had read the horror stories about the eBay blackouts, they wanted to make sure that they had the capacity—purchased at a high price from one of the publicly traded development firms. As a result they spent way too much on developing their Web sites and back-end to support levels of demand that had yet to be proved.

> *In one case, a company got an estimate from one of the publicly traded Web-developers for $1.5 million, then an estimate in the Denver area for around $500,000. The $1.5-million site would have been more robust and maybe even have led to more conversions at the margins—but this was not the key to success. The key to success was generating the demand.*

In most cases there are ways of dealing with demand overload. If you get too many orders at Christmas, you can probably recruit friends and family to pack boxes for a couple of evenings. If the back-end isn't fully automated, you can shuffle papers around and send faxes to suppliers. So long as the front-end experience of your customer exceeds expectations, you can struggle through the back-end issues with some low-tech ingenuity and save substantially on your development costs.

Missed Deadlines

The first few missed milestones usually don't seem like too big a deal. You are optimistic and a lot of unforeseen opportunities and problems impinge on the time resources that might have been used to meet those now-missed milestones.

These missed milestones can easily lead to trouble in ways that are less than obvious. The obvious way is that they represent falling behind, which may have broader implications. Perhaps there is a change in equity based on meeting your milestones that requires that, if you miss certain milestones, equity is transferred from the founders to the investors. You might run out of money before you get to a value-enhancing milestone or sales. You might miss a market window or you might miss a season (e.g. Christmas) or a major sales-event (e.g. Comdex).

Less obvious problems of missed milestones are that they show that you are failing either to plan or to execute. Not many things can be done instantaneously and virtually everything that needs to be done will take some time. You have limited resources and usually everyone in the company has many things that they need to get done. Also, at the early stages, you are trying to do many things for the first time and you have to allow for some missteps along the way. An inability to plan can lead to many problems, some of which have been mentioned above. But it also shows that management may not be as capable as you would like. It will lower the confidence of your customers in your ability to deliver quality service or to deliver a product at all. It will lower your odds of follow-on investment because of lower confidence in the team.

The failure to execute is even a more serious problem. This one almost always is a failure of management at some level. In more detail, it can be caused by poor communication, poor strategy, unreasonable expectations, poor leadership, poorly utilized resources and so on.

Another problem that is not obvious about missed deadlines is that, if they are missed on a regular basis, this leads to a cynicism about milestones in general. When milestones are proposed and even written down, they are accepted with a smirk and a nod but with no real commitment to meeting them. When they are missed, it becomes hard to punish the person most responsible because everyone is missing milestones and the company *always* misses milestones. It's quite insidious as it is happening and very hard to turn around. The process of turning this around almost always leads to a lot of people finding out that their permanent employment was more temporary than they thought.

> *I remember management meetings at one company that was notorious for missing milestones. Whenever one of the executives presented status on various projects and what his schedule was, the CEO immediately and without exception would say "You need to do better than that, it shouldn't take that long." It got so bad at times that executives would ask "When would you like it done," get a number from the CEO and then even agree to it while knowing full well they could not meet the deadlines. They would rather go through this foolish and demeaning exercise than enduring the less foolish but even more demeaning exercise of dealing with one of the CEO's outbursts. This company eventually got to production four years late, never met a sales forecast and sold its business at a fraction of the capital invested in the company.*

Infrastructure

This was introduced above. In general, the idea is to focus on what matters. You can use folding tables for desks for a while but you may want good-looking conference-room furniture. This stuff is not rocket science and after a couple hours at office supply and furniture stores you will have this figured out. On some of the high-dollar items you might consider a lease rather than purchase and look for brokers and refurnishers to buy good, used furniture and equipment.

I'm usually not a big fan of checklists, but here is one place where one is appropriate. These are some of the infrastructure items you'll need:

- ❑ copy machine
- ❑ fax machine
- ❑ computers
- ❑ server
- ❑ wall covering (pictures, posters, etc.)
- ❑ whiteboards
- ❑ feng shui consultant (just kidding)
- ❑ firewall

- network wiring
- mobile phones
- business cards
- letterhead
- envelopes
- filing cabinets
- workplace posters (minimum wage etc.)
- insurance
- cleaning crew
- utilities
- phone company
- high bandwidth
- kitchen
- coffee maker
- refrigerator
- lobby furniture
- plants
- conference-room furniture
- office furniture
- printers
- accounting software
- MS Office or equivalent per computer
- locks and/or alarm service
- office
- dishwasher
- vacuum
- informational Web site.

Functional Teams

There are entire books written on this very subject and so I will stick to a few key points here. Functional management-teams have a few very important qualities:

➢ constructive conflict

➢ quick decision-making

➢ action orientation

➢ results orientation

➢ a supportive attitude to decisions.

Constructive Conflict

Constructive conflict means that, when an issue arises, the team members engage and participate actively in expressing opinions. They have reasons for their opinions, which they can articulate, and they stay on topic and never attack individuals. Nonetheless, an environment exists in which people are comfortable expressing disagreement. They feel comfortable pointing out potential problems along with solutions. Notice that this is reasoned disagreement directed to solutions and results. It is not whining, it is not finger pointing, it is not arguing for argument's sake and it is not personal.

… this is reasoned disagreement directed to solutions and results. It is not whining, it is not finger pointing, it is not arguing for argument's sake and it is not personal.

Quick decision-making

Quick decision-making means that, after getting input or even taking some exploratory action, a decision is made on what to do.

Action Orientation

Action orientation is in contrast to information or process orientation. Rather than delay in taking action while more and more information is gathered, a functional team knows when it makes more sense to act than to study. Rather than develop a process that action must follow, it takes the most prudent action even while a plan, not a process, is being developed.

Results Orientation

Results orientation means that the team decides in advance of taking an action or making a decision what a successful outcome will be. It decides what feedback is appropriate to measuring whether the action was on the path to the company's success.

... once a decision has been made, the team gets behind the action and works to achieve the targeted results—regardless of what disagreement they may have had in the past.

Supportive Attitude to Decisions

Most importantly, once a decision has been made, the team gets behind the action and works to achieve the targeted results—regardless of what disagreement they may have had in the past.

Networking

On the one hand, there is a lot to be gained by networking with people with whom you have some common interests and from whom you can learn as well as whom you can teach. Wholesale networking, on the other hand, can eat up a lot of time for little benefit and it can become unbalanced—with people constantly asking you for something. Also, networking is like marketing: the more targeted and focused it is the better.

In most moderately populated areas that have some entrepreneurial activity there are many groups that offer networking opportunities to their members. They are of varying quality and have different focuses. The more general networking events, such as generic leads groups, are of limited value.

Networking works best where there is reciprocation. Try to add value to the people you talk to and likewise expect them to do so.

> *I have seen entrepreneurs all over the map in their networking. On one extreme are people who have a networking event almost every day or every evening of the week. At the other end of the spectrum are entrepreneurs that get so caught up in their companies that they don't network at all. The hazard in doing this is that you cease to hear new ideas in new contexts. You may miss economic trends or even trends within your industry.*

Moderation and focus are the keys. Limit the amount of time that you spend networking and make it quality networking. Rather than going to a leads group and collecting business cards, go out of your way to meet someone in a similar business. Find out how other people are running their businesses, what kind of feedback they are getting from customers, what CRM (customer relationship management) package they are using, what law firm they recommend and why, whether they know where you can hire a system architect. I have found that people are quite happy to share information and ideas and give you some of their time if you reciprocate. Sometimes this will take some time on your part—but if you are networking with people that can add value to what you are doing then it can be well worth it.

Copy What Works

This sounds like very simple advice but its amazing how often even small companies fall into NIH—not invented here— syndrome. Other companies have spent fortunes developing products and services and you can take advantage of their hard work. Take a look around you and copy the best of what you see.

Other companies have spent fortunes developing products and services and you can take advantage of their hard work. Take a look around you and copy the best of what you see.

> *If you are building an e-commerce company, you might look to Amazon.com and how it interacts with its customers after an order is placed. If you are providing a service, you might look at all of your competitors' marketing materials to see if there are elements of their messages that make sense for your business as well. Read some of the direct mail that you receive for good and bad examples.*

This notion of copying what works also goes beyond marketing and delivering products and services. If you are forming business relationships, you can see some great ideas by reading agreements that other companies have done.

> *For example, you might talk to your attorneys about a business relationship you are considering and ask them to send you some agreements their firm has done that might be relevant (with names taken out). You can go through these and usually identify the motivation for each of the terms and therefore get some clever ideas that someone else may have paid tens of thousands of dollars to figure out. You can also get such information*

and documents from board members and strategic partners. For example, a strategic partner might give you copies of several of their vendor agreements that you can comb through for ideas. (An excellent source of free sample documents is www.tannedfeet.com.)

When copying parts of what your competitors are doing, you are getting some "second mover advantage".

If you become good at copying you can save a lot of time and money that can be put to better use developing what is truly unique about, or core to, your business. When copying parts of what your competitors are doing, you are getting some "second mover advantage". And this offsets, to some extent, the "first mover advantages" that they might have in recognized brands, customer lists or existing business relationships. Put in this light, Toys-R-Us was the first mover and eToys was the late-mover.

The point is that you don't need to reinvent the wheel in every aspect of your business and there is a lot you can learn from related companies and especially from your competitors.

Plan Your Planning

Plan in advance to revise your plans and input real data. This is one of those instances in which a meeting can be the most efficient means. If you have a business plan, then this is the ideal vehicle for reconnecting with your plans. It is an opportune time to revise these plans and add to them from the real-world data you have been collecting.

For startups and early-stage companies, doing this every quarter is usually adequate and in most cases this can be done in a couple of hours if people have prepared for an hour or two beforehand. Preparation would include reading the business plan and testing the assumptions and projections against reality. Where there is a difference, take a moment to reflect on why to see if there is a lesson there.

If a team member has new ideas or thinks that there should be some significant changes then they should take the time to prepare proposals. These aren't 20-page, written proposals. Rather, depending on the culture of your company, they can be as simple as white-board diagrams or as formal as some overheads. Proposers should however have clear views of what they are proposing. They should also be able to make business cases for the proposals. Sometimes this will, of necessity, have to be subjective, but if it can be quantified, so much the better. The objective of the proposed action, measuring its success and objective pros and cons should also be presented.

A series of charts or sections might progress as follows:

➢ Problem

➢ Solution alternatives with pros and cons

➢ Recommendation

➢ Rationale and business case

➢ Action plan, metrics for success

By preparing this information the proposer makes it more likely that a decision can be made quickly in the meeting, rather than becoming an ongoing process for days or weeks, or getting dropped entirely because it seems like too much effort.

Plan Your Next Move

This is about you as much as about your company. It is about matching your strengths with the needs of the company. After reading this book and with some of your own experiences, you will know a lot about everything from motivation to finance to operation.

However, even if you know something and are good at something, this doesn't mean that is where your greatest strength is, nor does it mean that is where you add the most value.

There will be many times that you will need to work beyond the scope of your strengths. In a startup, there are so many things that need to be done and so few resources with which to do them.

> *There will be many times that you will need to work beyond the scope of your strengths.*

However, at some point, if you are working most of your time outside of your strengths, you will hold back your company and you will be doing a disservice to yourself. One option is to grow your company into one that matches your individual strengths very well. If you don't have any investors, this is a viable option. The trick then is to know your strengths and what this company should look like. Alternatively, if you have investors or shareholders, they have every reason to want the company to maximize their ROI—regardless of what satisfaction this provides to you or where you are in your comfort zone.

Another option, and usually the only one that treats investors fairly, is for you to have some idea of when you need to change roles or change companies. This shouldn't be as traumatic as it often becomes. This transition often results in a lot of board turmoil, inside politics, secrecy, distrust and, in some cases, lawsuits. Instead, many entrepreneurs are now thinking about this transition from the start. Rather than viewing this transition as some sort of failure, they see it as a natural occurrence.

Some people are best in the startup phases with less than 50 employees, others are great at running companies that have thousands of employees.

These transitions are usually much smoother if you think about them in advance. Otherwise they can result in a year or more's hiatus in the progress of the company.

> *In one company the CEO was absolutely awesome through the startup phases. Her strengths were finding good people, developing strategy, raising money and opening doors with customers. She was great at keeping people excited about what the company was doing and the progress the company was making in changing an industry. As the company grew, her fire-drill style, need to control and need to be the center of attention became anchors pulling against the company's forward motion. This company had received considerable venture-capital and the board meetings were pretty rough at times. But, since the CEO would not voluntarily make a transition, the board was faced with an awkward choice. It could replace the CEO involuntarily and cause much turmoil within the company or take the CEO's word that she could change. They chose the latter course—for a while. Eventually they replaced the CEO, but too late. The company had missed several windows of opportunity and had raised too much money for what they had done. The company ended up being shut down.*

There is an excellent book on knowing your strengths that I strongly recommend: *Now, Discover your Strengths* by Marcus Buckingham and Donald Clifton (The Free Press, A Division of Simon and Schuster, New York, New York, 2001). It is helpful, but you will have to work on trying to figure out where your strengths result in added value to your company, and to which growth phase they are best suited. If you have been part of building several companies, then you probably already have a good idea of where you fit best.

You can transition in a number of ways:

➢ Leave the company and go do something that is a better fit.

➢ Stay with the company and create a position for yourself in which you add the most value.

➢ Hire people that can complement you so that you can stay in the same position but change the nature of the position to match you better.

If this is your first time through the startup adventure, then you will have to pay attention to yourself. You will find that some activities are energizing and that you lose yourself in them. You could do these things for hours and not even notice that time had passed. Other activities will sap your energy, you will want to postpone them, and you find it difficult to make yourself do them. Now match what your company needs with what you find energizing. Think about where there is a match and try to envision the needs of the company through its life.

Now match what your company needs with what you find energizing.

You can actually turn this into an exercise. List the things that you like doing and do well. List things that you are certain you would like to do but need to do some learning to do well. Now list what the company needs now and in the future by identifying some stages. Suggestions are startup and pre-sales, sales ramp-up, rapid growth, operational excellence and so on. Where is the match between what you enjoy doing or want to do and what the company needs, this will tell you a lot about what you need to do. It will tell you in what areas, and when, you will need help, need to make a transition or need to leave. For those things that you want to do but can not yet do well, you can hire consultants to help you learn quickly. Most things aren't all that hard if you have desire and aptitude, and someone can show you through the subtleties so that you don't have to make all the mistakes on your own.

Most things aren't all that hard if you have desire and aptitude, and someone can show you through the subtleties so that you don't have to make all the mistakes on your own.

Playing Rough

If your experience is anything like mine has been, you will find overwhelmingly that the people that you meet through your business are wonderful, and that in most cases everyone scores a win in your business relationships.

However, there will come a time when someone tries to take something from you. They might sue you, steal your intellectual property, not pay you or breech a written or verbal agreement. You need to be prepared to play rough with these people or else they will continue to steal from you. In a sense, when the relationship becomes that adversarial it really is you or them.

You will need to find a way to play rough in that part of your business while not letting that negative energy bleed into all of the positive aspects of doing business.

9. REAL ENTREPRENEURS

In this chapter are the "stories" of two entrepreneurs. These stories will give you a sense of what it is like to be an entrepreneur and even though the entrepreneurs talk openly about the good *and* the bad you will see that they really would not, or could not, do anything else. You will also see how colorful and interesting these people are.

Although these entrepreneurs are in two very different businesses and the details of their journeys and their backgrounds differ, there are certain fundamentals that are common to both of them—namely:

➤ resourcefulness

➤ intuitiveness

➤ results-orientation

➤ integrity

➤ clarity

➤ accountability

➤ self-assurance

➤ humility

➤ sense of urgency

➤ drive.

Not only are the fundamentals pretty constant from one good entrepreneur to another but they are also relatively constant over time. I could have inserted the story of my father and his journey in starting his first business and it's unlikely that you would notice that 35 years had passed since the events, nor would his comments and lessons learned be very different from the entrepreneurs presented here.

Joshua Hanfling

Joshua Hanfling (CEO of Quicksign in Denver, Colorado) has been starting ventures since he was a youth. He has tried many things—some of which have worked out better than others. Much of his experience has been with traditional industries including his current company, Quicksign in Denver, Colorado. However, he has also worked on some technology ventures such as Aartronics.

Background

While Joshua had the usual "childhood" businesses such as shoveling snow, mowing lawns, paper routes and lemonade stands, he put his own entrepreneurial twist on these ventures. He hired other neighborhood kids to do the work for him for his paper route and he borrowed the money for a lawn mower from his father and paid it back by doing his family's lawn.

"... intrigued with the process of starting something new ... with the anxiety and tension of starting a business."

Another unique aspect of Joshua's childhood included exposure to his father's consulting work; entrepreneurs would come to his house on the weekends and seek his father's advice on starting companies. He would overhear the conversations and was "intrigued with the process of starting something new ... with the anxiety and tension of starting a business".

Yet another unique aspect of Joshua's background was his exposure to wealth and what that could do for one's lifestyle. He is quite comfortable in stating that he is motivated by a desire for wealth, the independence of lifestyle that it brings and the things one can spend it on.

Joshua is interesting in that he has such a healthy, well-balanced and frank approach to wealth. While he wants and even expects to become wealthy through his efforts, he is in no way greedy. He looks to long-term gain through long-term relationships, rather than trying to maximize every transaction in dollar terms. He also is conscientious in giving his time and money to charitable causes that he deems worthwhile. Not because he feels any need to "give something back" as he hasn't taken anything, but because he believes it is the right thing to do and he finds it personally rewarding. Wealth creation is a legitimate motivation and if it is one of yours then you might as well know it rather than denying the fact because it is politically incorrect.

Many kids have entrepreneurial parents and have childhood businesses, so where is that turning point that distinguished Joshua as a future entrepreneur rather than a future bureaucrat? In interviewing Joshua, I found that that turning point was when he recognized an opportunity at his temple while he was raising money for his youth group. He then organized and managed a group of other kids to execute that unique opportunity.

Joshua saw that families were spending a fortune on event planners and caterers for bar mitzvahs. The opportunity he saw was that he and other kids at his temple could do the job. He even had a novel business-model that benefited his temple while creating performance incentives for himself and his staff—he split the profits between his team and his temple.

After high school, Joshua attended Babson College, where he majored exclusively in entrepreneurial studies. He said that this pure focus on entrepreneurial studies "ensured that I was unemployable upon graduation." He liked the fact that the instructors had business experience that they could pass on to the students through real-world, rather than hypothetical, case-studies. He graduated with a bachelor's degree and relatively low in his class. When I asked him why he didn't get an MBA, he stressed that he wasn't a student and that his focus was on business.

In his junior year at Babson, Joshua started a business with a partner in Virginia, where there was a lot of construction at the time. His company would charge to receive wood waste such as tree stumps, then grind it and mulch it, and in many cases then sell the product to the same companies that had paid them to take the waste in the first place. They made $1 million in sales in their first year.

Joshua went back to Babson in his senior year and left his partner to run the business. One of Joshua's comments about the experience: "... we split that company 50/50. Don't ever, ever split a company 50/50. Its better to let somebody else take control than to have nobody take control. Disaster, disaster!" Ultimately the company was dissolved after some problems with his partner surfaced.

"Its better to let somebody else take control than to have nobody take control."

After graduating, Joshua worked for a number of companies in the Washington D.C. area, helping with planning and financing while he was looking for a venture into which to sink his teeth. An opportunity arose in Denver, Colorado with a company that was developing PC diagnostic hardware. Joshua moved to Colorado to work with the company and ended up running it when the founder left after it was discovered that he was working full time for another company. Not long after that, the investor that was funding the company filed for bankruptcy and Joshua had to look for another way to make Aartronics into a business. He landed a government contract that put the company at breakeven while it tried to run its sales and marketing on a shoestring—something it found unworkable for entering the consumer-electronics arena. At the end of the government contract the company shut down without filing for bankruptcy.

Joshua started consulting to Denver-area companies that were looking for financing as the Internet was getting hot. During this period he also started a travel agency in Washington D.C. that is still going strong with $6 million in annual bookings. He also founded and invested in a bar that was sold at a gain to investors.

The Journey

While consulting, Joshua saw the wealth that was being created by Internet entrepreneurs and wanted to jump into the fray. He started writing down ideas for companies and when he was visiting a friend's sign-shop he saw how the customer experience could be greatly improved on the Internet. He developed a plan and detailed financial models for an online sign-company and recruited an executive team that would join him upon funding.

Joshua met with tens of venture capitalists but found no takers. However, one of the objections that arose repeatedly was that he didn't have domain expertise; i.e. he didn't have any experience in the sign industry. One way Joshua saw to resolve this objection was to ally with bricks-and-mortar sign-companies, so he met with the president and VP of sales at such a company. The president of that company didn't want much to do with the "new economy" vision that Joshua had. However, Art Wollenweber, the VP of sales at that company, called Joshua the next day and arranged a meeting at which he expressed his interest in joining Joshua's management team. This solved the domain-expertise problem but did not solve the funding problem.

... it looks like a classic example of an entrepreneur making his luck.

Joshua said "it was pure luck" to find his guy (Art) with domain expertise in this way. However, to me it looks like a classic example of an entrepreneur making his luck. Granted, recruiting a VP of sales was not the goal of Joshua's meeting with the sign company. However, Joshua made the contact, set up the meeting, and pitched his vision so well that the VP of sales called the next day to talk to Joshua. Moreover, Joshua had enough vision, ability and leadership that this VP of sales joined Joshua when he bought Quicksign and put his Internet plans on hold.

As is often the case, resolving investors' primary objection only brought their secondary objections to the surface. The most common secondary objection was that Joshua didn't have facilities for manufacture and that such facilities would require a lot of capital. So Joshua went to work on a deal with yet another bricks-and-mortar sign-company. In the originally envisioned deal, Quicksign would supply to the online company until a second round of funding was received, at which time the online company would purchase Quicksign.

It turned out that this still wasn't enough to obtain a commitment from venture capitalists. So Joshua stepped back and asked himself whether the sign industry was fundamentally a good one to be in. He saw that it was horribly fragmented and that Quicksign, with its history and capital equipment, would have an edge. He decided to try to purchase Quicksign even without venture capital to fund the Internet strategy.

Joshua arranged an SBA (small business administration) loan, which provided 80% of the capital. Joshua contributed to the deal and the seller carried back 10%. Joshua was then owner of Quicksign.

In our interview, Joshua reflected on the mistakes he had made and the things he might have done differently in buying the company. He said that he would have done more due-diligence. As he put it, "Historical sales were not what I had been led to believe." He said, "I started without enough working capital." "The employees didn't do quality work ... I didn't know enough about the company on day-one to make changes ... If I had known then what I know today, I would have laid some people off right away and I would have changed pricing right away."

Words of Wisdom

To get some idea of how Joshua's mind works and how he is always looking for a new opportunity consider this quotation: "There's a huge opportunity here [in the sign industry] and I'm in the process of buying another company that has some capabilities and technologies that we need. It's a clean deal with a large crossover in the customer base."

When asked how he spends his time, Joshua said: "I probably do more networking and schmoozing than I

"I spend a lot of time looking at numbers ..."

should, I'll go to lunch for an hour and a half with customers that I'm courting or I'll go to lunch someplace where I'll see potential clients and customers. Right now, unfortunately, I'm on the phone with vendors a lot because I have to deal with when they're going to get paid, which is a distraction. I put out a lot of little fires. I'm trying to reorganize my business. I walk around a lot. A lot of it is writing plans because I'm trying to get the new company done. So I'm with lawyers a lot and getting the plan done for that. I spend a lot of time looking at numbers, for example right now I'm looking at switching to a cost-plus pricing method."

When asked what he thought about planning, Joshua said, "I'm a big believer, but things are never going to turn out the way you want. If you had asked me last year I would have told you that I would have a branch in another city by now.

"The problem with planning is that you want to do it before you buy a business but once you're in there it all goes right out the window. Then you just have to keep readjusting the plan. My favorite is to use whiteboards—it's the easiest way for me to keep track of my plans. For me the best way of planning is through spreadsheets. For example, for the company I am buying I have a twenty-page spreadsheet with historicals factored in but I haven't finished an executive summary yet. I always start with the model because I can understand the numbers better than if I write.

"When I do my projections I focus on cash flow. I don't care about the balance sheet, I don't care about owner's equity. That'll all work itself out."

"Plus, I honestly think that it's the most important part. I think that if you get a rock-solid spreadsheet and you've really thought through the assumptions properly, then, if you've built the model in the correct way and one of the assumptions changes, you very quickly know how it affects your whole business. It'll tell you when you need to hire and who you need to hire. I love the visual part, the graphs.

"When I do my projections I focus on cash flow. I don't care about the balance sheet, I don't care about owner's equity. That'll all work itself out. What really matters is cash flow. The day I figured out how cash flows worked in college was one of the coolest days of my life. Because once you've figured out the cash flows, you know exactly how much money you're going to need. It just shows that you've thought it through."

When asked what advice he would give to entrepreneurs, Joshua said:

➢ "Put some money in the deal but put some money away. There has to be a point where if you can't get somebody else to put something into a deal then maybe its not a good deal."

➢ "Read *Atlas Shrugged* over and over."

➢ "Fire quick."

➢ "Don't take yourself too seriously."

When asked what the biggest surprise was, Joshua said, "Before I bought this company I had been doing deals. This was another deal. The difference was that when this deal closed, I had to go to work the next day and I had twenty-five employees and I was a million dollars in debt. I was not prepared for that and I hadn't even thought about it. It took me months to adjust—to get my mind in the game.

"I love business, I love going there every day, I love knowing it's mine. If it does great it's mine, if I fuck it up it's my fault—nobody else's."

Takeaways

➤ People first: One of the lessons learned is that it always comes down to people first. If you don't have the right people on board, then the best vision and strategy are worthless.

➤ Due diligence: Before starting a venture, do your research and your planning. There are always surprises and plans are not reality, but with enough research and planning you can adjust quickly to reality.

➤ Think it through: Think downstream about what you are getting into and be prepared to adjust your lifestyle—usually this means making some sacrifices for a while.

➤ Ensure accountability: Someone needs to be in charge and be accountable for the success of the company. Consensus and diffused responsibility rarely work for very long.

Jerald Golley

Jerald Golley is CEO of Ami Visions and Mango Fish (among other companies) in Lakewood, Colorado—near Denver. As the youngest of eleven children, he defies the statistical entity of "typical entrepreneur". In addition, he "loved the military" of all things when he was younger. Like most entrepreneurs, he has had successes and failures, but his persistence and ability to adapt have meant that the successes have outnumbered the failures.

Background

Jerry was the youngest of eleven children and one of the two of those children who graduated from university. He tinkered with electronics and, as he said, "I don't know if I ever fixed anything but I took a lot of stuff apart." However, he was not especially entrepreneurial as a kid. Rather, he developed ways of getting what he wanted that would serve him well as an entrepreneur.

"You get something in your mind and you just go for it. You figure out what the first thing is that you have to do and you just do it!"

After he graduated from high school he joined the military because he wasn't sure exactly what he wanted to do and it supported his long-time goal of becoming a pilot. As Jerry points out, one of the consistent themes in his life is: "You get something in your mind and you just go for it. You figure out what the first thing is that you have to do and you just do it! I've never really had a complete map of what my future would look like. All I can figure is, this is my goal, and before I can get to there the very first thing I have to do is apply."

In the process of applying to flight school, Jerry was befriended by a West Point officer who offered to help him apply to West Point. The process took about two years, but in the end he was accepted to flight-school, West Point Prep School, and had orders to Germany, all at the same time. He took his flight-school physical in June but decided that he would go to West Point because they had an age limit and he could go to flight school after graduating. In August he took a separate physical for entry into West Point Prep School, where he became a cadet.

At the ripe old age of nineteen, Jerry was thrown a huge and unfortunate curve. He was pulled out of classes after only two and a half weeks because he was diagnosed with leukemia and given three to six years to live. He was given the option of receiving a bone-marrow transplant, but was warned that there was a 50% chance of not surviving the transplant and subsequent treatment. He decided that he had hardly yet lived and decided to forgo the transplant to take advantage of his military retirement and educational benefits by going to college.

> *It seemed odd to me that someone who has turned out to be such a great entrepreneur could have ever had such a love for a bureaucratic, traditional and authoritarian environment as the military. Jerry put it in perspective for me. He told me that he entered the military at seventeen and really hadn't experienced much, but, by virtue of the jobs he had, he was exposed to people and thoughts that he never could have experienced as quickly as a seventeen-year-old in any other way. Much as many people learn a great deal at large companies, Jerry took advantage of his exposure to learn as much as he could in the Army.*

As Jerry puts it "… but what do you study at college when you're terminally ill? You take the classes that are fun." While taking "fun" classes he developed interests in Geography and programming. Geography because of its breadth and mathematical nature, and programming because, quite simply, he liked the teaching style and sense of humor of a professor that offered a series of courses in programming. Jerry took every one of the programming courses offered by that professor.

In his third year in college, Jerry had a live-in girlfriend and a lot of friends and decided to have the transplant. He said the transplant went smoothly and he lost only a semester before returning to college. He continued in Geography in graduate school and completed his master's degree with close to a 4.0.

After completing an internship at National Geographic, he received a job offer from American Management Systems. There he did programming in geographic information systems (GIS). After about two years, the GIS work slowed and he was put on another project in 1992 to manage data and applications for the changes required by the Clean Air Act.

Jerry built a prototype of a system for permit management in a programming language called PowerBuilder. As the lead developer he was also the lead salesperson. Through this new role he learned a number of things—such as sales skills, listening to the customer, consulting and public speaking—that would benefit him later. Jerry made sales of $7 million and the project was a great success in all respects—except for one …

"I was twenty-six years old at the time and I felt that I should be the project manager. When I went to my boss, he said you probably deserve the job but you don't have enough experience. He told me, 'I'm going to make you the technical lead on the project, we're going to bring in a database lead and another person to be the administrative project manager.' It's probably a decision that I would make today, but at the time I was furious. And, it didn't work at all because he didn't put one person in charge of the project and so it became a triangle of power that was really ugly. I think within two months all three of us had quit."

"... it didn't work at all because he didn't put one person in charge of the project."

The Journey

Jerry received a cold-call about a job in Colorado Springs doing contracting for MCI. He got the job following a phone interview, but it wasn't to last: "I got fired from MCI because I was making decisions I really wasn't authorized to make and stepped on some manager's toes." He decided he really wanted to move to Denver and he called around and got a contract job with Lipper Analytical Services.

Lipper wanted to migrate from Cobol to PowerBuilder. Jerry earned the trust of his boss in New York and was soon running the project, which was going smoothly until his boss got a new boss that insisted a contractor should not lead the project—effectively demoting Jerry to programmer. Meanwhile, the complicated system migration started to unravel, so Jerry approached his boss with a proposal to put things back on track.

As Jerry put it: "I approached my boss and the local VP and said that I could outsource some work and do it on my own. And I told them I would do the work on a fixed bid. The first project I did for Lipper was for $10,000 and worked out really well. I did it by myself in my spare time—I worked around the clock essentially, but I got it done and delivered it to them and they were really happy. They said, 'That worked well and would you consider more?' And it was actually their suggestion that I start my own company."

"... it was actually their suggestion that I start my own company."

Jerry then started Ami Visions in 1996.

"They gave me a small project of about $40,000 and I hired one person to help me with it. I was still working hourly on projects so I was basically working two jobs. The next project was approximately $140,000. In the first year they [Lipper] were my only client. We started the company in June and by the end of the year we did approximately $60,000 of work. In the twelve months after that we did another $600,000 of work and I had grown the company to about nine or ten people ... About a year after I started the company I realized that I needed another client ... My second client was BI ... they had software that managed inmates. By the time we were two years old we probably had twenty-five clients and twenty to twenty-five employees."

Ami Visions grew to $1.8 million in sales by 1999 and exceeded $3 million in sales in 2000.

In about 1999, Jerry saw that he needed to transition Ami Visions away from client-server work and decided to start doing Web-development work. He realized that PowerBuilder was becoming a dead language and needed to change course. Making the transition was complicated by the fact that it is hard to get business without experience and it is hard to get experienced people without the projects. Jerry solved both problems by hiring a woman who brought with her a client and several other developers. This solved the near-term problem and started the transition in earnest.

[Jerry] found a next step in the direction of his goal by hiring a woman that brought a client. He then took the next step towards his goal by recognizing opportunity in a lift line at a ski area.

Jerry had one of those apparent chicken-and-egg problems that leave many entrepreneurs stuck for a while. However, as a good entrepreneur, rather than concede, he found a next step in the direction of his goal by hiring the woman that brought a client. He then took the next step towards his goal by recognizing opportunity in a lift line at a ski area.

The element that completed the transition resulted from a chance meeting. Jerry met Brian Muncaster, CEO of BuyChoice.com, in a lift line at Winter Park (a ski area). At the time, the BuyChoice.com site was built on static HTML and needed to be converted to more scalable technology, which of course was exactly what Ami Visions could do for Brian. BuyChoice.com was then doing annual sales in the low hundreds of thousands and Jerry told Brian that his company could build them a Web site that would scale to $20 million in annual sales. Jerry wanted the work to train his people and to build his portfolio; Brian wanted a quality Web-site.

At the time, however, BuyChoice.com could not afford Ami Visions' services. In fact, Jerry insists that Brian almost threw him out of the office when he heard how much the Web site would cost.

In spite of that near-miss, Jerry and Brian were able to reach agreement. Jerry took the risk of doing the work for BuyChoice.com in exchange for some ownership in the company. This has been a hugely successful and healthy business-relationship, with BuyChoice.com sales now approaching ten million dollars.

The relationship between Ami Visions and BuyChoice.com signaled the end of the client-server days for Ami Visions and its conversion into a Web-development company. Interestingly, the success of the BuyChoice.com business-relationship has led Jerry in yet another new direction with Ami Visions and the formation of his new company, MangoFish. Jerry's insight was that the BuyChoice.com/Ami Visions model could be replicated for other Web-related companies that needed help in getting traction.

In 2000, Jerry started Ultimate Currency, which was a single-product company selling a time-management and billing system. It was unable to sell the product and has now abandoned that business although Ami Visions continues to use the product internally. Jerry also started another single-product company called Project Notes that sold a suite of tools for managing complex projects. That too was abandoned because a market could not be created for the product.

In about 1999, Jerry started a company called One of Eleven, to purchase a building into which Ami Visons could move, but which also had other tenants. This real-estate investment and the BuyChoice.com relationship turned out to be great buffers for 2001, which was a horrible year for other Web-development revenue.

"An interesting twist on this whole thing is that I bought the building because Ami was doing so well in 1999 so I could leverage the growth and the profitability of Ami to buy the building. Once I owned the building and Ami was having problems, I was able to leverage the building to get the financial resources I needed to keep Ami going."

Words of Wisdom

> Get Help: "The reason I am successful is that I'm not trying to do anything alone. There are a lot of people involved in any venture when you want to be successful. So I think a key is getting a smart and synergistic group of people involved and just get started. Don't plan too long, too much planning and nothing will get done. Paraphrasing Patton: a good plan executed today is better than a perfect plan executed perfectly next week."

> Leverage Opportunities: It is important to find and leverage opportunities because "opportunities are everywhere and it's a matter of seeing them and taking them and then pushing through them."

> Let Go of Perfection: "Another thing is letting go of perfection. Perfection will never ever happen. Recognize when good enough will work."

"What has been easy is what has been fun. It's been fun challenging myself, growing the business and enhancing my business. I think one mistake I made in growing so fast is that I lost sight of what is most important about growth—and that's profit. It used to be that my profit was directly tied to the number of people I had because business was so unlimited that so long as I could hire and retain the people, I could get the business and be profitable. What happened in this downturn in the market is that I held on to some employees too long; I mistakenly considered body count, instead of the bottom line, as my measure of success."

Takeaways

> Get help from great people: This comes up over and over again. Jerry has developed relationships with many talented people with whom he can join forces for a given opportunity.

> Take action: Determine your goals and figure out what action you can take in the direction of any goal. Then do it, even if you don't have the exact plan mapped out.

> Leverage: Recognize opportunity and then take advantage of it. For example, find ways to use financial stability in one business to buffer another during difficult times.

> Be agile: In Jerry's case this has been a strong theme. If a technology is dying, move to another one. If a product won't sell after a reasonable amount of effort, abandon it.

10. IN CLOSING

We have covered a lot of ground in this book—taking you from inside-out so-to-speak. From a close look at yourself, to a look within and without to vet opportunities, to venturing out to plan a business, then to trying it on for size by interacting with customers, then to taking the final steps and putting it all into results-oriented action.

Starting a company is one of the most rewarding things that a person can do. Creating value through the will and ability of you and your team. Taking the incredible potential of a group of people and turning it into something so valuable that people will pay for it. In almost all cases you will have moved yourself and society forward a notch or two simply by starting your company.

I sincerely hope that this book has provided you with insights and wisdom that will help make your business life both enjoyable and successful. I invite your feedback through the "contact us" section of the ROI Press Web site (www.ROIPress.com).

Now, startup!

RESOURCES

Books

Crossing the Chasm by Geoffrey Moore and Regis McKenna (HarperCollins, New York, New York, 1991). The book to read on how to bring technology to the mainstream market.

Five Temptations of a CEO: A Leadership Fable by Pat Lencioni (Jossey-Bass, Inc., San Francisco, California, 1998). The book is written as a fable to convey the insights and wisdom that can be distilled into the five temptations. Incredible clarity in both the writing and the key points.

Flow: The Psychology of Optimal Experience by Mihaly Csikszentmihalyi (HarperCollins, New York, New York, 1990). Wordy at times, but an excellent book about finding and living in life's sweet spot.

Growing Pains by Eric Flamholtz and Yvonne Randle (Jossey-Bass, Inc., San Francisco, California, 2000). The classic book that not only discusses the transitions through the various phases of a company but also provides useful information on how to manage and organize people through those phases.

High Tech Startups by John Nesheim (John Nesheim, Saratoga, California, 1997). A great source if you are looking for venture capital. It appears a little dated following the burst of the bubble because some of their advice and information is unique to that period. Still, if you calibrate it to the present there is much useful information in this book.

Inside the Tornado by Geoffrey Moore (HarperCollins, New York, New York, 1999). Takes another step beyond the crossing of the chasm and provides great insights on the transitions of technology-based products in various phases of adoption.

Startup: A Silicon Valley Adventure by Jerry Kaplan (Penguin Books, New York, New York, 1996). An entertaining, true-life story of the rise and fall of a pen-computing startup. The story predates the Internet bubble so it isn't just another dot-bomb story. Just plain fun to read.

Working Together by Olaf Isachsen and Linda Berens (Institute for Management Development, San Juan Capistrano, California, 1988). While there are many books on Myers Briggs tests and their interpretations, this one is narrowly directed at the workplace and is useful in a work setting.

Periodicals

Redherring. A twice-monthly magazine with excellent writing on startup business, technology and venture capital. See also www.redherring.com.

Business 2.0. Good writing on new-business formation, trends and technology. Broader and more variable than Redherring. See also www.business2.com.

Wall Street Journal. The source for daily information on business.

Harvard Business Review. While many of the articles are more appropriate to General Motors than to a startup, you will find many articles that are both relevant and insightful. A good way to keep in contact with new and useful thinking.

Notes

Notes

Notes